STORIES IN A NEW SKIN

APPROACHES TO INUIT LITERATURE

KEAVY MARTIN

UMP
University of Manitoba Press

University of Manitoba Press
Winnipeg, Manitoba
Canada R3T 2M5
uofmpress.ca

Printed in Canada
Text printed on chlorine-free, 100% post-consumer recycled paper

16 15 14 13 12   1 2 3 4 5

Cover design: Jessica Koroscil
Cover image: "Shaman Revealed" (2007) by Ningeokuluk Teevee,
lithograph, 20.25" x 18", reproduced with the permission of Dorset Fine Arts.
Interior design: Jessica Koroscil

Library and Archives Canada Cataloguing in Publication

Martin, Keavy
Stories in a new skin : approaches to Inuit literature / Keavy
Martin.

(Contemporary studies on the north, ISSN 1928-1722 ; 3)
Includes bibliographical references and index.
ISBN 978-0-88755-736-1 (pbk.)
ISBN 978-0-88755-426-1 (PDF e-book)
ISBN 978-0-88755-428-5 (epub e-book)

1. Inuit literature--Canada--History and criticism. I. Title.
II. Series: Contemporary studies on the north ; 3

PS8075.5.M37 2012   809'.889712   C2012-902600-X

The University of Manitoba Press gratefully acknowledges the financial
support for its publication program provided by the Government of Canada
through the Canada Book Fund, the Canada Council for the Arts, the Manitoba
Department of Culture, Heritage, Tourism, the Manitoba Arts Council,
and the Manitoba Book Publishing Tax Credit.

FSC
www.fsc.org
MIX
Paper from
responsible sources
FSC® C016245

For my angusiaq,
Joseph John Nashalik-Suvissak;
for his anaana, Karen;
and for our ataata, Inuusiq Nashalik.

And for nîcimos, Richard...

CONTENTS

ACKNOWLEDGEMENTS

THIS BOOK WOULD NEVER HAVE HAPPENED without the generous support of many communities.

I am forever indebted to the University of Manitoba's Pangnirtung Summer School, which first took me to Nunavut and changed what I thought about everything. I am equally grateful for the patience and humour of my many Inuktitut teachers, especially Alukie Metuq, Saila Michael, and Karen Nashalik. The community of Pangnirtung continues to awe and humble me deeply, and I would like to say *qujannamiippaaluk* in particular to elders Evie Anilniliak, Jaco Ishulutaq, Annie Maniapik, Inuusiq Nashalik, Taina Nowdlak, and Joanasie Qappik, and also to Sim Akpalialuk, Silasie Anilniliak, Ooleepeeka Arnaqaq, Seemeeonie "Moe" Evic, Ooleepa Ishulutaq, Petrosie Kakee, Kelly Karpik, Corina Kuluguqtuq, Paulette Metuq, Henry Mike, Rev. Louee Mike, Margaret Nakashuk, Caroline Nashalik, Oleepika Saullu Nashalik, Maryann Shoapik, Sakiasie Sowdlooapik, and Peter Young for their generosity, hospitality, friendship, and good teachings. I was fortunate, also, to meet Marie-Lucie Uviluq from Igloolik, who taught me a great deal in a short time. I would like to honour the late Noah Metuq and the late Towkie Etuangat, both kind and patient teachers, and both gone too quickly. And I would also like to acknowledge the late Thomas Kimeksun Thrasher of Tuktoyaktuk, who believed in the power and the future of Inuit literature. I am grateful to have known you.

In its early stages, this project was supported by a SSHRC Canada Graduate Scholarship, which allowed me to travel to Nunavut. I am likewise indebted to the many scholars and experts who very generously took the time to provide me with feedback, advice, and to lend me materials. Thanks to Richard Dauenhauer and Nora Marks Dauenhauer, Louis-Jacques Dorais, Maurizio Gatti, Kenn Harper, Peter Irniq, Peter Kulchyski, Frédéric Laugrand, John MacDonald, Mick Mallon, Terry and Leslie Ryan, Susan Sammons, Marianne Stenbaek, and

Andrew Stewart. Robin McGrath and one other reviewer provided invaluable feedback on the manuscript, as did Warren Cariou and Jean Wilson. I have also learned a great deal from Christopher Trott, who kindly reviewed the manuscript and who continues to put up with my questions. And without the support and encouragement of the wonderful team at the University of Manitoba Press, this book would still be a bulky and neglected file on my computer. My heartfelt thanks go to David Carr, Cheryl Miki, and my editor, Glenn Bergen. My research assistant, Cynthia Spring, greatly eased the final stages of revision.

In addition, the friends and mentors who supported, questioned, fed, and consoled me made the process of producing this work not only manageable but also enjoyable. At the University of Toronto, I was privileged to work with Alana Johns, who first introduced me to Inuktitut and kept me learning; with Linda Hutcheon, who inspired me with her wisdom and kindness; and with Daniel Heath Justice, who supplied me with laughter, good music, and straight talk when I needed it. I would especially like to express my fond thanks to my supervisor and mentor Ted Chamberlin, who first got me thinking about stories and songs. I would have been lost without him. The Centre for Comparative Literature provided me with a community in which my curiosity could thrive, and my colleagues and students at the University of Alberta have taught me the welcome lesson that real learning begins *after* the PhD. And I am blessed to work in a field with such talented and thoughtful people; Warren Cariou, Renate Eigenbrod, Daniel Morley Johnson, Sophie McCall, Sam McKegney, Sharron Proulx-Turner, Deanna Reder, Niigaanwewidam J. Sinclair, Gregory Scofield, Christine Stewart, and Pauline Wakeham, you continue to inspire me.

My parents and their wonderful partners have provided me with unfailing support and inspiration: thanks to my mom, Lindsay, and her husband, Jay, for their big hearts and their faith in me; to Nadia for her kind help with French; and to my dad, Michael, for many thoughtful conversations—and also for his trusty editing. Thanks to my brothers, Tom and Samuel, for keeping me young. To my grandmothers, Margaret and Shelagh, I am so grateful to have found you again. Finally, *mahsi cho* to the love of my life, Richard, whose encouragement allowed me to get this book done—and who reminds me daily that there is more to life than working all the time.

PERMISSIONS

I would like to thank the authors and publishers who granted permission for the use of their materials: Tom Lowenstein (for *Eskimo Poems from Canada and Greenland*), Nunavut Arctic College (for *Perspectives on Traditional Law*), and

Igloolik Isuma Productions (for *The Journals of Knud Rasmussen and Unikkaat Sivunittinnit*). The maps were kindly provided by *The Canadian Encyclopedia*, Inuit Tapiriit Kanatami, Statistics Canada, McGill-Queen's University Press, Parks Canada, and Natural Resources Canada. *Nakurmiik* to Dorset Fine Arts and to Ningeokuluk Teevee, whose beautiful lithograph appears on the cover. Some sections of the introduction appeared in *Studies in Canadian Literature* 35, 2 (2010) and are used with permission from the publisher. An earlier version of Chapter 1 was published in the *American Indian Culture and Research Journal*, volume 34, 2 (2010) and is reprinted here by permission of the American Indian Studies Center, UCLA © 2010 Regents of the University of California. A French translation of an earlier version of Chapter 2 appeared in *Littératures autochtones* (2010) and is reprinted with permission of Mémoire d'encrier. Some sections of Chapter 3 were published in the Spring 2011 issue (208) of *Canadian Literature* and appear here with permission. Finally, an earlier version of Chapter 4 appeared in the *Canadian Journal of Native Studies* XXIX, 1&2 (2009) and is included here with persmission.

All proceeds from this publication will go to the Nunavut Bilingual Education Society.

A NOTE ON LANGUAGES

Inuit languages are written in a variety of ways. Much of Nunavut has adapted a version of the syllabic system that was first used for the Cree language and later brought north by the Reverend Edmund Peck. The Western dialects of Inuinnaqtun and Inuvialuktun, however, are written in the roman alphabet, while Labrador uses the orthography of the Moravian missionaries. A thorough overview of these variations can be found in Kenn Harper's "Inuit Writing Systems in Nunavut: Issues and Challenges." One of the challenges relevant here is that Inuktitut words written in roman letters are rendered in a range of spellings, and even proper names can vary immensely. Inuktitut also differs quite substantially by dialect, and there is no standardized version of the language in Canada. In discussing texts from different regions, then, I have attempted to preserve the spellings used in the texts themselves. As a result, my spelling of names (such as *Ivaluardjuk*) or terms (such as *unikkaaqtuaq*) may vary. I may also at times exhibit a bias for Eastern dialects, as I am most familiar with the language of the Qikiqtaaluk (Baffin) region.

Unless indicated otherwise, all translations from French are my own.

MAP I

POLITICAL MAP OF NUNAVUT

Reproduced with the permission of Natural Resources Canada (© 2012), courtesy of the *Atlas of Canada*.

MAP 2

INUIT REGIONS OF CANADA

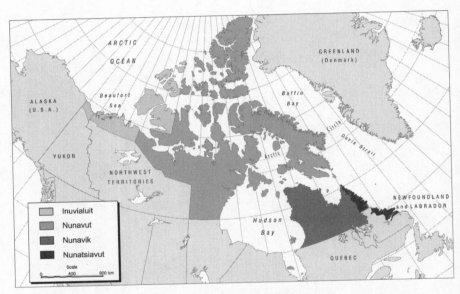

Reproduced with the permission of Inuit Tapiriit Kanatami (© 2008), www.itk.ca.

MAP 3

ETHNOGRAPHIC MAP OF THE ARCTIC

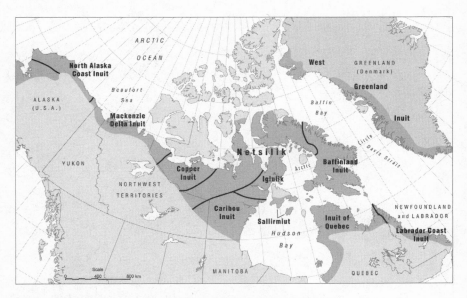

Reproduced with the permission of *The Canadian Encyclopedia* (© 2009).

MAP 4
-MIUT GROUPS OF NUNAVUT

Source: Parks Canada and McGill-Queen's University Press, courtesy of Susan Bennett and Graham Rowley (*Uqalurait: An Oral History of Nunavut*). Reproduced with permission.

INTRODUCTION

SILATTUQSARVIK
A Place (and Time) to Become Wise

DURING AN INTERVIEW WITH FILMMAKER Zacharias Kunuk and environmental scientist Ian Mauro, elder Rita Nashook (Iqaluit) made the following observation: "Southerners don't want to understand Inuit ways. They're ignorant about our culture, don't consider our opinion and treat us like we know nothing. Inuit culture is oral and we keep knowledge in our minds. Even without text, our culture is full of wisdom." Nashook spoke passionately about the clash between Inuit knowledge and the prevailing opinions of southern scientists, particularly with regards to issues like wildlife management in Nunavut. In the resulting 2010 documentary *Qapirangajuq: Inuit Knowledge and Climate Change*, a series of interviews in the Nunavut communities of Iqaluit, Pangnirtung, Igloolik, and Resolute Bay revealed that across the Qikiqtaaluk (Baffin) region, elders are observing the same kinds of drastic changes in their world. In a time when the impact of climate change on Inuit communities often takes a back seat in the media to southern concerns about the health of polar bear populations, the film acted as an important reminder of the human impacts of climate change—and of the expertise that exists in Northern communities.

The observations made by elders in *Qapirangajuq* challenge scientists in a profound way. Not only do they point out that polar bear populations are actually increasing, but they also observe that the sun, moon, and stars have shifted their positions drastically.[1] Although an awareness of the reality that southern activities are responsible for these climatic shifts does not feature prominently in the film, several elders maintain that it is *the actions of the scientists themselves* that is endangering Arctic wildlife—and Inuit communities. As Nathaniel Kalluk of Resolute Bay observes, polar bears wearing radio collars cannot hunt effectively at seal breathing holes; Simon Idlout, also of Resolute Bay, mentions that the bears' sensitive hearing has been damaged by the noise of scientists' helicopters. As the bears' ability to hunt is threatened—again, not by the reduced sea ice, but by interference of this kind—they cause more and more problems for Inuit on the land and in the communities. The late Jamesie Mike, an elder from Pangnirtung, noted that "bears that are tagged and handled act more aggressively." While scientists may believe they are providing data that will lead to policies that protect the "fragile" Arctic environment, Simon Idlout points out that they are in fact breaking a vital Inuit law about the mistreatment of wildlife. As Inuusiq Nashalik of Pangnirtung observes, "[Bears] are constantly tampered with, by Southerners, who only know them by what they read and have never interacted with them. We know our wildlife intimately."

The academy—along with other southern institutions and, to some extent, the public—is slowly awakening to the reality that it must contend seriously with Indigenous knowledge, and not only out of a sense of postcolonial obligation. As the Nuu-chah-nulth scholar and hereditary chief Umeek (E. Richard Atleo) states, "These [non-Indigenous] visitors have made their gifts of science and technology evident and recognizable to all, while our gifts of relationality and *isaak* (respect for all life forms) have only now begun to emerge" (134). Indigenous and non-Indigenous scholars, some working within the discipline of Native Studies, have laboured to create space both in classrooms and in research programs for Indigenous perspectives to be prioritized. As the Dakota scholar Waziyatawin (Angela Cavendar Wilson) writes, "reclamation of Indigenous knowledge is more than resistance to colonial domination, it is also a signifier of cultural revitalization and mounting Native nationalism" (Wilson 84). Yet in *Qapirangajuq*, elders demonstrate that bridging the knowledges of the academy and the community may require more than a simple willingness, on the part of the academics, to "integrate" some samples of Indigenous "content." Rather, elders like Inuusiq Nashalik question the very methods that the academy employs—not only in its interactions with polar bears, but in the acquisition of knowledge itself. What do we do when the experience of elders—whose livelihood, as the film points out, has depended on careful and detailed observation of their environment—fully and forcefully contradicts what the academy "knows" to be true?

The study of literature may consider itself to be somewhat more benign than wildlife biology, as the findings of literary scholars seldom influence policy decisions (like hunting quotas). But in reality, literary critics now face the same kinds of challenges. In a discipline in which community consultation is nowhere near the norm, how can our work create positive impacts for Indigenous communities, both rural and urban? How can Indigenous literary studies take seriously Indigenous knowledge, "traditional" or otherwise? How do our methods—our ways of thinking about and reading texts—converse with Indigenous traditions and contemporary concerns? Do categories like "literature" or practices like "critical analysis" tie our work inextricably to European traditions—and perhaps prevent us from seeing other ways? And how, in seeking to think deeply about traditional knowledge—or the comparable yet distinct concept of *Inuit Qaujimajatuqangit* (IQ)—do we account for crucial and ever-present Indigenous adaptations of "tradition"?

This book demonstrates a series of ways of thinking about Inuit "literature," a diverse body of stories, songs, life writing, oral history, poetry, fiction, and film. Following principles of Indigenous intellectual sovereignty, I seek to locate interpretive strategies within these texts and to consider the ways in which *Inuit Qaujimajatuqangit*—"what Inuit have known for a very long time" or "*the Inuit way of doing things: the past, present and future knowledge, experience and values of Inuit Society*"—contains principles that can guide students and scholars of Inuit literature ("First Annual Report" 7, emphasis in original). In other words, I seek to locate—inasmuch as it is possible for an outsider to do so—examples of Inuit literary criticism. While Inuit texts have, for the most part, remained notably geared toward Inuit (and often Inuktitut-speaking) audiences, they also contain crucial and instructive challenges for literary studies as it is practised in southern (or Eurowestern) institutions. This capacity for adaptation, known under the IQ framework as *qanuqtuurniq*, or a quality of resourcefulness in problem-solving ("First Annual Report" 8), allows Inuit texts to enter academic settings—and likewise challenges literary scholars to begin to reconsider their own ways of doing things.

In the first years of this project, I often framed it as an attempt to rectify a major oversight on the part of the literary establishment; Inuit literature, I argued, is a rich and extensive tradition, but it has tended to be underrepresented within literary studies. As the Nunavik politician and columnist Zebedee Nungak writes:

> Since Inuit traditions are oral and not literary, Inuit have had to process through a transition to find a suitable "zone of comfort" in the field of written literature. In past times, writing seemed to be something for "others" to do, and was not at all a preoccupation of Inuit. For a long time, it seemed that Inuit were neither meant, nor expected to be, writers. That is, in the way that Qallunaat have been authors, poets, and producers of written works for centuries.
>
> From the late 1950s onward, Inuit have proven themselves more than capable as writers ever since magazines, newsletters, and other publications have been available to them across the Arctic. But for the most

part, Inuit writing has yet to make its presence memorable in the world of mainstream literature. Several Inuit have pioneered the literary trail as published authors, but these are still far too few. Inuit writers have yet to attain such "firsts" as making the bestseller lists, or winning mainline literary prizes for written works. (64–6)[2]

Indigenous literature courses and anthologies now often include work by the late Alootook Ipellie, or perhaps Igloolik Isuma Productions' *Atanarjuat (The Fast Runner)*. On the whole, however, many students and scholars profess a certain degree of ignorance about the Inuit literary tradition. They are often unaware of the autobiographical writings of Abraham Ulrikab, Peter Pitseolak, Minnie Aodla Freeman, Alice Masak French, and Anthony Apakark Thrasher; they do not know the poetry of Aqqaluk Lynge or Taqralik Partridge; they have not read the fiction of Markoosie Patsauq, Rachel A. Qitsualik, or Michael Arvaarluk Kusugak; and they have not browsed the extensive collections of oral histories and traditional stories and songs that are being recorded and published at the community level.

Yet while it is crucial that we continue to challenge the biases that haunt our classroom syllabi, publishing houses, and literary award committees, I am becoming more and more skeptical of "underrepresentation" as a scholarly rhetorical strategy. After all, does the canonization of predominantly English-language Indigenous novels, short stories, and poetry truly constitute the privileging of Indigenous intellectual traditions? Or is this a mere extension of the Enlightenment principles of the university, which continue to encourage scholars to "contribute to knowledge" by gathering more and more remote content into the benevolent halls of learning? Scholarly attention and recognition *does* have its benefits; Indigenous students in pursuit of their degrees deserve to see their traditions respectfully represented in the curriculum, and non-Indigenous students need to be taught about the extensive intellectual traditions that have shaped the land that they are guests on. But in order for the academy to truly decolonize, it must radically shift its understanding about the nature and location of knowledge. And it must recognize that its "attention" can also harbour methods and ideologies that, in Indigenous contexts, are not always appropriate.

I first visited the community of Pangnirtung in 2007, as a student of the University of Manitoba's annual "bush school." Very quickly, I learned that my years of postsecondary education, my accreditations, and the reading that I had done about Nunavut meant very little in Pangnirtung; knowledge, as Inuusiq Nashalik stated in *Qapirangajuq* (and made clear to me personally), is based on real, lived experience. In this, I was lacking. In Inuktitut, the word that is used for Nunavut Arctic College is *silattuqsarvik*: a place (or, depending on context, a time³) of working to acquire *sila*. The word *sila* has multiple significations, most commonly, it refers to the environment, such as in the phrases *silami qa-nuippa?* (how's the weather?) or *silaup asijjipallianinga* (climate change). The other meaning of *sila*, however, refers to wisdom, or cleverness, as in *silatujuq* (he/she/it is intelligent, sensible, or wise). The etymological explanation for the correlation of these two concepts may be more complex than the conclusion that wisdom is predicated on a knowledge of one's environment, but practically speaking, this seems to be the case.⁴

The *sila*—both the wisdom and the environment—of Pangnirtung taught me that I was missing many of the skills that are crucial to good living. Having devoted the bulk of my recent energies to the demands of my PhD program, other skills, like my ability to be self-sufficient, to be a good member of my community, and to read and make use of my environment, had remained infantile. As a repeat visitor to Pangnirtung, and as a student of Inuktitut language, I have been privileged—thanks to the generosity of my teachers—to gain some basic experience with Inuit ways of doing things. More importantly, Pangnirtung has taught me the meaning of community—in particular, the responsibilities that come with it. As a faculty member at the University of Alberta, I now work (and, often, struggle) to put these teachings into practice. I try to understand that my students and colleagues are whole human beings whose intellectual autonomy should be respected. I seek to remember that we should share resources freely with one another, that we should always help each other (ideally without being asked), and that whenever possible, we should seek out and speak from experience, rather than relying always on secondhand knowledge. Yet I continue to grapple with the geographical and conceptual distance between these two worlds; this book, in many ways, is a product of that struggle.

In 1994, the Osage scholar Robert Warrior published a book entitled *Tribal Secrets: Recovering American Indian Intellectual Traditions*, in which he introduced the concept of "intellectual sovereignty." The study of Indigenous texts, he demonstrates, need not only draw upon methodologies originating in other places; rather, it should consider Indigenous texts in the context of work by other Indigenous writers, both past and present (87). "How does construing the field in the terms of intellectual history change the critical landscape?" Warrior asks (xiii). He was soon joined in this project by other scholars in the field of what is now known as American Indian or Indigenous literary nationalism. In many ways, the project of Indigenous literary nationalism is a project of renaming: the use of the term "intellectual traditions" to describe Indigenous writing and storytelling transforms these texts in the minds of the readers and listeners; instead of remaining ethnographic artifacts or historical curios, they become literary and critical masterpieces. By using the terminology of the academy, then, Indigenous scholars have translated these traditions into forms that the institution can recognize. As Daniel Heath Justice (Cherokee) explains, "the stories told both *by* and *about* Indian people are vital to the processes of peoplehood, as they help to give shape to the social, political, intellectual, and spiritual dimensions of tribal life. Stories are never far from their contexts, as words give shape the world. 'Sovereignty' is a story, as are 'self-determination' and 'nationhood.' These stories challenge others, like 'Manifest Destiny,' 'savage,' 'assimilation,' 'genocide'.... [W]e can use the academy's resources and cultural capital to serve both the pursuit of truth and the dignified decolonization of Indigenous peoples" (*Our Fire* 207–208).

As many scholars have pointed out, Indigenous peoples have always adapted useful concepts and technologies without fear that their cultural purity might be compromised. Tradition, as Audra Simpson (Kanien'hehaka) notes, is "profoundly contemporary" (though its signifier often fails to convey as much).[5] Craig Womack (Muskogee/Cherokee), meanwhile, asserts that the idea of the "traditional" might be reworked to mean "anything that is useful to Indian people in retaining their values and worldviews, no matter how much it deviates from what people did one or two hundred years ago.... Only cultures that are able to adapt to change remain living cultures; otherwise they become no longer relevant and are abandoned" (*Red on Red* 42). Despite this progressive thinking, however, the traumas of forced assimilation and ongoing marginalization continue to fuel uncertainty about the appropriateness (or, often, certainty about the *in*appropriateness) of Eurowestern concepts, tools, and people in Indigenous studies. For Jace Weaver (Cherokee), the dangers of this power imbalance extend to what he calls "Eurocentric comparisons, such as that which asks with plaintive arrogance, 'Where is the African Proust?' or that of Albert Schweitzer, who dubbed South Asian Nobel laureate Rabindrinath Tagore 'the Indian Goethe.' In each case there is the clear implication that persons who need the adjectival modifier are something less than their Western counterparts, the 'actual' Proust or the 'real' Goethe" (*That the People Might Live* x). Is the comparison implied in the use of terms like "literature" or "intellectual traditions," then, likewise problematic? In other words, is the translation of Indigenous writing and storytelling into forms that that the academy will recognize a strategic tactic—or a sell-out?

In thinking about this question, I look to a trope from Inuit storytelling traditions, which have much to say about the challenges and potential of adaptation. In 1958, a Kugluktuk (Coppermine) man named Louis Qajuina told a story to the Oblate missionary Maurice Métayer about a group of hunters who paddle upriver to look for caribou but never return.[6] A second group of hunters sets out to search for them, but they too go missing, and the community is at a loss until a poor orphan boy decides that he will head out to find the men. Borrowing a kayak, he heads up the river until he comes to a group of very large snow houses. He looks inside for the lost hunters, but finds no one there. Suddenly, though, he hears footsteps approaching, and he soon discovers that the settlement into which he has stumbled is not a village of men, but of bears, and that he is therefore in great danger. Here, Métayer annotates the story, adding that "many times the boy had heard stories of these beasts who lived in igloos like people and *who could take off their outer skins whenever they were inside their own homes. When they were out hunting[,] the bear-men wore their skins and were very, very dangerous*" (Métayer, *Tales* 26, emphasis added). Having wounded one of the bears, the boy tries to hide in a different snow house, but finds two old bear-women inside. Without hesitation, he kills them both quickly and immediately begins skinning one, dressing himself in the fresh skin just as the other bears enter the house. Thus acting the part of the old bear-woman, he is able to escape detection until he has a chance, at last, to escape.

The idea of animals *wearing* their skins—much as humans wear skin clothing—features prominently in Inuit stories. Another story recorded by Métayer tells of a wolf couple who take off their skins and appear in human form in order to kidnap a human baby (*Tales* 73–77). The hero Kiviuq, meanwhile, is said to steal the skin of a fox-woman and to refuse to return it until she agrees to become his wife.[7] "Shaman Revealed," a 2007 lithograph by the Cape Dorset artist Ningeokuluk Teevee (and the cover image of this book), depicts a woman who has unzipped her human skin, clothing and all, to reveal the head of a fox. Inspired by the story of Kiviuq's fox wife, she says, "I wanted to show how people could change from one thing to another but still be the same person" (Lalonde et al., *Uuturautiit*). In another episode of this story cycle, Kiviuq is married to a wolf whose mother becomes jealous, murders her daughter, and dresses in her skin in order to seduce her son-in-law.[8] Skins and skin clothing are obviously of enormous importance in Inuit tradition, as they symbolize the Inuit reliance on and interconnection with the animal world. Indeed, the idea of harvesting and adapting the skin of an animal evokes the ingenuity and skill that have enabled Inuit to live in an environment that—to the rest of the world—is astounding in its extremes.

In framing this study, then, I am interested in the ways in which Inuit intellectual traditions might similarly dress in new "skins" for the purposes of infiltrating the academy—and likewise, in the ways in which the wrongs of the southern institution might similarly be "re-dressed." This metaphor is in no way benign (or merely celebratory); with its complex connotations of kinship and transformation, and also of violence and coercion, it represents both the possibility and the discomfort of adaptation. Again, many Inuit stress that adaptation is central to Inuit culture; in the words of the Igloolik writer Rachel A. Qitsualik: "Inuit are the embodiment of adaptability itself, and other peoples who direct eyes toward the Arctic...would do well to emulate such plasticity" ("*Nalunaktuq*"). Ideas of Indigenous continuance, furthermore, have formed a valuable framework for Native studies, articulating an important counternarrative to all-too-pervasive stories of victimization, assimilation, and helplessness. Frédéric Laugrand and Jarich Oosten, for instance, argue that the introduction of Christianity to the Arctic, rather than initiating a profound break with the shamanism (*angakkuniq*) of the past, "represents a stage in a complex process of cultural transformation, one that testifies to the resilience of Inuit culture and its capacity to integrate external influences" (*Inuit Shamanism and Christianity* xviii). Yet the shedding or acquiring of skins is still a risky or unsettling activity: a difficult but sometimes necessary process whereby new relationships are forged and new experiences are acquired. With this danger and potential in mind, this book explores the ways in which Inuit texts adapt to new contexts and, in doing so, powerfully challenge the academy to rethink its own ways of being.

The first chapter experiments with the idea—or the "skin"—of "nationhood." The term "nation" is almost never applied to or used by Inuit, in part because of the enormous size of the Inuit homeland and the diversity that exists within it. Are literary nationalist readings—interpretations that take Inuit intellectual traditions and political concerns as their primary framework—therefore possible? While no singular or homogenous definition of Inuit identity exists, political organizing by groups such as the Inuit Tapiriit Kanatami (ITK) and the Inuit Circumpolar Council (ICC) have drawn upon the notion of a common land, language, and culture—what some might call a "peoplehood"—in order to establish an international presence.[9] Following their lead, I argue that a "national" literature of sorts exists in the shared, though variable, traditions of stories. In particular, I compare community tales about the Tuniit (or Dorset—the people displaced by the Thule Inuit) with Rachel A. Qitsualik's imagining of an Inuit/Tuniit encounter in her 2005 short story "Skraeling." I argue that these texts work to articulate a kind of national consciousness, or a sense of what it means to be Inuit. In doing so, they both complicate the idea of the "apolitical" Inuit and provide the foundations for literary nationalist readings of Inuit literature.

The second chapter looks at *unikkaaqtuat*—classic tales, or "traditional" stories—and discusses the lessons that they contain for students and scholars of Inuit literature. Through a reading of the late Thomas Kusugaq's story "Angusugjuk and the Polar Bears," I explore the implications of the prominent moral about following instructions. Although Angusugjuk clearly does not understand his situation fully, he carefully follows his mother-in-law's advice—and is rewarded for doing so. This parable, I argue, presents a challenge for literary scholars, who are accustomed to prioritizing a particular kind of critical thinking. Is it possible to practise the faith—and respect—that Angusugjuk models in our own reading practices? These lessons, I find, assist readers in understanding the work of Thomas Kusugaq's son, the writer Michael Arvaaluk Kusugak, who adapts the *unipkaaqtuat* in the writing of his young adult novel, *The Curse of the Shaman*. The *unipkaaqtuat* not only constitute literary "classics," therefore, but they can also usefully guide the reading of other texts in the Inuit tradition.

Chapter Three explores the song traditions recorded by the Greenlandic Inuk ethnographer Knud Rasmussen during the Fifth Thule Expedition of 1921–1924 along with their later iterations in the work of Igloolik Isuma Productions. As Sophie McCall points out, many of the old songs have been presented as lyric poetry—and thereby transformed into decontextualized ethnographic fragments. Although this is a legitimate political concern, I seek to complicate the perceived problem of removing songs from their context by exploring the tradition of *ikiaqtagaq*: the "splitting" or borrowing of songs from previous owners. As we see in Isuma's 2006 film *The Journals of Knud Rasmussen*, Inuit songs are occasionally decontextualized and even exported to serve as tools and trade items: they might then take on a spiritual power, function symbolically to evoke a particular place or ideology, and they can in some cases be bartered for, or bought and sold. As Tom Lowenstein points out, the language and imagery of the songs often underscores this objectification: songs are depicted as craft objects, or as prey, constantly sought (xix–xxii). As such, I suggest, they might put to rest some (though not all) of our anxieties about the ethnographic record and southern adaptations of Inuit traditions.

The final chapter examines one of the most prominent genres in the Inuit tradition: *inuusirmingnik unikkaat*, stories from experience or life history. The many autobiographical texts produced by collaboration between Inuit and *qallunaat* (southerners) have more recently been supplemented by the publication of oral history projects, which derive primarily from interviews with elders. In imitation of the Nunavut government's commitment to *Inuit Qaujimajatuqangit* (IQ)—Inuit "traditional knowledge"—I consider these elders to be scholars of their tradition, and I therefore seek to locate literary critical elements in their stories. In particular, I explore the generic distinction between *inuusirmingnik unikkaat* (life stories) and *unikkaaqtuat* (traditional stories). The boundary between these two forms, though permeable, depends upon the distinction between stories told from personal experience and those told from hearsay. In the latter category, language or the style of expression takes sudden prominence; in this, I argue, we might find a sense of the "literary" which is not beholden to Eurowestern definitions. I explore this thesis with reference to Minnie Aodla Freeman's autobiography *Life Among the Qallunaat*, a text that likewise hovers between personal testimony and reported speech, and thereby contributes to a sense—or a "skin"—of the literary, and of literary scholarship.

This book cannot be comprehensive in its discussion of Inuit literature; nor does it seek to have the last word on the subject. In reading the selected texts, I have tried to consider carefully not only their social, political, and literary contexts, but also the language—especially the original language—of their expression. While I do not speak Inuktitut fluently, thanks to my teachers I am able to consider these texts in their original language, and I do my best here to convey the beauty and complexity of their Inuktitut expression. The necessity of looking at Inuktitut-language texts, however, has required me to limit the scope of the project to a representative selection of work produced by writers and storytellers in the Eastern Arctic (whose Qikiqtaaluk or Baffin dialects I am most familiar with).

That said, publications like Alootook Ipellie's *Arctic Dreams and Nightmares*, Salomé Mitiarjuk Nappaaluk's *Sanaaq*, Markoosie's *Harpoon of the Hunter*, Alice Masak French's *The Restless Nomad*, Anthony Apakark Thrasher's *Skid Row Eskimo*, *The Diary of Abraham Ulrikab*, and the memoirs of Lydia Campbell and Elizabeth Goudie are regretfully not discussed here. Texts from Greenland, Alaska, and Siberia—such as *Words of the Real People: Alaska Native Literature in Translation* (eds. Ann Fienup-Riordan and Lawrence Kaplan), Lela Kiana Oman's *The Epic of Qayaq*, *From the Writings of Greenlanders/ Kalaallit atuakkiaannit* (ed. Michael Fortescue), and Aqqaluk Lynge's book of poetry *Taqqat uummammut aqqutaannut takorluukkat apuuffiannut/The Veins of the Heart to the Pinnacle of the Mind* are also unfortunately absent. Interested readers should likewise seek out the publications of newer Inuit writers like Taqralik Partridge, Mosha Folger, Norma Dunning, Jordan Carpenter, and Reneltta Arluk, whose work is sure to provide both northern and southern audiences with much to talk about. It is clear, though, that further studies—especially by Inuktitut-speaking

Inuit scholars—are needed in this field, and I hope that this work may be useful in furthering that conversation.

As an outsider, I remain wary of imposing perspectives on the material; indeed, the goal of this project has been to seek Inuit methods of interpretation, as embodied by the texts themselves. And although these texts are at times made familiar by the use of Eurowestern labels like "literature," readers should keep in mind that these implicit comparisons are strategic and therefore imperfect. Like the borrowing of skins, they function as a disguise and can be as misleading as they are helpful. If the traditions have been mislabelled or mis-clothed, then, I hope that it is in the way in which metaphor is also a mislabelling. As in a figure of speech, this disjuncture is meant to be productive or transformative—to allow for a new way of seeing, and of being seen.

One of the most prevalent *unikkaaqtuat* (traditional stories) is the one about Aningaat, the blind boy whose mother is cruel to him. In the version told by the late Thomas Kusugaq of Repulse Bay, Aningaat asks his sister to lead him down to the lake where the loons are.[10] Once he is alone, a loon takes him by the hand and dunks him under the water until he chokes. It then administers an excruciating eyeball-licking. Even when he begs it to stop, it continues, asking whether he can yet see the blades of grass on the smoking hill in the distance. Eventually, after several rounds, Aningaat emerges from the lake with the sharpest of vision.

In navigating Inuit intellectual geographies, I find this story itself to be a useful guide. Learning to see well, it says, can be a painful process and might require you to put your trust in something unfamiliar or even uncomfortable. But as Rachel Qitsualik suggests, southerners might look to Inuit society—which has endured many challenges and many transformations—as a model of prudent and successful adaptation. Elisapee Ishulutaq of Pangnirtung observes in *Qapirangajuq* that "Our environment is changing. And so are Inuit. All of us are changing." Indeed, climate change—for better or for worse—reveals the ways in which the Inuit and *qallunaat* worlds are unavoidably connected. And as the Inuit world adapts, the academy's *sila*—its wisdom—must change, too.

ONE

"IT WAS SAID THEY HAD ONE SONG":
"Tuniit" Stories and the Origins of Inuit Nationhood

My father had a short wave radio, and I remembered how my grand-mother Jeannie enjoyed listening to the radio and twisting the dial for signals. Living in the bush there were not many radio programs to find. Once in a while, she would come across the BBC and some-times they would play Greenlandic Inuit songs. Greenlanders are well known for their singing and they have beautiful songs. She would call us to gather around the radio, saying, 'You have to listen to this. These are our relatives who live in faraway lands.' And while we listened to these songs, she would tell us that even though they live in a distant place called Akukituk (Inuktitut for Greenland), we were all one people and that someday we were all going to get together.
  —Mary Simon, *Inuit: One Future—One Arctic*

The process of 'story-making' and the process of nation gathering may be one and the same.
  —Lisa Brooks, "Afterword: At the Gathering Place"

INTRODUCTION: THE "APOLITICAL" INUIT
In the year 1999, the implementation of the Nunavut Act created a new ter-ritory in the Canadian Arctic: a political entity that encompassed the largest land claim in Canada's history (the Nunavut Land Claims Agreement).[1] Tradi-tional Inuit territory, however, extends far beyond these new borders: it reaches westward through the Northwest Territories to Alaska and Siberia, and eastward to northern Quebec, Labrador, and Greenland. *Inuit Nunaat*—the Inuit home-land—spans four countries and almost an entire hemisphere. Because of the vast-ness of this region, descriptions of Inuit people and communities often use terms like "scattered," "widespread," and "far-flung"—passive expressions that construct an image of a people fated to isolation from the world and from each other. In the imagination of southerners—"southerners" being people living below the

treeline—this idea of the Arctic as a vast, barren, and empty space often translates into impressions of Inuit as a people without history or politics, and certainly without any unified sense of nationhood. As Robert G. Williamson wrote in 1974, "traditionally, though the Eskimo conceived of themselves generally and generically as *Iniut* [sic]— 'The People,' they never had any strong sense of total ethnic-group loyalty, still less of a sense of identification on a pan-Eskimo or national scale. Social commitment is intensely toward the extended family, somewhat less toward the camp group, which is a changeable constellation, and moderately toward the dialect group as a whole. Beyond the dialect group, the Eskimo felt very little sense of commitment" (31).

Yet in 1977, Inuit representatives from Alaska, Arctic Canada, and Greenland gathered in Barrow, Alaska, for the inaugural meeting of the Inuit Circumpolar Council (ICC).[2] This was a key moment in Arctic politics; following the decline of the fox fur trade, southern administrations had developed a new interest in other kinds of northern resources, such as oil, natural gas, and mineral deposits. Decades of government intervention into Inuit communities meant that a new generation of Inuit leaders was preparing to pursue land claims settlements. Mary Simon recalls that "as a means of insuring [sic] protection of Inuit culture and the Arctic's resources, [the delegates at Barrow] believed it necessary to establish a unified position on…issues that might affect their people and homelands" (*Inuit: One Future* 15). The newly formed ICC thus laid down a series of resolutions, which began as follows:

WHEREAS, the Inuit of Greenland, Alaska and Canada are *one indivisible people with a common language, culture, environment and concerns*; and

WHEREAS, the Inuit of the circumpolar region declares [sic] the oneness of its culture, environment and land and the wholeness of the homeland and that it is only the boundaries of certain nation states that separate us; and

WHEREAS, we have met in the first Inuit Circumpolar Conference held in Barrow, Alaska, from June 13–18, 1977, to discuss our communal aspirations and concerns; and

WHEREAS, we wish to reaffirm our right to self-determination; and

WHEREAS, there is a need for an international organization of Inuit to study, discuss, represent, lobby and protect our interests on the international level;

NOW, THEREFORE, BE IT RESOLVED:

That the Inuit Circumpolar Conference is formed…. (Inuit Circumpolar Council, emphasis added)

For Michael Amarook, then-president of the Inuit Tapirisat of Canada,[3] this
declaration marked a change in Inuit self-perception: "for the first time in history," he said, "we have become one people" (qtd. in Lauritzen 26). This newfound
cohesiveness found expression in the use of the term "Inuit," often loosely translated as "the people,"[4] which would not only gradually replace the now-outdated
term "Eskimo" but would also function to unite peoples known by many other
names (Therrien, *Le Corps* 144). As André Légaré explains, "the generic term
'Inuit' was used by [regional] groups only when they were confronted, in traditional times, with Indian groups or more recently, with Europeans" (159).
Alaskan "Inuit," meanwhile, are still more commonly known as "Iñupiat" and
"Yupiit," while residents of the Mackenzie Delta region are "Inuvialuit." Even in
central and eastern areas where the term "Inuit" is broadly used, the more meaningful labels are the often region-specific -*miut* appellations.[5] But in 1977, the
umbrella term "Inuit" served to bolster solidarity; as Michèle Therrien explains,
"according to [the Inuit gathered at Barrow], [the ethnonym 'Inuit'] could be
used without undermining local designations. This choice was made in response
to a situation where it seemed important to emphasize the unity, and not the
disparity, of a large cultural group concerned with its future as a distinct society"
(*Le Corps* 144). [Selon (les Inuit réunis à Barrow), (l'ethnonyme "Inuit") pouvait
être utilisé sans porter atteinte aux désignations employées localement. Ce choix
répondait à une logique de situation au moment où il apparaissait important de
souligner l'unité et non la disparité d'un large groupe culturel soucieux de son
devenir en tant que société distincte.]

Like Amarook, many southern scholars have understood the declaration at
Barrow to be prescriptive, rather than descriptive; rather than depicting a pre-
existing reality of Inuit nationhood, the ICC seemed to be trying to call it into
being. Some scholars, however, have viewed this shift in the political climate as
representing a political debut or awakening, largely based on the presupposition
that pre-colonial Inuit life had little need for politics. In the latter half of the
twentieth century, Inuit adapted—out of necessity—to the political structures
of the Canadian state: they formed regional, national, and circumpolar asso-
ciations, established organizations, elected leaders and spokespeople, advocated
for hunting and fishing rights, negotiated land claims settlements, and won the
right to self-governance.[6] In pre-colonial Inuit life, many of these activities did

not take place in the same way, largely because they were unnecessary. Thus, Mary T. Loughlin remarked in 1943 that "[Eskimo] winter camps number no more than two to five families; they need no national rules nor government" (qtd. in Morice 11). More recent commentators have persisted in this belief; Marybelle Mitchell's *From Talking Chiefs to a Native Corporate Elite: The Birth of Class and Nationalism among the Canadian Inuit*, for instance, tracks "the transformation of Inuit relationships from relatively egalitarian, *apolitical*, family-based units to ethnoregional collectivities" (ix, emphasis added). And Robin McGrath, author of an important 1984 dissertation on Canadian Inuit literature, notes that "formerly, it would have been impossible to talk about the Eskimo political consciousness because such a thing did not exist.... Traditional Inuit society had no politics" (*Canadian Inuit Literature* 60).

This chapter demonstrates, however, that Inuit political consciousness was not merely conjured out of thin air by the declaration at Barrow, nor was it the result of contact with European culture. While the threat of southern colonialism has certainly inspired Inuit leaders to reformulate their cultural and political identities into shapes which non-Inuit will recognize and respond to, Inuit nationalism, I argue, has roots that go much deeper. Although the Inuit homeland is a vast region that traditionally was never regulated by a centralized government, an articulation of peoplehood—of a uniquely Inuit humanity—is apparent in the traditions of songs and stories that Inuit communities share. The Greenlandic Inuk ethnographer Knud Rasmussen sought out this unity in the 1920s, noting during his three-year journey across the Canadian Arctic that "it would be natural for the language and traditions of the various tribes to have lost all homogeneity. Yet the remarkable thing I found was that my Greenland dialect served to get me into complete understanding with all the tribes" (*Across Arctic America* xxxvi). As a people, Inuit may have been composed of widespread regional groups, but their language and literary traditions told a different story: they spoke of a connection that surpassed geographical and historical distance. The idea of "nation" or unified peoplehood, then, is a "skin" that Inuit adopted in 1977, but it was not an entirely new or unfamiliar one.

In a book chapter entitled "Reading the Oral Tradition for Nationalist Themes: Beyond Ethnography," the Muskogee/Cherokee scholar Craig Womack argues that classic Indigenous stories have a deeply political aspect; they serve—and have always served—to articulate a national identity (*Red on Red* 51–74). As Womack puts it, "oral traditions—legends and myths, if you will—performed in their cultural contexts have always been nationalistic and are told for the purpose of cultivating a political consciousness" (61). Stories provide listeners with a sense of communal identity; they describe "what it means to be from a clan, a town, a nation" (62). Following the "Indigenous literary nationalist" approach developed by Womack and others, this chapter will demonstrate that Inuit literature from a range of historical periods and genres is likewise involved in the project of describing the nation. Texts from the Inuit oral tradition, along with contemporary Inuit writing, take as a central theme the idea of what it means to be Inuit—often by describing what it means to *not* be Inuit. This, I argue, constitutes a declaration of nationhood that long precedes the 1977 meeting at Barrow. Despite regional divisions, Inuit form an "imagined community," as old as the stories themselves.[7]

THE MEANING OF NATION

In an 1882 lecture given at the Sorbonne, Ernest Renan asked the question "*Qu'est-ce qu'une nation?*" or "What is a nation?" In the resulting essay, he discusses the factors of shared race, language, religion, and "interests," and one by one eliminates them as the defining feature of nationhood. Geography, he concedes, is an important factor; however, the true core of the nation lies in a kind of shared consciousness amongst its members—in "the possession in common of a rich legacy of memories...[and in] the desire to live together, the will to perpetuate the value of the heritage that one has received in an undivided form" ("What Is a Nation?" 19). This idea that nationhood is determined not by a set of shared characteristics, but rather by a kind of imaginary covenant between members, was later expanded upon by Benedict Anderson. The nation, Anderson said famously, "is an imagined political community" (6). It is based on a constructed narrative of a shared common history, identity, and often a common enemy. As Renan put it, "forgetting, I would even go so far as to say historical error is a crucial factor in the creation of a nation.... [T]he essence of a nation is that all individuals have many things in common, and also that they have forgotten many things" (11). Anderson, however, frames this idea differently, asking why scholars of the nation have "assimilate[d] 'invention' to 'fabrication' and 'falsity,' rather than to 'imagining' and 'creation'" (6).

However, Renan, like Anderson, is in fact concerned with a particular kind of nation: the nation-state. Along with theorists like Ernest Gellner, Renan believes that "nations, in this sense of the term, are something fairly new in history. Antiquity was unfamiliar with them" (9). An invention of the "modern," industrialized era, nation-states are political bodies defined by a "fusion of their component populations" (Renan 10). In other words, the nation-state is a political entity that can encompass multiple "ethnic" nations and is usually endowed with various institutions for managing its citizens. As Max Weber argued in his essay "Politics as a Vocation," "a state is a human community that (successfully) claims the monopoly of the legitimate use of physical force within a given territory" (78). Defining a nation as a political group outfitted with the trappings of statehood, however, dismisses the possibility of nationhood among non-industrialized peoples. Yet while the idea of the nation has certainly undergone changes, it has been around much longer than the era of industrialization. The Latin root of the term, *natio*, refers to birth and evokes a group of people connected by kinship ties. As such, a nation is literally a group of people linked by common descent, rather than a centralized administrative system ("Nation"). Thus we get a more general usage of the term, which refers to a group of people, regardless of their political configuration. By this definition, the nation is a concept as old as humankind.

Tom Holm, J. Diane Pearson, and Ben Chavis observe that "over the years, anthropologists, political philosophers, and Western academicians in general have developed a hierarchical set of definitions of the ways in which human beings organize themselves socially and politically. The lowest and, to use Western terminology, the most 'primitive' form of human organization is the band" (15). From the band—a small group of hunters and gatherers—societies "progress" to the tribe, the chiefdom, and the state (Holm, Pearson, and Chavis 15–16). These "evolutionary or developmental paradigms," as J. Edward Chamberlin points out, "are pretty well discredited now"; however, the idea that human societies exist in hierarchical formations continues to be pervasive. "Scarcely a day goes by," Chamberlin says, "that I don't hear one or two traces of it in conversation" ("From Hand to Mouth" 139–40). It is assumed—often subconsciously—that the destiny of every people is to practise agriculture and commerce rather than hunting and gathering and to develop a written literature as a way to avoid reliance on the seemingly untrustworthy spoken word.[8] Similarly, the assumption goes, in order to have a political life, and in order to be sovereign, a society must progress out of tribal obscurity and eventually form (or preferably join, or be subsumed by) a state (Holm, Pearson, and Chavis 15–16).

This pervasive narrative may explain why scholars have had such difficulty acknowledging the political nature of pre-colonial Inuit life. Given a moment's consideration, the idea that *any* people might exist without politics—that is, without forms of social organization, without systems of authority, without relationships and conflicts with other peoples, without struggles for power—is difficult to entertain. Inuit elders, furthermore, recall the complex systems of law

and governance that were in place before the intervention of southern administrations; for instance, the second volume of Nunavut Arctic College's Interviewing Inuit Elders series, *Perspectives on Traditional Law*, provides an introduction
to complex legal concepts such as *tirigusuusiit, piqujait,* and *maligait.*[9] Many
non-Inuit, however, have been hampered by the difficulty of recognizing cultural institutions in unfamiliar forms; as Indigenous scholars consistently point
out, the academy itself has a chronic difficulty in recognizing Indigenous intellectual traditions and in engaging with them in responsible ways (Womack,
Red on Red 1–24). This is one of the reasons why Indigenous scholars like Lee
Maracle (Stó:lō), Simon Ortiz (Acoma), Craig Womack (Muskogee/Cherokee),
Jace Weaver (Cherokee), Robert Allen Warrior (Osage), Daniel Heath Justice
(Cherokee), Lisa Brooks (Abenaki), Christopher Teuton (Cherokee), and Scott
Richard Lyons (Ojibwe/Dakota) have found a nationalist lens to be useful in formulating critical approaches to Indigenous literatures. Both the classics of the
oral traditions and more recently created works of Indigenous literature, they
argue, can be understood as articulating and bolstering the sovereign nationhood of Indigenous peoples. In this political motivation and utility, Indigenous
literatures are nationalist.

The term "nationalism," however, comes with baggage, and Indigenous
literary nationalists have been careful to distance themselves from the often-
insidious nationalism of nation-states. As Daniel Heath Justice explains in his
Cherokee literary history, *Our Fire Survives the Storm*: "assertions of Indigenous
nationhood should not…be necessarily conflated with the nationalism that has
given birth to industrialized nation-states, for the distinctions are significant.
Nation-state nationalism is often dependent upon the erasure of kinship bonds
in favor of a code of patriotism that places loyalty to the state above kinship obligations, and emphasizes the assimilative militant history of the nation (generally
along a progressivist mythological arc) above the specific geographic, genea-
logical, and spiritual histories of peoples" (23). Here, the nationalism of nation-
states is revealed as inherently assimilative. When Renan referenced this ability
of civic nations to "fuse" divergent ethnicities into the project of statehood, he
lauded it as part of a political entity's journey to "full national existence, such
as we see it blossoming today" ("What Is a Nation?" 10). Meanwhile, "ethnic"
nations within the state must engage in what Said called "nationalist anti-impe-
rialism" ("Yeats and Decolonization" 76). Indigenous nations, therefore, oppose
the nationalism of the American and Canadian states, which time and again
have attempted to subsume them. To quote Justice again: "Indigenous nation-

hood is a necessary ethical response to the assimilationist directive of imperial-
ist nation-states" (*Our Fire* 8).

In order to better articulate their distance from the ideologies of the nation-
state, and perhaps to escape the baggage of terms like "ethnic nationalism," some
scholars have employed the concept of "peoplehood" to define Indigenous nations. As explained by Holm, Pearson, and Chavis, Indigenous peoplehood is
dependent on four intertwined and equally important factors: a shared language,
sacred history, ceremonial cycle, and place, or territory (12). This model takes
important steps towards complicating understandings of tribal nationhoods; in
particular, it avoids the emphasis on ethnicity, or blood, that prevails in discussions of "ethnic" nationalism.[10] The term "peoplehood," then, is perhaps a better
description of Indigenous political groups than the term "nation," as "nation"
can either be dismissed as a generalized ethnic grouping, or confused with a
"nation-state." However, I will continue to make use of both terms, in the hope
of keeping the political aspects of peoplehood in the foreground. Holm, Pearson, and Chavis explain that peoplehood "predates and is a prerequisite for all
other forms of socio-political organization.... It is the basis of nationalism and
the original organization of states" (17). On its own, however, I would argue that
peoplehood is also deeply political—it is the core of social organization, and the
source of a community's authority among other groups. Indeed, the peoplehood
matrix reveals that Indigenous nationhood is rooted in more than a gene pool;
like nation-states, Indigenous nations are imagined communities. As Womack
reminds us, "to exist as a nation, the community needs a perception of nationhood, that is, stories (like the migration account) that help them imagine who
they are as a people, how they came to be, and what cultural values they wish to
preserve" (*Red on Red* 26). Even if a people inhabits a large territory and makes
use of localized rather than centralized systems of governance, its nationhood
is affirmed in its intellectual and artistic traditions—in the stories that it tells.

The use of nationalism—even Indigenous literary nationalism—as a lens
through which to understand Inuit intellectual tradition is not without its problems. Inuit are legally, politically, and culturally distinct from First Nations and
American Indian nations; Inuit have no historic treaties, no reserves, and the Indian Act does not apply to them. The historic relationship between Inuit and *allait*—Indians—has often been tense. Indigenous literary nationalism, then, risks
following in the footsteps of the numerous other foreign methodologies through
which scholars have attempted to understand the Arctic. Yet at the core of Indigenous literary nationalism lies the requirement that Indigenous literatures
must be considered within the framework of their own intellectual histories—

and this is not a foreign concept in Inuit territory. Indeed, the adoption of *Inuit Qaujimajatuqangit* (IQ)—or, 'what Inuit have know for a very long time'—as a guiding principle for the territory of Nunavut resonates strongly with the literary nationalist project. Literary nationalism performs the important function of highlighting the ways in which Inuit literary and political histories are ancient, intertwined, and of ongoing significance to contemporary Inuit life. Echoing the 1977 declaration by the ICC, this chapter employs nationalism as the first "skin" in which Inuit literary tradition may be dressed.

READING TUNIIT STORIES FOR NATIONALIST THEMES

The classic Inuit stories cover a wide range of topics, yet a consistent theme is the presence, and sometimes the threat, of other (non-Inuit) beings. As the editors of *Uqalurait: An Oral History of Nunavut* point out, "Inuit folklore is full of stories about the murderous nature of strangers" (Bennett and Rowley 130). Even when they are not murderous, these others are characterized by a wonderfully disconcerting weirdness. In the brother and sister stories,[11] for instance, a pair of travelling siblings visit the land of the *kukilingiattiaraaluit*, the "ones with the long nails," and the *itiqanngittut*, the "ones without anuses" (Kublu 171–177). Other stories tell of visits to villages of bears (Spalding 1–14) and of a whole range of *uumajuit* (animal spirits) and *inurajait* (human-like beings) (Aupilaarjuk et al., *Cosmology* 51). This latter category includes *ijirait*[12] (shapeshifting land spirits, or "hidden ones"), *inukpasugjuit* (giants), and *inugarulligaarjuit* (little people), to name only a few (Aupilaarjuk, *Cosmology* 51; Bennett and Rowley 150–9). These others often live in ways that parallel Inuit life, but they also inevitably reveal some (frequently horrific) difference, which marks them as distinctly non-Inuit or non-human. Aside from fantastic beings, the classic stories are also populated with non-Inuit people, like the *Iqqiliit* (Dene), the *Allait* or *Unaliit* (Cree),[13] the *Qallunaat* (white people),[14] and the Tuniit—the people who inhabited the Central and Eastern Arctic prior to the arrival of the Inuit.

Chamberlin points out that "we all have stories that hold us in thrall and others at bay" (*If This Is Your Land* 2). Indeed, stories of others are an effective way of defining who we are by reminding us of who we are not. This is particularly the case for national groups that have a great deal of internal diversity, as Inuit do. Inuit speak of their difference from Inuit of other regions; however, this is not the same difference that separates them from non-Inuit. Simon Anaviapik, a Tununirmiut elder, tells a story about travelling as a child to the Nattilik region.[15] At first, his family was struck by the strangeness of the other Inuit: "They seemed almost like animals to us in their own dialect" (qtd. in Bennett and Rowley 126). However, similarities quickly became apparent and the strangeness fell away: "It did not take very long for the language difficulty to clear up," Anaviapik says. "That's how it is when you're all Inuit; problems are easily solved" (qtd. in Bennett and Rowley 126).

When different Inuit regional groups encountered each other, it was likely that they would know many of the same stories, and those stories would remind them of their shared peoplehood. In particular, the various tales of the Tuniit[16]—the people who inhabited the Central and Eastern Arctic prior to the arrival of the Thule (the ancestors of contemporary Inuit)—provide many examples of narrative nation building. Tuniit appear in a variety of Inuit literary genres, whether in narratives collected by anthropologists and retold by contemporary elders, or re-imagined in recent fiction, such as in Rachel Qitsualik's short story "Skraeling." As all of these accounts demonstrate, Inuit representations of the Tuniit—also known as the *Sivullirmiut* (the "First People")—are complex and sometimes incongruous constructions (Brody, "Land Occupancy" 186). At times, the difference of the Tuniit is emphasized through descriptions of their apparent primitiveness, or strangeness. At other times, the stories convey a sense of admiration for and even kinship with the first people. Both of these tactics contribute to a sense of distinct Inuit humanity and entitlement to the land—in other words, to a sense of peoplehood.

Few southerners will be familiar with stories of the Tuniit, although some may know them as the people memorialized in Al Purdy's 1968 poem "Lament for the Dorsets." Here, they are imagined with a kind of prehistoric majesty—and expiration date:

> ...the Dorset giants
> who drove the Vikings back to their long ships
> talked to spirits of earth and water
> —a picture of terrifying old men
> so large they broke the backs of bears...
> they couldn't compete with little men
> who came from the west with dogs
> Or else in a warm climatic cycle
> the seals went back to cold waters (Purdy, "Lament" 3–7; 18–21)

The Dorset people, or "Dorset Paleo-Eskimos," first caught the attention of southern archeologists in 1925, when Diamond Jenness reported a discovery of archaeological evidence of a "new" Arctic people (Sutherland 1).[17] Since that time, archaeologists have attempted to better understand the identity of the Dorset people, the nature and extent of their interaction with the Thule Inuit, and the cause of their disappearance.

Archaeologists date the arrival of the Thule, or "Neo-Eskimos"[18]—the ancestors of contemporary Inuit—in the Eastern Arctic at around 1000 AD (Sutherland 12), and the disappearance of the Dorset in the thirteenth or fourteenth century (Pitseolak 31). Another theory regarding the fate of the Tuniit, entertained both by southern archaeology and by Inuit oral tradition, is that the Sadlermiut, or Sallirmiut—the inhabitants of Southampton Island—were in fact the last of the Dorset (Eber, *When the Whalers* 77–83; Sutherland 13–14). The story of the Sadlermiut fits with the general theme of the disappearance that characterizes tales of Dorset and Tuniit alike: in 1902, the remaining Sadlermiut were wiped out by disease when they came into contact with European whalers (Eber, *When the Whalers* 77). Others believe that the Dorset may have intermarried with the Thule Inuit, adopted their technologies, and eventually ceased to be a distinct people (Qitsualik, "Bones" 14). But in archaeological circles, the history of the Dorset remains something of a mystery.

Inuit oral tradition, however, contains a great deal of information about the Tuniit, or *Sivullirmiut*—the "First People" (Brody, "Land Occupancy" 186). Their stories are told in many versions in the Central and Eastern Arctic, and their descriptions vary from place to place. Sometimes they are described as being exceptionally large, almost giant; elsewhere, they are short and stocky (Mathiassen, *Archaeology* 188). In either case, they are extremely strong, one Tuniq being able to carry a walrus or bearded seal by himself (Bennett and Rowley 143). Tuniit hunters, they say, used to keep lamps under their coats, and their stomachs would often be burned and scarred when, paying no heed to the scalding oil, they moved to kill a seal (Inuksuk 36; Bennett and Rowley 144). Evidence of their enormous strength can be seen in the remains of their houses—found all over Inuit territory—which are built with stones far too heavy for an average person to lift. Often it is told that Tuniit slept with their legs elevated, so that the blood would drain out and make their feet light and quick (Bennett and Rowley 144–5). Although strong and fast, they were thought to be timid and not especially bright (Qitsualik, "Skraeling" 40; Bennett and Rowley 146). Their speech was understandable, but different—less articulate; Peter Pitseolak (Cape Dorset) describes the Sadlermiut as "talking like small babies, unable to pronounce correctly" (33). Simon Qirniq (Gjoa Haven) describes the limitations of the Tuniit in a different way: he writes, *"pisiqaqtunnguuq atausirmik"*—"it was said they had [only] one song" (37). In short, Tuniit are often represented as a kind of primitive people: physically powerful, but developmentally deficient.

Interestingly, echoes of this representation—of Tuniit as primitive artists on the verge of extinction—can be heard in Purdy's "Lament for the Dorsets." Despite their physical strength, the Dorset seem to lack the intellectual ability necessary for adaptation. When Purdy hypothesized the seals out of the polar waters ("Or else in a warm climatic cycle / the seals went back to cold waters"), his "puzzled Dorsets scratched their heads / with hairy thumbs around 1350 A.D. / —couldn't figure it out /…And died" (20–21; 22–29). Like Arctic Neanderthals, they seem to be caught in the riptide of evolution. Qirniq's description of a people with only one song is apt here; it seems to portray the Tuniit as having a knowledge system of very limited range. Perhaps if they'd had other songs, they might have known what to do when the climate changed or when the people out of the west arrived. If you have only one song, a key change can mean irrelevance and death. Similarly, in Purdy's poem, we see "the last Dorset" starving in his tent; instead of one song, he seems to have only one shape—a swan, which he carves over and over. Purdy imagines his name to be Kudluk—an appellation which (if pronounced a certain way) could translate to "thumb"[19] and perhaps emphasizes the physical strength, stubbiness, and isolation of the Tuniq carver. Like much art, Kudluk's swan is useless, and fails to save him from extinction.

Like Purdy's telling, Inuit accounts of the fate of the Tuniit vary; however, all seem to agree on the cause of their disappearance: the influx of Inuit into Tuniit lands. Therkel Mathiassen recounts a version of these events that was told to Rasmussen by the Netsilingmiut: "Once the Tunit lived at Qingmertoq (Adelaide Peninsula); there the land was taken from them by the Ugjulingmiut. The Tunit fled eastwards to Saitoq but, when they reached Naparutalik, they threw off all their clothes and swam over Kingarsuit. On the little island Pagdlagfik they reached land, but they were so exhausted that they fell forward and died. They also lived at Itivnarsuk, Back's River, and wept when they were driven away from this good hunting ground" (qtd. in Bennett and Rowley 147). Kuppaq tells a very similar story in *We Don't Live in Snow Houses Now: Reflections of Arctic Bay*: "There used to be a camp called Sannirut, near Pond Inlet. The people who lived there were known as Tuniit by the Inuit. The Inuit took their land and the Tuniit had to leave. As they were leaving their camp they cried, because the seal hunting was so good there all year round" (qtd. in Innuksuk and Cowan 15). Other versions are more ambivalent about Inuit responsibility in removing their predecessors from the land and suggest that it was the timid nature of the Tuniit that caused them to flee. Aipili Inuksuk (Igloolik) writes that "the Inuit think [the Tuniit] ran away. Yes, perhaps they ran away, maybe they got scared of the Inuit" (36). As Atoat (Arctic Bay) tells it, "the Inuit frightened [the Tuniit] away. I suppose they were teasing the Inuit and the Inuit got annoyed, so they tried to scare them, and scared them right away" (qtd. in Innuksuk and Cowan 17).

Some accounts even go as far as to depict the Tuniit giving the Inuit their blessing as they flee. In Rasmussen's collection of Netsilingmiut oral tradition, a story told by Samik reports that:

> malerualiŋme nunaqA·rtualo·galuAramik nuna·ER-
> At Malerualik they once had a large settlement, but the land
> tauʃut   suna piblugo tusa·manäŋ·icɔq. nu-
> was taken from them what for has not been heard. But
> na·ERtaublutiŋɔq qima·lERamik
> when the land was taken from them, it is said, and they ran away,
> ima tɔrLulaʃunaluit:
> this they cried:
>
> ʽmalERuarLugitle sunasuArpäk·abtigo, male-
> *'By keeping on following them we used to hunt, by keeping*
> ruArLusiukle sunasuArpagumatlra·'jaivArse!' tuktut
> *on following them you must now do your hunting!'* They meant
> piblugit.
> the caribou. (426, emphasis added)

Louis Uqsuqituq's (Repulse Bay) account, however, pulls no punches: "before there were any Inuit, the first people were called Tuniit. They were strong, but the Inuit killed them and took the land away" (qtd. in Brody, "Land Occupancy" 186).

A people who were powerful, yet lacking in technological advancements, who were driven from their land, who disappeared, and who entrusted the newcomers with their legacy: this discourse is oddly familiar. Indeed, the body of Tuniit stories has many parallels with European colonial representations of Indigenous peoples.[20] This may place contemporary readers—who are likely under some degree of influence from postcolonial studies—in a difficult position; as Chamberlin writes: "postcolonialism is…extremely uncomfortable addressing what might be called the internal colonialisms of a tradition" ("From Hand to Mouth" 134). In the case of European colonization, dehumanizing characterizations of Indigenous peoples have the effect of validating the newcomers' claim to the land; as such, they laid the foundations for a new nation. Yet the characterizations of Tuniit in

Inuit stories, though invented to offset the humanity of the "real" people, are by no means straightforward. For one thing, in the versions quoted above, it can at times be extremely difficult to determine the tone in which the story is told. When Louis Uqsuqituq stated that the Tuniit "were strong, but the Inuit killed them and took the land away," he may have been speaking with pride, or with sadness (qtd. in Brody, "Land Occupancy" 186). While reading a translated and decontextualized fragment, we are unable to determine which. Part of the difficulty of interpretation, then, lies in the challenge of encountering oral tradition on the page, particularly when reading across a cultural divide. The decision as to whether Uqsuqituq is speaking of the demise of the Tuniit with regret or with relief, however, need not be paralyzing; rather, the possibility of multiple meanings is appropriate and natural for such a varied tradition of stories. It adds layers of nuance to the Inuit understanding of Tuniit, and therefore to the Inuit articulation of self. Indeed, I would argue that within the body of Tuniit legends there exists a tension between antagonism and sympathy, between differentiation and identification. In short, there are moments where the boundaries between Inuit and Tuniit—the boundaries of the nations—become blurred.

The story "Tunijjuaq" ("Big Tuniq") by Joe Patiq (Rankin Inlet), which was published in a 1987 edition of *Inuktitut* magazine, contains an interesting comment on the nature of encounters with Tuniit: "It is said that when you meet them you forget them as soon as you part. You cannot remember anything about them.... When an Inuk remembers and starts to tell about it, happy to be telling about meeting such a being, the person just ends up crying a lot. It is said that the person will start to say, 'Look, I met this...' then right away the person will start to cry" (39–40).[21] This passage demonstrates the complexity of Inuit representations of Tuniit. If a person meets a Tuniq, Patiq tells us, he or she will not be able to tell others of the encounter; once they part, the Inuk will mysteriously begin to forget. This forgetting may be a symptom of a lack of understanding; after an encounter with the unfamiliar, the teller discovers that he or she lacks the ability to represent it. It sounds, however, as if this affliction may be a measure of the Tuniit's own powers of self-preservation: just as they flee to avoid encounters with Inuit,[23] they have the ability to slip from memory as well. Such a skill would ensure that their image remain autonomous, rather than at the mercy of strangers' re-imaginings. Patiq goes on to say that even when the Inuk does remember the meeting, he or she is once again mysteriously silenced—this time by the sudden onset of weeping. The cause of this sorrow is unclear, and possibly multifold. Perhaps the weeping is both a cause and a symptom: the teller is both struck dumb by grief and grieving at his or her inability to tell the tale. After all, crying here constitutes another kind of forgetting, as the tale will be lost if it cannot be passed on. This idea of forgetting, then, evokes the central trope in Tuniit stories: their fleeting nature, and their tendency to disappear. Patiq's statement can thus be read as a sample of literary criticism, as it foregrounds the challenge of remembering and of *representing* the ones who came before.

Perhaps it is appropriate that the teller's only articulation is of his sorrow—that speechlessness is caused by tears, rather than uncontrollable laughter, or maybe a sudden drowsiness. Tuniit stories, after all, are often sad stories. As seen in the examples given above, they are usually stories of exile and of death. Perhaps, then, the teller grieves simultaneously for both the remembrance of the Tuniit as well as for the forgetting. In any case, the result is that in place of a story about Tuniit, a profound sorrow is conveyed. Even if the teller is trying to describe the defeat of an enemy, he or she expresses an involuntary sympathy and cannot help but identify with the subject of the tale. As Patiq's statement indicates, Tuniit stories are heavily nuanced and often contain multiple and conflicting attitudes toward the first people. At times, Tuniit are fearsome enemies, barely human; elsewhere, they are almost kin.

When I first went to Pangnirtung in the summer of 2007, one of my fellow *qallunaaq* classmates had an interest in Tuniit, particularly in the various theories of their disappearance. As I mentioned earlier, some believe that the Inuit and Tuniit most likely intermarried, and that the Tuniit were gradually assimilated into Inuit culture (Qitsualik, "Bones"; Sutherland 11–56); however, this is not a hypothesis that is readily entertained by the Tuniit stories of the oral tradition. Nonetheless, this student had made a habit of discussing it with local people, asking, "don't you think it's possible that the Tuniit and Inuit intermarried, and so—*that your ancestors might be Tuniit?*" On this particular occasion in the kitchen, a young man replied rather emphatically to the student's suggestion: "I am not a Tuniq!" Yet a few weeks later, at the campsite called Sannirut just outside the mouth of the Pangnirtung fjord, elder Joanasie Qappik was speaking about the four types of *inuksuit*, some of which were made by the people who inhabited the land before the Inuit. He told us (with the help of our interpreter Marie Uviluq) that one of their old campsites was nearby, and before we knew it we had piled into the boats and were heading out into the sound. Ten or fifteen minutes along the shoreline, we got out and walked a short way, over a rocky beach, through a boggy, low-lying field. Impossibly, the bleached remains of a large tree were resting there. We stopped on the hillside in an area scattered with large rocks. I could see no signs whatsoever of human habitation, until Joanasie pointed out that we were in fact standing over the remains of a house. Suddenly it became clear—the oval-shaped ring of stones, the raised sleeping platform, the entranceway. Joanasie and Uviluq, along with Jaco Ishulu-taq and Noah Metuq, began telling us about the people who had built these houses. They were very strong, as we could see from the size of the stones they had moved. Noah mentioned that they used to sleep with their feet up against the wall to make them lighter—faster—and that this was why the bed platforms were so short. One of the students asked Joanasie how he knew about this place, and Uviluq translated his answer: he knew about this place because this was his country, and he knew it intimately. As for the way these people lived, Uviluq said, he knew "by instinct." They had no metal tools, and no guns, but they had been extremely resourceful, and they had thrived.

In the first incident, the idea of Inuit having been descended from Tuniit was likely offensive because it was informed by a tradition of storytelling that describes the first people as timid, slow-witted, technologically inferior, and ul-timately doomed to extinction. In the second story, however, there was no trace of derision that I could detect; rather, those ancient people were spoken of with admiration and perhaps even with a sense of kinship. This sense of connection or sympathy with Tuniit, interestingly, is almost as common as the character-izations of the first people as primitive and beast-like. In fact, there are many accounts in which the firm lines of differentiation between Inuit and Tuniit be-come blurred. In an article entitled "In the Bones of the World," Rachel Qit-sualik describes Inuit and Tuniit as long-lost cousins who failed to recognize one another. "It is interesting," she says, "that Inuit tradition has always referred to the Tunit as a separate people—to be completely honest, a separate species altogether, when in fact there is a great deal of archaeological evidence to dem-onstrate that Inuit and Tunit derive from the same root culture." Joanassie Ilka-lee of Qikiqtarjuaq (Broughton Island), meanwhile, recognizes the humanity of the first people: "I've heard that Tuniit ran to the north," he says, "away from this part of land, because of war. *Yes, they were Inuit*, but they were very strong people" (qtd. in Brody, "Land Occupancy" 186, emphasis added).

Other Inuit accounts likewise suggest a link between the ancestors of the contemporary Inuit—the Thule—and the Tuniit. Qikiqtani Inuit Association has created an online compilation of the characters in Inuit legends, and the section on the Tunit/Tunitjuat contains the following statement, which seems to combine both the sense of derision and of association found in Tuniit stories: "If you ever come across a thick and strong person dressed in skins and *using the tools of our ancestors*, it might be the Tuniit! If this being speaks to you, answer slowly and don't use big words" (Qikiqtani, emphasis added). The reference to the ancestors in this context is somewhat surprising; it emphasizes the intellectual inferiority of Tuniit, yet suggests that they live in ways that parallel the lifestyle of the Thule. It is highly unlikely that this is meant as a slight toward the ancestors; rather, it seems to subtly acknowledge a certain esteem for the first people. The Tuniit, like the Thule ancestors, lived on the land without the convenience of European products, such as guns or gasoline. This in itself earns the respect of many contemporary Inuit, especially in a time when there is a resurgence of interest in the *inummariit*—the *real* Inuit, or those who have a strong knowledge of Inuit traditions and skills. Rachel Qitsualik points out that "in the story of Inuit meeting Tunit, west meeting east, it is the Tunit who are most 'traditional'" ("Bones"). In this context, then, the Tuniit take on a new significance; as "traditional" people, they become a source of pride. As such, "when the Inuit of today tell their stories, talk about the past and about the first occupants of the Arctic, they are also talking about themselves" (Brody, "Land Occupancy" 186).

This blurring of the boundaries differentiating Inuit from Tuniit can also be observed in the varying forms of particular stories. The second Tuniit story told to Rasmussen by the Netsilingmiut, for instance, describes a lazy Tuniq who, instead of hunting, would lie down and rub his *kamik* (boot) soles against a stone, thereby creating the impression that he had been walking all day (Rasmussen, *Netsilik* 426–7). However, when Maurice Métayer copied down this story from the "Copper Eskimos" (people of the Kitikmeot or Central Arctic region) the main character was not a Tuniq, but an Inuk—a "lazy son-in-law" (*Tales from the Igloo* 113). Now, it is not clear which version of this story came first—perhaps it was a story about a lazy Inuk, who was replaced by a Tuniq when the story travelled east. Or perhaps the original Tuniit identity of the character was lost, and he became marked merely as lazy, rather than as Tuniq. In either case, this shift in the identity of the protagonist further demonstrates the malleable nature of the classifications "Inuit" and "Tuniit."

Perhaps it is this fluctuating sense of difference between Inuit and Tuniit that allows Patiq's storyteller (the one who could only weep when trying to recall the Tuniq he or she had met) to find his or her words again. After all, although the representation of Tuniit is said to be prevented by forgetfulness and weeping, the very existence of Tuniit stories indicates that some tellers must have been able to break the spell. Patiq himself demonstrates this incongruity: he writes of the impossibility of remembering and telling, and then moves seamlessly into a dry-eyed rendition of a Tuniit tale. Perhaps this is because the tellers recognize that the stories they are telling are not really about Tuniit, but (as Brody says) about themselves ("Land Occupancy" 186). The Tuniit of the stories, then, are not "real" Tuniit; they are constructed characters who work to contribute to an articulation of Inuit identity. As such, while the sense of connection between Inuit and Tuniit may seem antithetical to the process of describing a distinct national Inuit group, I would argue that it is a strategic identification: it is another means of articulating Inuit nationhood. By establishing a sense of kinship with the first people, Inuit storytellers represent themselves as the inheritors of Tuniit territory—as another manifestation of the original people.

Despite all of their complexity, though, Tuniit stories challenge contemporary audiences with their unsettling resemblance to the very colonial rhetoric and mimetic strategies that have been inflicted upon contemporary Inuit. Yet to shy away from the problematic or "colonial" aspects of Tuniit stories is to play into the idea that pre-colonial Indigenous societies were peaceful utopias, without their own complex histories of political conflicts and alliances. And this, I would argue, amounts to yet another erasure of Indigenous politics. We should be cautious, however, about constructing an unproblematized comparison between Inuit and European colonizers; after all, it is debatable whether the Thule Inuit, following game into the East and engaging in intermittent conflict with local people in 1000 CE, constituted a colonial force. Unlike the Europeans, Inuit were not extracting resources from the new territory to support the economy of a distant motherland. To imagine Thule Inuit as a colonial force, furthermore, is to use European colonization as a fallback referent for all other land-centred conflicts, regardless of their historical period or cultural context. Indeed, in light of the extent of European colonial violence and wrongdoing, international Indigenous conflicts have often been eclipsed; Indigenous societies are often cast as the victims, rather than the instigators, of conflict and war. However, the idea of pre-colonial North America being a peaceful paradise—although tempting— is ultimately disempowering, as it assumes that both politics and the idea of nationhood are European imports. One function of the Tuniit stories, problematic though they may be, is to prove otherwise.

THIS IS NOT A TUNIQ

I would like now to turn to a contemporary telling of a Tuniit tale—the short story "Skraeling" by the Igloolik writer Rachel A. Qitsualik—and to examine its critical engagement both with the classic representations of Tuniit and with the process of nation-building more generally. The setting for "Skraeling" is Baffin Island in 1000 CE—the era in which the Thule Inuit were beginning to move into the Tuniitlands. Qitsualik begins by contextualizing this time period; she describes the concurrent goings-on in a variety of locations around the world: the Mayan empire, Egypt, Ghana, China, France, Russia, Norway, and Denmark. These are times, she implies, in which many young nations are coming into being and struggling with other groups for dominance. By providing her story with this international context, she effectively removes it from "prehistoric" times (read: the time before Europeans were present), which is where some readers might automatically place it. As the ITK publication "Inuit History and Heritage" declares: "when we speak about the origins and history of our culture, we do so from a perspective that is different from that often used by non-Inuit who have studied our past. For example, in our culture we do not divide the past from the present so we do not like to use terms such as prehistory. Our history is simply our history and we feel that the time has come for us as Inuit to take more control over determining what is important and how it should be interpreted" (4). Qitsualik, in agreement, emphasizes the idea of the Inuit people as a young nation engaged in the process of defining themselves, exactly like the other "great" civilizations referenced.

Qitsualik's main character is Kannujaq, a young man travelling alone, eastwards, into the land of the legendary Tuniit. Kannujaq has heard stories of these other people, as well as of the "Iqqiliit" (Indians), who live among the trees in the West. When Kannujaq first finds himself in Tuniit country, he is extremely apprehensive. Even the sight of the *inuksuit*, raised in order to direct the caribou into kill zones, gives him the chills (37). This sensation is only intensified by a sudden chorus of wolf howls and the realization that it is the Tuniit who are howling, trying to drive the caribou. Notably, Tuniit are not visible at the beginning of the story; rather, their presence is indicated by simulations: the *inuksuit*—stand-ins for humans[23]—and the mimicry of wolf song. Not only does this removed presence evoke the mysterious and elusive nature of the Tuniit characters, it subtly hints that even the Tuniit who do appear to Kannujaq may not be real, but rather may likewise be imitations of Tuniit—simulations based on legend and filtered through the words of storyteller and author alike.

Kannujaq's understanding of the Tuniit is based on what he has heard in stories: "Tunit—while immensely strong—were supposedly cowards, running whenever they saw real people. They might resemble humans, albeit shorter, more squat, but they were little more than beasts" (40). Both relieved and disturbed by this knowledge, he leaves the place where the still unseen Tuniit are hunting, and continues on his journey. With a storm gathering, he is relieved to see a settlement up ahead, but once he is close enough to be noticed, he has the alarming realization that the figures running towards him are not Inuit at all:

"He, like his dogs, no doubt, had assumed this was a human encampment. What a mistake. Now he would be ripped apart by Tunit" (41). What follows is the process by which Kannujaq learns to see through—at least partially—the prejudices and fears that have been instilled in him, and which inform his first impressions. Initially, Kannujaq perceives people with "dark faces twisted up in fear," with "shabby, sooty tops" and "short, squat frames" (41). The community has, in fact, just been brutalized by Viking raid. But when Kannujaq sees the bodies of the dead, "who lay like so many seals dragged up from the shore," he assumes that the Tuniit are involved in some kind of "feud" with another group (42, 43). "*This is a place of murder*," he thinks, suggesting—despite the evidence—that the Tuniit are the killers, rather than the victims (42, emphasis in original). The grief of the survivors, rather than being humanizing, seems to only heighten Kannujaq's sense of the Tuniit's uncivilized behaviour, as all around him people weep, stagger, and clutch (43, 47). Even those who seem to have some control over themselves nonetheless fall short of civilized: the boy who attempts to speak to him is incomprehensible and overly aggressive, while the village leader Angula is corpulent, tyrannical, and clumsily pretentious (41, 43, 50).

After these initial perceptions of barbarism, however, Kannujaq gradually begins to rethink his first impressions. The story progresses via moments of realization, as the Inuk begins to perceive that not all aspects of Tuniit society are unfamiliar. Since Kannujaq arrived, the young boy has been attempting to speak to him, but the Tuniit dialect is too foreign. However, as Kannujaq witnesses the chaotic state of the community, the word that the boy has been repeating at last becomes clear: "*He's saying 'Help,'* Kannujaq suddenly realized. *It's 'Help'*" (43, emphasis in original). Such moments of clarity and understanding are layered over and under Kannujaq's impressions of primitiveness. Gradually, though, the glimpses of Tuniit humanity become more frequent. As he watches the young boy weep over the body of a murdered friend, Kannujaq thinks, "*A dead person was not very much like a seal, after all*" (45, emphasis in original). Although struck by the Tuniit's strangeness, Kannujaq comes to see that "*they are human, after all*" (46, emphasis in original).

In writing this encounter, characterized as it is by Kannujaq's oscillating impressions of the Tuniit, Qitsualik reproduces the opposition that is present in the Tuniit stories of Inuit oral tradition: she alternates between depicting Tuniit as unavoidably primitive and different and as nearly human—even sympathetic. As Kannujaq begins to gain understanding of the Tuniit beyond what he knows from his people's stories, Qitsualik—it could be argued—offers a critical commentary on the tradition of Inuit representations of Tuniit. The Tuniit of Inuit stories, she acknowledges, are not fully developed characters, and there is a humanity and a complexity to the first people that is beyond the scope of outside depictions. Yet although Qitsualik recognizes this shortcoming, she does not attempt to rectify it in her own story, indeed, there are no fully developed, "human" Tuniit characters in "Skraeling." The young boy Siku turns out to be the son of an Inuk mother and a Viking father. Qitsualik creates sympathy for Kannujaq, for the boy, and for both of his parents; meanwhile, the Tuniit remain in the background, largely un-narrated. Perhaps Qitsualik recognizes the impossibility of fully representing the Tuniit, as her attempts will always be second-hand, based on Inuit stories, archaeological data, or her own imaginings. The focus of her tale reaffirms the message of the earlier accounts of the first people: that Tuniit stories are in fact Inuit stories.

These mimetic limitations are appropriately reflected in Kannujaq's own inability to completely shed his prejudices toward the people he is visiting. Although Kannujaq comes to recognize the humanity of the Tuniit, he persists in viewing them as timid and incapable—almost childlike. While this may be problematic, I believe that it is also intentional. Because the opinions of Qitsualik should not be confused with those expressed by her main character; she might even be understood as writing a commentary on the difficulties of overcoming cultural prejudice. For all his good intentions, after all, Kannujaq is a kind of Inuk cowboy. Out of a sense of pity for the poor Tuniit, he stays to solve the community's problems. He kills the despotic Tuniq leader Angula in self-defence, and then teaches the people how to defeat the marauding Vikings with guile: by drugging and then ambushing them. In the meantime, Kannujaq learns the story of the boy's mother, Siaq, who stands out immediately amongst the Tuniit: "Kannujaq saw the first beautiful thing that he had seen since coming here. It was a woman, one with eyes like dark stones beneath sunlit water… This was no Tunik! This was a woman of his own kind" (51). Apparently, Siaq's husband had died, and she was beginning to starve when the Tuniit found her. She was taken in by them but made to work for the cruel Angula, who valued her superior sewing skills. At the story's end, when Kannujaq offers to take her away, Siaq refuses, saying "that she was no longer comfortable among her own" (65). In other words, she has "gone Tuniq."

When one considers the plot from this angle, it reads remarkably like an Arctic *Dances with Wolves*. The lone hero visits a misunderstood and exotic people, assists them with their struggles, dazzles them with his foreign goods, and falls for a woman of his own kind—a sweet surprise in an unfamiliar place. At the end, the tone of nostalgia dwindles into a poignant sense of the impending downfall

of the host community. The "wolves" whom Kannujaq is "dancing" with here signify both of the non-Inuit peoples in the story. At the beginning, as you may recall, Kannujaq hears the Tuniit imitating wolves, and shudders at their beast-like
behaviour (39–40). Later in the story, the Vikings are referred to as wolves, prey-
ing on the herd of helpless Tuniit "caribou," and Kannujaq kills them in the same
way that his people hunt wolves—by using their own greed and gluttony against
them (61). The reason for this association between Tuniq and Viking becomes
apparent at the end of the story, when Kannujaq is haunted by the image of the
Viking leader floating away on his ship, helpless and alone, unable to manoeuvre
the vessel by himself. The Tuniit will likewise disappear, Qitsualik tells us, to exist
only in the legends of the Inuit (66). Notably missing in this account, of course,
is any mention of possible Inuit responsibility in the disappearance of the Tuniit.
Elsewhere, Qitsualik has imagined that the Tuniit had simply assimilated into
Inuit culture, attracted by "the benefits of 'Thule' cultural innovations" ("In the
Bones"). "It is possible," she says, "that many of the Tunit themselves did not care,
embracing the Inuit lifestyle until the end; until those last few Tunit wept when
they could no longer remember the old songs sung by their great-grandparents."
In this account, the Tuniit seem to be largely responsible for their own decline.
Either that, or they are victims of an inevitable assimilation: a side effect of an
encounter with a more technologically advanced culture.

Once again, the temptation here is to view the Tuniit story as a colonial ana-
logue. And in this case, for once, the association may be appropriate, because
a critique of colonial tactics is undoubtedly one of the aims (or results) of this
story. It is unlikely, after all, that Qitsualik would have failed to notice the similarity between Kannujaq's feelings about the Tuniit and *qallunaat* attitudes toward
Inuit; after all, Qitsualik grew up witnessing the European colonization of the
Inuit homeland. Her depiction of Kannujaq's misconceptions and continued cultural bias, therefore, might be read as a reflection on the dangers and challenges
of cross-cultural encounters more generally. Europeans, after all, are present in
this story not only in the form of the murderous Vikings, but in the cultural
makeup of the readership, with which Qitsualik is in constant negotiation. In her
preface to the story, for instance, she declares that she is quite purposefully *not*
providing a great deal of autoethnographic information, because, she says, "if
the reader wants to understand a people, he or she has to live with those people
for a while. And a story is the ultimate magic by which this may occur" (36).
Throughout the story, then, Qitsualik works to maintain an Inuit perspective
and to not cater to the understanding of her non-Inuit readers. That said, the
story is peppered with explanations, whether they be translations of Inuktitut

terms[24] or more lengthy cultural commentaries.[25] This constant awareness of the gaze of *qallunaat* readers makes European colonization part of—or at least analogous to—the subject matter of the story.

In view of the long history of *qallunaat* misrepresentations of Inuit, stories such as "Skraeling" become instruments by which Inuit articulate their own identity as a people. The Tuniit, meanwhile, become a tool to facilitate this process. It may seem ironic that in order for Inuit storytellers to articulate a sense of self, they have to dehumanize another group. Qitsualik, however, is able to use this irony as a tool in her story; by telling a Tuniit tale to a mainly *qallunaat* audience, she is able to subtly critique the cross-cultural misconceptions that are so prevalent in southern discussions of the North. As readers witness the persistence of Kannujaq's prejudice, they may perhaps recognize the shortcomings of their own assumptions about other peoples. Although classic representations of Tuniit may be problematic, Qitsualik demonstrates the way that they may be used to simultaneously establish a sense of Inuit nationhood *and* to critique colonial attitudes in general.

At the end of the story, when Kannujaq and Siku are leaving the community (Siku, Qitsualik says, "had never felt comfortable among the Tunit"), the boy asks Kannujaq: "What…am I to say my mother is, if not a Tunik? *What are we?*" (65, 66, emphasis added). "'I don't know,' Kannujaq replie[s]. But he thought about a word his grandfather had used. 'Perhaps we are *Inuit*'" (66, emphasis in original). In this moment, it is clear that although the year is 1000 CE, it is also 1977, when the ICC declared the "oneness" of the Inuit people. One might imagine that Qitsualik is writing an antecedent to the meeting at Barrow—that she is positing a much earlier origin of Inuit national consciousness. Note, however, the difference in tone. The resolution at Barrow was full of certainty and couched in a particular legal style. Kannujaq, however, speaks the Inuit nation into being with words of a casual, speculative quality: "*Perhaps* we are Inuit," he says (66, emphasis added). It is as if he is trying out the term—testing for its active properties. The readers know that he has chosen the right word. But what exactly has Kannujaq conjured with this utterance?

The term "Inuit" is deceptively simple. It is a term whose meaning shifts depending on context, and within these multiple meanings there is a message of nationhood. Spoken in Inuktitut, the primary meaning of "Inuit" is often simply "people," or human beings. It is the plural of *inuk*, "person." In some contexts, then, it can reference humans without specifying their national or cultural origins. But spoken in another context (including when it is used in the English language), the word "Inuit" becomes a marker of ethnicity and therefore a political statement, containing the subtle semantic possibility that those who are not Inuit are not people—not human. As Chamberlin points out, "the names of many native nations…mean 'the people,'" and they carry with them a sense of predominance— of being "*the* people" (*If This Is Your Land* 15). As the Tuniit stories demonstrate, those who are not Inuit are literarily "not human."

Yet the significations of the term "Inuit" do not end there. When Kannujaq first speaks it, the word has little meaning for Siku, other than the idea of being neither Tuniq nor Viking. Kannujaq explains: "it means something like 'those living here now'" (66). This is a definition that Qitsualik has insisted on elsewhere, as well: "Now, I have read too many interpretations of 'Inuit' as meaning, 'Humans' or 'The People'.… However, having been a translator for 30 years, I can guarantee you that 'Inuit' is a specific term. It precisely means, 'The Living Ones Who Are Here.' It denotes a sense of place, of having arrived, a memory that Inuit knew they had kin somewhere else" ("'Eskimos' or 'Inuit'?"). Indeed, the term *innujunga* (composed of the root *inuk* + *-u-* ("to be") + the first person declarative ending *-junga*) can mean, depending on context, "I am a person," "I am an Inuk" (e.g., a member of the Inuit people), and "I am alive." Michèle Therrien, in her book *Le Corps Inuit*, mentions other core meanings of the term: "habitant" and "propriétaire" ("inhabitant" and "owner") (146). Furthermore, in the possessive form *inua,* the word designates the soul (both human and animal, depending on the region) (Therrien 146).[26]

It is difficult for a non-native speaker of Inuktitut to understand the extent to which these various meanings are entertained in the mind simultaneously. The meaning of the term *innujunga* is highly dependent on context and can no doubt be quite straightforward. However, it does seem as if there would be great potential for punning or for subtext—for instance, in declaring "Inuitness," a people might also be asserting their (superior) humanity, or their survival—their state of being alive. As Therrien argues, in Inuktitut "the non-Inuit human being appears de-centred, the linguistic system sets it apart: the terms that designate it do not refer to the idea of humanity" (164). [L'être humain non-inuit apparaît décentré, l'organisation linguistique le situe à part: les termes le désignant ne réfèrent pas à l'idée d'humanité.] As such, she claims emphatically that "through their language, and in reality, Inuit *invade* and *saturate* the field of the human" (164, emphasis added). [Au travers de leur langue, et dans la réalité, les Inuit envahissent, saturent le champ de l'humain.]

Such a thing would be a political coup indeed; however, the idea that the Inuit language holds strangers to be non-human is complicated by the multiple meanings of the root *inuk*. After all, to say that someone *inuunngittuq*, that he or she is not *inuk*, could mean that the person is not Inuit and not a human being, but it could also mean that he or she is *not alive*, and it is frankly unlikely that this connotation is intended. (Similarly, when an Inuk dies, he or she does not lose his/her membership in the nation. A corpse, or *inuviniq*, is a "former person," not a former Inuk, as if the body had somehow changed its ethnicity in its last moments.) Furthermore, as Therrien says, "the foreigner can, in certain circumstances, be promoted to the rank of Inuk" (149). [L'étranger peut, dans certains circonstances, être promu au rang d'Inuk.] As in the peoplehood matrix, "Inuitness" is not fully determined by ethnicity; almost every southerner who has worked in Inuit country has a proud story about the moment when somebody first told them that they were an Inuk—or better, an *inummarik* (a real Inuk). The category of Inuit, then, is not so reified as to be impenetrable, and the boundaries of Inuit peoplehood are not rigid. This use of the term "Inuit," then, is hardly the dehumanization of the Other as practised by expansionist nation-states.

Perhaps this is why Qitsualik is so emphatic about "Inuit" meaning "those living here now" ("Skraeling" 66). Such a definition is inclusive, not jingoistic; technically, it excludes only the non-present and the non-living. And, as Qitsualik says, "it also betrays the fact that Inuit once knew they were not the original peoples of their lands" ("'Eskimos' or 'Inuit'"). Like Qitsualik's story, then, this definition of the term "Inuit" attempts to *acknowledge* rather than to deny the peoplehood of former inhabitants—and perhaps even attests to its own role in their displacement. The term "Inuit" thus refers to a highly complex and self-consciousness nationhood: it defines itself against the foil of subhuman others yet simultaneously acknowledges an affinity with them. These nuances point to the complexities of Inuit peoplehood; to have any hope of understanding it, as Qitsualik demonstrates, one has to go much further back than 1977 or the arrival of the *qallunaat*.

CONCLUSION: THE "PROBLEM" OF INUIT DIVERSITY

Tuniit stories, as I mentioned earlier, are told in the Central and Eastern Arctic; as such, they are not universal to Inuit. Indeed, although we can look to shared tales as evidence of a national consciousness, it would be impossible to find stories which are told in exactly the same way throughout the Inuit homeland, and which therefore encapsulate a homogenous Inuit identity. However, I would argue that homogeneity is not essential to the literary articulation of Inuit nationhood. The more important national trait is the tradition of telling of stories that work to define Inuitness by raising the spectre of Otherness. The classic and contemporary Tuniit stories thus point to a tradition of self-articulation that *is* common to all Inuit groups. I would argue, furthermore, that national self-definitions based on a shared difference from Others might even allow for more flexible *internal* definitions of national identity: Inuit can maintain all kinds of regional differences while still agreeing on their shared distinctness from Tuniit, Allait, and Qallunaat. This, therefore, has the potential to be a nationhood, and a national unity, that does not necessarily demand homogeneity.

Still, if Inuit stories are so diverse and regionally specific, why emphasize their commonalities? Why is cohesion—whether of a people, or of a literature—so politically compelling? In other words, why does a monolithic tradition get more attention than a fragmented or miniscule one? Is it part of an aesthetic sensibility—a desire for narrative unity? Or is it pure military strategy: a nation that spans four countries is formidable, and the same goes for its literature; that kind of breadth, we think, must equal value, or at least a respectable design. If nations and literatures are large and organized enough, then it is clearly unwise or impossible to ignore them. On the other hand, the current need for cohesion—or a broad view—in studies of Inuit literature might simply be a side effect of the material's obscurity in the mainstream. The possibility of learning about Inuit literary traditions might be appealing to many students, especially with the groundwork laid by Indigenous studies and Igloolik Isuma Productions.[27] However, the availability of Yupiit, Iñupiat, Inuvialuit, Nattilingmiut, Aivilingmiut, Iglulingmiut, Nunavimmiut, Nunatsiavummiut, or Kalaallit literatures for study might be a bit overwhelming for most southern students; indeed, it might send them back to the comforting embrace of Milton or N. Scott Momaday.

Robert Warrior, in his discussion of Indigenous literary nationalism, points out that "[Edward] Said understood nationalism as something problematic, but also something necessary to the mobilization of groups of people toward political goals" (*American Indian Literary Nationalism* 180). The imagining of literary traditions can be similarly strategic; this we know already from reading national literary histories, which play a key role in affirmations of nationhood. However, the danger is that in articulating national literatures strategically—in order to resist the assimilationist tactics of the colonial nation-states—critics may inadvertently downplay the diversity that exists *within* Indigenous traditions. The dangers of emphasizing coherence and unity exist whether the critic is imagining nations or literatures; indeed, the possibility of creating totalizing narratives is one that literary history as a discipline has struggled with.[28]

Stories from the various regions of Inuit Nunaat do have remarkable similarities; this alone might indicate the possibility of a unified vision of the literature. However, attempts to make stories from one region harmonize with stories from another will always require some selective listening—and will, by necessity, downplay the unique cultural and political contexts of the different regions. A more acceptable strategy for a study, therefore, might be to consider the way in which the form and function of the literature—rather than its content—remain consistent. As works of Inuit literature from different regions and historical periods endeavour to describe what it means to be Inuit, they are involved in the process of nation building. And this is the thread that might pull them together—or if not together, at least in the same direction.

The idea of an Inuit nation may not be the primary political framework of Arctic communities; indeed, it might only flicker to life in moments of encounter, as people recognize their differences from others or their similarities to each other. The rest of the time, it might be the more tangible, local realities that take precedence: the questions of Nunavut identity, of Labrador dialect, or of Alaskan oil-drilling. But those occasional moments of unification—that theoretical sense of peoplehood, or nation—might be justification enough for an Inuit literary nationalism. Indeed, let's not forget that this tying together—this search for connective sinews, or threads[29]—is strategic, ultimately, as nationalisms always are. Like the ICC's declaration of unity, the idea of a coherent Inuit literary tradition has the potential to confer a sense of sovereignty onto Inuit literature, and to "re-affirm [its] right to self-determination" (ICC). In other words, this kind of study might encourage students and scholars to recognize Inuit literature as an autonomous aesthetic and political tradition, equipped with its own critical methodologies.

The usefulness of the narrative of Inuit unity—or nationhood—does not negate the need for specific, regional studies that take the full complexity of local history and geography into account. I look forward to celebrations of the literary traditions of the Inuvialuit Settlement Region, of Igloolik, or of Cumberland Sound. Yet in an age where southern power-holders continue to look north and see vacant polar landscapes, isolated communities, and exploitable resources, it remains important to point out that the Inuit homeland—despite its diversity—is a region united by shared intellectual traditions. And as the following chapters demonstrate, these traditions contain a series of principles that can guide understanding and encourage many readers to question their own first impressions. Students of Inuit literature would do well to pay attention to these teachings; otherwise, like Purdy's Dorsets, they may be doomed to recreate the same tired image, sadly repeating their only song.

TWO.

"TAGVANI ISUMATAUJUT"
[THEY ARE THE LEADERS HERE]
Reading Unipkaaqtuat, *the Classic Inuit Tales*

It is an assumption that understanding sophisticated oral traditions comes naturally to the sympathetic ear. It doesn't. Just as we learn how to read, so we learn how to listen; and this learning does not come naturally.

—J. Edward Chamberlin, *If This Is Your Land, Where Are Your Stories?*

Native languages, traditional stories, and written texts contain incredible insights into what it means to be a human being, what it means to write, and what it means to participate in a thinking world. On all of the ideas cultural theory seeks to understand, to deconstruct, or to reconstruct, our traditions have much to say.

—Lisa Brooks, "Digging at the Roots: Locating an Ethical, Native Criticism"

INTRODUCTION: EIGHT INUIT MYTHS

In the winter of 1950, a man named Thomas Kusugaq told eight *unipkaaqtuat*—eight "myths," or traditional stories—to Alex Spalding, a Hudson's Bay Company clerk working in Repulse Bay (Aivilik/Naujaat). These stories include one about the blind boy whose sight is restored by the loons, about the unlucky hunter whose fortunes are changed when he earns the help of a bear spirit, and about the quick-tempered hero Kiviuq, and his long journey far from home.[1] They were eventually published in 1979 as *Eight Inuit Myths: Inuit Unipkaaqtuat Pingasuniarvinilit*—or Canadian Ethnology Service Paper No. 59—as a part of the National Museum of Man (now the Canadian Museum of Civilization) Mercury Series. It is one of the rare collections of Inuit stories that includes the text of the original Inuktitut telling, along with two English translations—one "morphemic," and one "literary." Unfortunately, *Eight Inuit Myths* was never meant for wide distribution. With its drab, bureaucratic cover, it can be found primarily in university libraries (where it often does not circulate) and is long out of print. And while this obscurity may have saved Kusugaq's stories from the kind of rigorous editing that might be thought necessary to prepare them for mainstream audiences,[2] it has also caused a valuable resource to go largely unnoticed.

As the editor of this collection, Spalding appears to be interested in Kusugaq's stories at least partially as linguistic evidence—or perhaps as language lesson. In the preface, Spalding explains that "while these myths were related to me in Aivilik (Repulse Bay) dialect, the dialogue or speech of the mythical characters was most often given in Nassilik (Pelly Bay, Boothia, King William Is.) dialect and, because of this, the glottal stop (') was sometimes employed where normally it would be absent if speaking *Aivilingmiutitut*"[3] (vi). This kind of commentary seems to be aimed at readers who have some background in Inuktitut linguistics. Likewise, Spalding's morphemic parsing, while of great use to Inuktitut-language learners, is not the kind of feature usually found in translations of literary texts.[4] Spalding's preface, however, actually devotes very little time to linguistic commentary; instead, he crosses into the field of literary criticism,[5] reflecting at length on the aesthetic value and meaning of Kusugaq's stories. "The quality of these myths," Spalding says, "is of the first magnitude or the first water. They come bathed from a depth of the human spirit where the most grievous travail and the most glorious achievement of a people are complemented and fused with one another, where the banal and the profane is raised to the level of the special and the miraculous, and where, embodied in the accounts of everyday pursuits and customs, the most important and mysterious spiritual quests and battles have their rise and fulfillment" (v).

Although Spalding's ear is certainly that of a linguist, he seems to have the heart of a poet. We might think, here, of John Swanton, the young linguist who in 1900 arrived at Haida Gwaii, intending to spend six months studying the language. As Robert Bringhurst describes it in *A Story as Sharp as a Knife*, "The linguist found himself confronted by great art, great devastation and great literature. His teacher had forewarned him to expect the devastation and the visual art as well. It was the literature that took him by surprise. And so for three and a half years he did nothing whatsoever but transcribe, translate and study Haida mythtexts, stories, histories and songs" (13). Alex Spalding seems to have been struck with a similar wonder. "Of the first water"—the phrase he uses to describe Kusugaq's stories—is an old expression from the gem trade; it denotes the highest quality of diamond ("Water"). Spalding reiterates this geological metaphor later in his commentary: "in the words of Shakespeare," he says, "[these myths] have 'suffered a sea change into something rich and strange.' They are surely the diamonds, pearls, and sapphires of the Inuit spirit" (*Eight Inuit Myths* vi). Here, we are led to envision the stories as existing underwater, or underground, and to imagine that they have been forged by mysterious and unseen forces, only now to float to the surface, or to be pulled from the rock. Although Spalding's figures of speech ring strangely and prophetically of the language of resource extraction, and although he seems to imagine Kusugaq's stories as being endowed with a kind of "primitive" purity,[6] his appreciation for the aesthetic calibre of the material is never in doubt.

Spalding went on to earn a PhD in English literature at McMaster University, where he chose to write his doctoral thesis on "Wordsworth as a Pastoral Poet." The year was 1974, and Spalding was fifty years old. After receiving his degree, however, he returned quite quickly to his work in Inuit studies and went on to publish a North Baffin dialect grammar (1979, 1992), a book of poetry entitled *The Polar Bear and Other Northern Poems* (1993), a memoir on his time spent in Repulse Bay (1994), and an Inuktitut dictionary[7] (1998). After Spalding passed away in Toronto in early 2002, his ashes were sent back to Repulse Bay, and that is where he was laid to rest ("Inuktitut Linguist"). When looking back over a life and career so devoted to Inuit language and culture, though, one has to wonder good-naturedly why Spalding chose to spend his years in graduate school studying English Romanticism. Did he ever consider the Inuit literary traditions, which he had spent years listening to and documenting, as a possible dissertation topic? Or did the climate of a Canadian English department in the 1970s make it necessary for him to devote his research to the work of a canonical writer?[8]

There was a time when traditional Indigenous stories, after all, received comparatively little attention from literary scholars; more often, they were studied by anthropologists not for their artistic merit, but rather to illustrate the features of a society. Indeed, this is the method which Spalding falls back upon after his initial praising of the aesthetics of Kusugaq's tales: "within [these myths] is a whole compendium of practices and customs which *bear authentic witness to their truth to Inuit life*," Spalding says, and then goes on to list their descriptions of distinctive customs, such as communal feasting, contests of strength, and the tattooing of women (*Eight Inuit Myths* vi, emphasis added). He also notes that the stories often contain satire, and that they have a didactic component[9] (vi). In other words, despite his interest in literature (as demonstrated by his later graduate studies), Spalding's evaluation of Kusugaq's stories *as literary works* is somewhat limited. Instead, he attempts an ethnographic reading; he is more concerned with evidence of wife swapping and drum dancing than with the aesthetics of the stories. Yet this is an interpretive lens that makes it difficult to see Indigenous storytellers as creative individuals who are continually re-inventing and extending the traditions that they have inherited. Rather, the tellers appear to be involved in a kind of semi-voluntary mimesis, reflecting their culture and worldview in a series of transparent tales. In a process common to many receptions of Indigenous culture, Art, here, is transformed into artifact.[10]

This chapter explores the challenges and potential of reading *unipkaaqtuat* like *Eight Inuit Myths* as literary texts. As many Indigenous scholars have demonstrated, oral stories function as an aesthetic and critical foundation for many Indigenous literary traditions. They provide scholars not only with crucial information about cultural and aesthetic values and therefore can function as the cornerstone of sovereign Indigenous literary criticisms. Here, I consider one of Kusugaq's stories, "Angusugjuk and the Polar Bears," for the lessons that it contains for readers of Inuit literature. We learn that like Angusugjuk, readers must demonstrate faith in the stories that are told, knowing that they contain important lessons that can be adapted to many circumstances—even the discipline of literary study. Putting this into practice, I consider the 2006 young adult novel by Thomas Kusaguq's son, Michael Arvaarluk Kusugak, which makes use of a Eurowestern genre—the novel—to innovatively expand on the didactic function of *unipkaaqtuat* in a time when Inuit and *qallunaat* alike are in need of good advice.

UNIPKAAQTUAT AS LITERARY TEXTS

An *unipkaaqtuaq* is not a "literary" text—at least, not exactly. Often translated as a "legend" or "myth," the precise identity of this genre is difficult to render smoothly into English. The root of *unikkaaqtuaq*,[11] *unikkaaq-*, means to "narrate," or "tell a story" (Dorais, *Parole* 170). *Unipkaaq* is a fairly general term for "story"; as Peter Irniq says, it "could be any story."[12] *Unipkaalangajunga*, you could say—"I am going to tell a story"—and it could be about the trip you took last week or about a time when your father was young.[13] *Unipkaaqtuaq*, however, is a more specific genre, and as soon as it is mentioned, the definition of *unipkaaq* seems to narrow. The glossaries of the Interviewing Inuit Elders series, for instance, define *unikkaaqtuat* as "traditional stories," "stor[ies] passed from generation to generation," "old stor[ies]," and "very old stories," while the definitions for *unikkaat*, which follow immediately after, are "modern stories" and "stor[ies] of recent origin" (Angmaalik et al. 213; Ekho and Ottokie 136; Attagutsiak et al. 318). As Peter Irniq explains, "Unipkaaqtuat are 'legends' such as Kiviu. They are from another time, at another place."

The distinction here at first seems to be temporal: perhaps *unipkaat* happen in time that people (or their grandparents) can remember, while *unipkaaqtuat* are located in a kind of mythological time, when the world was different? This hypothesis, however, is complicated by the ending that creates the latter term: *-tuaq*. Louis-Jacques Dorais explains that *-tuaq* is "a lexicalized form of *-tu-aqtaq* or *-tuagaq*. *-tuar-* is a frequentative ('does it frequently, or for a long time') and *-taq* or *-gaq* is the passive form. So, *unikkaqtuagaq* [became] *unikkaqtuaq* [meaning] 'which is told for a long time.'"[14] In *La parole inuit: langue, culture, et société dans l'Arctique nord-américain*, Dorais writes that "unikkaatuaq" designates "a good-length story, which recounts events that are either recent, or of a not-very-distant past" (toute histoire de bonne longueur rapportent des événements récents ou remontant à un passé pas trop lointain) (170). Here, the sense of *unipkaaqtuat* happening in the distant past vanishes in favour of a denotation that the story is simply very long. Saila Michael confirms this definition, explaining that an *unikkaaqtuaq* is a story that goes on for a very long time, *regardless* of its temporal setting.

The word "literature" fits imperfectly over this genre not only because "literature" refers specifically to "letters," and therefore to written language; literary scholars have for the most part come around to the idea that their field need not be restricted to the printed page or to the aesthetic productions of only select groups of people. The more challenging issue, I would argue, lies in the fact that *unipkaaqtuat*, like other Inuit genres, exist within their own intellectual framework whose protocols may differ drastically from those conferred by the English word "literature." Jaypetee Arnakak writes that "these longer stories teach knowledge of geography, community, history, and survival. They express what is to be remembered and were usually told to the group as a whole" (*Traditional Stories* 5). When an *unipkaaqtuaq* becomes a literary text, though, it becomes available for particular kinds of reading and engagement—methods that the Academy, for the most part, determines. The problem, then, is that "literature"—like "nation"—remains a foreign term that may potentially skew understandings of the subject at hand.

Yet "literature"—again, like "nation"—has also been a useful term, in that it provides a means (and indeed, an impetus) for scholars to think seriously about the aesthetic and critical value of Indigenous intellectual traditions. This is not a new project; beginning in the late 1960s, scholars like Jerome Rothenberg, Dell Hymes, and Dennis Tedlock—working in a field known as "ethnopo-etics"—devoted painstaking attention to the form of classic Indigenous stories and songs; they have since been criticized for removing the material from its social and political contexts and for failing to acknowledge contemporary Indigenous writing, as if it were somehow less authentic.[15] The 1980s and '90s saw a renewed interest in orality, but critics like Walter Ong were constrained by their sense that oral traditions represented an earlier stage in literary and cognitive development.[16] Successive work (by people like Richard and Nora Marks Dauenhauer, Julie Cruikshank, Simon Ortiz, and J. Edward Chamberlin) recognized that Ong's position was deeply problematic, and grappled instead with the difficulty—and the possibility—of putting oral literatures on the page.[17]

Despite this precedent, Richard Dauenhauer and Nora Marks Dauenhauer (Tlingit) comment on the ongoing "reluctance of the educational establishment to accept contemporary oral literature as serious, adult literature" ("Paradox" 24). In many ways, I believe, this results from the politics of naming. "Oral traditions," as a term, continues to conjure an image of something esoteric and obscure; as Christopher B. Teuton writes, "it now risks becoming mystical dogma disconnected from the contemporary lived experience of a community" (*Deep Waters* xvii). The name "literature," however, has an equalizing function; it works to dismantle the troubling binary between so-called "oral" and "written" traditions and insists that Indigenous traditions be taken seriously by the academic elite. As J. Edward Chamberlin writes: "I know of no other word that catches the way in which language—the medium of literature, after all—figures largely in these traditions…and no other word (than literature) that respects the 'writing without words' in woven and beaded fabric, in carved wood and stone, and in the intricate choreographies of dancing and drama, which are a central part of many performances" (Chamberlin, "Corn People" 72).

Scholars of Indigenous literatures, therefore, have employed the term "literature" strategically, drawing on its connotations of cultural achievement and sophistication to reconfigure the ways in which Indigeneity has been understood by the academy. Indigenous scholars, furthermore, work to counter the assimilative influence of the academy and its disciplines by formulating alternatives to mainstream literary theory, such as the postcolonial and postmodern approaches that have dominated discussions of Indigenous texts since they first made their ways into literary classrooms. Instead, they seek a more *autonomous* criticism—one that takes Indigenous intellectual traditions as its primary referent. In 1993, Kimberley M. Blaeser's (Anishnaabe) essay, "Native Literature: Seeking a Critical Center," spoke to the necessity of finding "a way to approach

Native Literature from an indigenous cultural context, a way to frame and en-
act a *tribal-centered criticism*" (53, emphasis added). The following year, when
Robert Warrior (Osage) published *Tribal Secrets*, he made a point of ground-
ing his interpretations in work by American Indian authors (xvi): Indigenous
critics, he demonstrated, might turn to the work of literary ancestors like Samson Occom (Mohegan) and William Apess (Pequot), rather than to the canonical Eurowestern theorists; in this way, Indigenous literary criticism becomes
self-referential, and increasingly self-sufficient. In *Red on Red*, Craig Womack
continued this project by commenting on the need "to articulate how the oral
tradition provides the principles for interpreting our national literatures" (76).
"When we have looked at enough of these stories," he writes, "we need to ask
ourselves what we have learned from them that might help us formulate interpretive strategies" (*Red on Red* 76).[18] As a result, other Indigenous scholars like
Lisa Brooks (Abenaki), Christopher B. Teuton (Cherokee), and Daniel Heath
Justice (Cherokee), have further demonstrated ways in which traditional stories
"offer crucial interpretive 'keys' that unlock meaning in Native-authored texts"
(Brooks, "Digging" 236).[19]

These scholars, then, have not only adapted the term "literature" to describe
diverse Indigenous intellectual traditions, but they also demonstrate the potential for this strategic renaming to bring about much-needed methodological
changes within Eurowestern disciplines. Rather than being tainted by affiliation with the academy, traditional stories are highly adaptable and continue to
provide important teachings in new contexts. In formulating critical approaches
to Inuit literature, I look here to the *unipkaaqtuat* as they don this new, literary "skin." Elders consistently emphasize the didactic function of *unipkaaqtuat*,
which contain important lessons about ways to live a good life. "If we listen carefully," says Bernadette Patterk (Rankin Inlet), "we'll pick up what we need" (qtd.
in Van Deusen 349). Here, then, I read one of Thomas Kusugaq's *unipkaaqtuat*,
"Angusugjuk and the Polar Bears," for the teachings that it contains regarding the
interpretation of Inuit literatures, both old and new.

"ANGUSUGJUK AND THE POLAR BEARS"
The first step in reading *unipkaaqtuat* is to have a clear sense of where—and to
whom—they belong in the world. The stories may take place in that "time im-
memorial" of traditional tales, but they were told to Spalding in a particular time
and place, under particular circumstances, and by a particular person: Thomas
Kusugaq. This context produces a much different experience than considering

these texts as generalized and dislocated "Inuit stories," which is how many of them have made their appearance in print. On the book's cover, for instance, only Alex Spalding's name appears, as if the great labour—or privilege of authorship—has been in locating and tapping into a source of oral tradition, while the teller, Thomas Kusugaq, is represented more like a natural resource than as a vital, individual interpreter of a tradition. Yet while some may think of Kusugaq as being Spalding's "informant,"[20] Spalding speaks of him primarily as a teacher and friend. In the preface, he recalls that Kusugaq "was...very patient for a young man and carefully explained customs and concepts to me when I showed in my manner that I was at a loss to follow.... Above all, he was my good teacher and I am always in his debt for that" (*Eight Inuit Myths* v).

Thomas (Thomasie) Kusugaq was originally Nassilingmiut,[21] but in 1950, he and his wife Kukik (Theresa Kusugak) were living in Repulse Bay.[22] The area had been a destination for European whalers for hundreds of years; that industry was later replaced by the fur trade and by the art industry. The Hudson's Bay Company had opened a permanent trading post in 1919, and it provided the Kusugaq family with some income, employing Thomas as a handyman and Kukik as a cleaner and washer of furs. They had a son, Arvaarluk (Michael Kusugak), who would later—perhaps not by coincidence—grow up to become one of the best-known Inuit authors and storytellers. In 1950, Kukik gave birth to the couple's second son, Amaujaq (Jose), who as an adult become the president of the Inuit Tapiriit Kanatami. Ten more children would follow. In his spare time, Thomas Kusugaq schooled Spalding in Inuit language and oral tradition; later, the two would collaborate in the production of an Inuktitut dictionary. One by one, the Kusugaq children went away to residential school in Chesterfield Inlet (Igluligaarjuk), and in 1960, Thomas and Kukik moved to Rankin Inlet, where a nickel mine had opened up. The mine closed only two years later, however, and in 1973, Thomas Kusugaq was killed in a boating accident. Kukik survived him until 2003.[23]

The decline of the fur trade in the late 1940s and early '50s led to a shift in administrative policy in the Arctic: while the government had been "promot[ing] traditional economies because it was thought this would avoid the creation of dependency," the loss of the Arctic's major source of economic income meant that "a more interventionist approach" was deemed necessary (Kulchyski and Tester 7). This meant the creation of permanent settlements, and, for the majority of Inuit, the transition off of the land and into a wage-based economy. In Repulse Bay, the year 1950—when Thomas Kusugaq told his eight tales to Alex Spalding—was a time bordering on immense. In this context, Kusugaq's telling of the old stories is a powerful testament to the history, culture, and future of his people.

While Spalding does not provide great detail about the setting or process of his recording (for instance, we do not know whether other Inuit were present during the telling), it is safe to say that his presence—as an informed *qallunaaq*, but an outsider nonetheless—in the audience (or as the audience) would have prompted Kusugaq to adapt his telling to the situation at hand. Spalding describes the narration as follows:

> [Kusugaq] knew these *unipkaaqtuat* by heart, having heard them many times as a child, and gave them to me with all the detail and relish he could bring to it, slowing down or repeating only because of the need to give me time to write. His delivery was spontaneous and enthusiastic and it was obvious that he was grateful and pleased to find someone who was willing to listen and take the trouble to set them down and relish their fine points just as I was grateful and pleased to find someone who would be patient and obliging in the transmission of them and to get them at first hand from a genuine source in the Inuit oral tradition. (*Eight Inuit Myths* 5)

Here, Spalding emphasizes the authenticity of Kusugaq's stories; again, he imagines—like most enthusiastic cultural preservers—that the material he has gathered is of the "first water." Yet we might also imagine the telling as containing specific lessons or information for Spalding, as Kusugaq takes the opportunity to educate the *qallunaaq* visitor. The anthropologist Pamela Stern recounts that during her fieldwork in the NWT community of Holman (now Ulukhaktok), her interviewees tailored their responses to include information that they believed she needed to hear, although they never overtly framed it as advice ("Learning to Be Smart" 511). Likewise, Spalding recalls that "in the course of our discussions on myth and language, [Thomas] brought me up straight when I was silly, teased me when I was over-serious or naive, was annoyed at me when I was over-taxing in my questions, or would just tell me that he couldn't take anymore and go off" (*Eight Inuit Myths* 5). Fortunately for Spalding, the *unipkaaqtuat* are full of lessons about good behaviour, especially—in the story that follows—for people who find themselves in unfamiliar territory.

The first tale in the collection, "Angusugjuk Nanuillu," or "Angusugjuk and the Polar Bears," tells the tale of Angusugjuk.[24] The story goes that he returns home from hunting to find a puppy in his doorway. Taking it inside, he is surprised to see a woman in his house. "*Qiturngara qaijjuk!*" she says, "Bring me my child!" (1). Angusugjuk, seeing an opportunity, refuses to give her the puppy unless she agrees to become his wife. She finally agrees, but after they are married, she exhibits strange behaviour, eating nothing but fat. One day, after being scolded by her mother-in-law, she leaves for the floe edge. Angusugjuk tracks her, noticing that while one of her prints is human, the other is the print of a polar bear. When he finally catches up with her, she is rolling on her back in the snow. She tells him that she is going out into the ocean to visit her relatives. Angusugjuk is determined to go with her, so she lets him ride on her back as she swims out to sea.

Partway through the journey, they reach some solid sea ice, and as they walk on it, the wife tells Angusugjuk that there is land ahead but because there will also be fierce bears, and that he should take her walking stick to defend himself. Thus warned, Angusugjuk rides on her back once again as she swims toward the land. Sure enough, as soon as they arrive at the camp, our suspicions about Angusugjuk's wife are confirmed—her people are bears, and they are coming out of their houses to attack Angusugjuk. He, however, follows his wife's instructions, striking the first bear in the jaws, and causing it to fall on its behind, and then to flee, "nothing but a skull [they say]" (5, 12).[25] After this initial confrontation, Angusugjuk and his wife go to visit her parents,[26] who are the "chiefs"[27]—the *isumatait*—of the community. In order to get a look at Angusugjuk, the other bears all then come to visit, and the biggest one seems to be eyeing him fiercely. And, indeed, as soon as that big bear has gone home, his wife comes to shout that her husband wants to challenge Angusugjuk to a contest of diving for jellyfish.[28] Angusugjuk's mother-in-law, however, advises against accepting this challenge, as "one's face keeps getting covered and because [jellyfish] are extremely ticklish" (13).[29] An alternate contest is proposed—a lifting match—and the mother-in-law advises Angusugjuk to accept, for she will tell him how to win:

> She told him that the big slippery lifting-stone was very round and wickedly smooth, and that there were absolutely no places on it to hold on by. She said, however, that there were four tiny indents on it, enough for two fingernail grips, and that these were the only dents. She said that, when he was about to pick it up, he must pretend to pat the surface of the stone lightly in order to find the little indents and that, when he found them, he was to draw the stone towards himself and carry it forward to the mark. If he was able to bring it back, she said, he was,

first of all, to carry it back and place it in its spot and then run very swiftly to enter the house and to refrain from looking back. (13)

Angusugjuk listens to her instructions, and during the contest, when even the big bear cannot lift the stone, he is able to carry it and place it back on its mark. As warned, he hears the "terrible biting and snapping noises" behind him as he flees to the safety of his in-laws' house (9).

Then, for the third time, the wife of the big bear shouts out a challenge: this time, the game is hunting seals. Once again, the mother-in-law gives him instructions (although Angusugjuk is already a "very great hunter" [12], here, it seems that he has to hunt bear-style and is therefore in need of advice). She tells him that there are three seal breathing holes, and that the big bear will wait over the middle one. Angusugjuk must dive down through the farthest hole, swim past the middle (without coming up for air, where the big bear might nab him), and reach the closest one. There, he must get the "little black thing" from the seal's nest, climb out of the hole, and run quickly towards home without looking back. And, once again, things go just as the mother-in-law said. He grabs the "little black thing" in his teeth, runs home with the "terrible snapping and biting noises" behind him, and gets "a pleasant surprise when he discovered that the little black thing was a seal which his wife placed up on the meat bench" (14). There the story ends, with Angusugjuk having survived the challenges—and even having brought home a meal for his new family.

At first glance, this story may seem to be like the large smooth stone that Angusugjuk must lift: difficult to get a grip on. For southern readers—and perhaps even for some younger or urban Inuit—its events may be strange, and its references unfamiliar. Indeed, the reader or listener, like Angusugjuk, is headed into strange territory—a potentially dangerous place, with different rules and customs. However, Angusugjuk is wise enough to listen carefully to the instructions that he is given, and when he obeys them, he finds that the surface of the lifting-stone is not as smooth as it appears: there are grooves where his fingers can get purchase. Attentive readers, then, will begin to locate fissures in a text—markers of a place where, with a bit of work, one can climb in or get a grip.

As a way of searching for a finger hold, I am going to think first about the ways in which this tale might function allegorically. As I mentioned, Kusugaq told this story in a time of great and often devastating change—the fur trade was declining, and more and more Inuit were being forced to move into permanent settlements, where the government could provide them with welfare services and the churches could educate their children. Interestingly, the story of Angusugjuk is also a parable of man making the transition into a strange new culture. In the village of the bears, there are different rules of behaviour, and the villagers are powerful and dangerous. But Angusugjuk is ultimately able to adapt, and by the end of the story, he has learned the skills that he needs to survive. Having learned a few bear-tricks, he bests Nanualuk (the "Giant Bear") and so maintains his role as Angusugjuk, the "Great Man"—a hunter and provider for his family. The story ends with the image of a stable and prosperous home, as Angusugjuk's wife lifts the seal up onto the meat bench of her mother's house. In the context of Repulse Bay in the 1950s, this is a story of great hopefulness: it prophesies successful adaptations that put conflicts to rest and result in strong, healthy families.

When we recall, furthermore, that Kusugaq's telling of this story was to an outsider, Angusugjuk becomes more than a role model for Inuit listeners; he has a thing or two to teach Spalding as well. Indeed, the tale of Angusugjuk may well have resonated with Spalding, as a fellow stranger in a strange land. Again, we might imagine that Kusugaq was subtly passing on pieces of prudent advice to the young Titirarti (Spalding's Inuktitut nickname).[30] In *Uqalurait: An Oral History of Nunavut*, Paallirmiut elder Margaret Uyauperk Aniksak refers to appropriate behaviour in visiting new territory: "It is said that, often the land is very sensitive to strange people. In the old days people who are strangers to the land used to offer small items as a token of peace. Strangers were required to produce the offering.... So whenever you step foot on a stranger's land, you must produce a small offering. That was our way of living at peace with the land" (Bennett and Rowley 131). No such offering is made by Angusugjuk, but he does display a humility and awareness in new surroundings, and he listens closely to the advice of the local people. By the end of the story, he even seems to have become bear-like, having adapted to customs that are impossible for a human: diving down through seal breathing holes, and catching seals in his teeth.[31] To tell this story to a visitor like Spalding, then, is to remind him to listen carefully, to be adaptive, and to show respect for local ways of being.

Recalling Bernadette Patterk's comment that "if we listen carefully, we'll pick up what we need [from *unipkaaqtuat*]" (qtd. in Van Deusen 349), I would like to experiment with one more allegorical reading—one that reflects my own needs as a *qallunaaq* student of Inuit literature. What happens if we read "Angusugjuk" as a parable for readers and listeners—in other words, for literary critics?

We know from early in the story that Angusugjuk is a reader. As his new wife leaves to return to her people and heads off toward the edge of the floe, she tracks a text into the snow, and it is half-human, half-bear.[32] The woman's writing resonates with the other signs of her bear nature: the fact that she eats only fat (as bears prefer to), her rolling in the snow, her ability to swim long distances in cold water. We might walk for a moment, though, with Angusugjuk as he trails his missing wife. As he follows her tracks, he reads a tale of departure, maybe even of sadness. Most of all, though, he is reading a mystery—how can a woman be half-human and half-bear? For the reader, this riddle is left unresolved throughout the entire story. Although we watch Angusugjuk climb on his wife's back as she swims through the icy waters, and although we learn that her village is a village of bears, we never actually *see* her in bear form—we never hear her bear body described. When Angusugjuk catches up with her at the floe edge, Kusugaq tells us that "*sunauvva sinaani nalajuq*"—"much to his surprise, she is lying on her back at the floe edge"[33] (2). Very notably, he does *not* say "Angusugjuk was surprised to find that his wife *had transformed into a bear*, and was rolling on her back in the snow." She is never actually *seen* walking on one human leg and one bear leg. Her dual nature is instead implied; her tracks seem to be symbolic, not literal. They are a signifier whose meaning seems to escape Angusugjuk, but which titillates the readers, who may be getting an idea of what the protagonist is heading into.

Indeed, readers or listeners familiar with a range of *unipkaaqtuat* will have a much easier time making sense of the events of this tale. As the stories' patterns and motifs begin to emerge and repeat themselves, things that were strange at first soon become the identifying features of a tradition.[34] For example, those acquainted with Inuit storytelling will find a very familiar motif in the opening scene of "Angusugjuk": the wooing of the animal-wife. Often, the protagonist of an *unipkaaqtuaq* will encounter a strange woman who has taken off her animal skin to reveal a human form; the protagonist can then hold the skin as a bargaining chip until the woman agrees to marry him. In the famous "Kiviuq" story (which happens to be the fifth story in *Eight Inuit Myths*), we hear the episode of the fox-wife: Kiviuq returns home to find that a fox is entering his tent while he is out and doing the tasks of a wife (Spalding 55–6, 64–5). She has also hung her skin up to freshen outside. Kiviuq seizes the skin and refuses to return it until she agrees to marry him.[35] This motif is repeated later in the "Kiviuq" cycle, when the hero woos his goose-wife.[36] The story of Angusugjuk is somewhat different, in that the hero is not apparently aware of the animal nature of his love interest (and, instead of her skin, he has her puppy-child). However, the appearance of a strange woman in his house, and the bargaining for her hand in marriage would certainly evoke for many listeners the tales of the animal-wives.

The interconnected nature of the *unipkaaqtuat* also means that while Angusugjuk travels to an unknown place, many of the listeners are headed somewhere familiar—and that place is signposted for them along the way. When Angusugjuk and his wife climb out onto the sea ice—a kind of threshold, or stopover, for the land that is their destination—the wife says: "Down there is the land of my relatives; they are down there now. The ones who come out of the next house are going to be giant bears."[37] [*Taunani nunataqarmat taima ilakka taunaniiliqput. Taima iglumit tugliqpaamit anijuqarniarmat nanualungnik* (Spalding 3).] *Taunani* ("down there") the speech begins, and before the phrase is over it appears again: *taunaniiliqput* ("they are down there now")—a rhythmic reminder of the place that is approaching and of the people who will be met. Lucien Schneider's translation of the word *taunani*, furthermore, adds an element that Spalding's translation is missing: *taunani*, it says, can mean "below there," but also "at sea," or "toward the sea."[38] The land Angusugjuk's wife is referring to is away, further out at sea, deep in the legendary space of the ocean. Imaginatively, the journeying listeners are shifting worlds—about to enter the most mysterious of places. Yet it is a place that they are uncannily familiar with, as the repeated word *taunani* conjures both the direction of the sea and also every tale that has happened down there: the legends of Kiviuq in his kayak, who in a sudden storm is swept far away from home, of the Qalupalik, who comes up from beneath to steal children, of the skeleton-woman, of the narwhal who was once the cruel mother of the blind boy, and of Nuliajuk, or Sedna, the vengeful spirit of the ocean-bottom who traps the sea-mammals in her free-floating hair. "That is where we are going," Angusugjuk's wife says, and the listeners shiver with excitement, or dread. "*They* are down there now."

Angusugjuk—like the listeners—is thus warned of what is coming, and this is a pattern that is repeated throughout the story. Throughout the tale, Angusugjuk spends a good amount of time listening to stories of this kind, as his wife and mother-in-law tell him about the challenges that he will have to face. The events of the story are consistently pre-narrated, and then they unfold—just as it was said that they would. Before both of the contests, Angusugjuk's mother-in-law tells him in detail what will happen, and what he must do to succeed. Yet this plot event is no one-liner; Kusugaq does not just say "Angusugjuk's mother-in-law told him how to defeat the great bear." Rather, we hear *in detail* what she tells Angusugjuk, and then we have the pleasure of seeing her words verified as the challenges unfold—in full detail, again. There goes Angusugjuk to the lifting-stone, and there he finds his grip—now watch as he heaves it forward and wins the challenge, just as she said he would. In this way, a clear lesson emerges: listen to your elders, and take their advice. This is doubly important if you are in unfamiliar territory.

Indeed, this trope of instructions acts as another unifying measure within the tradition; characters in the *unipkaaqtuat* often turn to extraordinary beings for assistance; think, for instance, of the orphan boy Kaujjarjuk training with the spirit of his brother,[39] the blind boy Aningaat being healed by the loons,[40] or the abused wife asking the moon-man for help. In "Ululijarnaat," the version of the latter story told in 1990 by Igloolik elder Hervé Paniaq, the moon-man takes the woman away with him, but he warns her that she will face a series of dangers (MacDonald 220–2). When they reach the moon, he tells her, she will go into a house where an old hag will visit and try to make her laugh: "When that happens she should place her hands under her own *kinniq* [the front flap of a woman's parka] and shape them into the form of a *nanukinniq* [a model of a polar bear] and imitate the sound of the bear" (221). She follows these instructions, and when she makes the sound of a bear the old hag rushes from the house. The woman learns that had she laughed, the old hag would have torn out her intestines. But when she fails to follow the moon-man's final set of instructions—that upon returning home she should not eat anything caught by her husband—she dies, along with her child.

Angusugjuk may know this story, as he never for a moment considers disobeying the instructions that he is given. Indeed, as a reader, Angusugjuk is not highly critical; instead, he exhibits total faith in the stories he is told, obediently grappling with the rock and diving down to capture what he apparently does not realize is a seal. While he listens carefully and follows his in-laws' instructions with diligence, he misses details—or fails to connect different parts of a story. Figurative language, for the most part, seems to pass him by; for instance, when Nanualuk's (the Giant Bear's) wife comes to announce that the third contest will be seal hunting, the word *nassiq* (ringed seal) is used twice (9). The mother-in-law's instructions, however, tell Angusugjuk that he must swim to the first hole and grab the "little black thing" (*qirniqtukulungmik*)[41] (10). Angusugjuk does as she says; he takes the "little black thing" in his teeth, climbs out, runs home, and drops it in the doorway (11). Then, Kusugaq tells us "*Sunauvvaguuq taamna qirniqtukuluk nassiunirmat*"—"*much to his surprise,* they say, that little black thing turned out to be a seal" (11).[42] Somehow, it seems, the rather transparent epithet for "seal" was lost on him.

For me, this is the most perplexing and also the most important moment in the story. Angusugjuk is given a set of instructions that seem bizarre, or at the very least, life threatening (for a human). Admittedly, in a community of bears, the activity of diving down into a seal breathing hole and rooting around in a den could be a very normal activity. While we are not privy to Angusugjuk's thoughts and feelings about the matter, he does not seem to question the instructions or even to wonder what the "little black thing" might be. He seems fully committed to the competition and to following the advice that he has been given. By this point in the story—and maybe also through his *unipkaaqtuat*-based education—he has perhaps come to trust such moments; he knows that his wife and in-laws have everyone's best interests at heart. As students of *unipkaaqtuat,* though, what lesson should we take away from this? How might we put a similar kind of trust into practice?

As a teacher of literature in a southern academic institution, I have learned that it is one of my responsibilities to teach my students critical thinking. As Stephen P. Norris explains, the purpose of teaching critical thinking is "to bring individuals to the point where their beliefs and actions are based justifiably upon reasons that they themselves have arbitrated" (200); in the words of Richard Paul, it cultivates "the free, rational, and autonomous mind" (qtd. in Norris 200). In other words, critical thinking is a way to liberate the student from some of the more oppressive aspect of his/her educational experience, which occasionally demands obedience and acceptance of the teacher's knowledge. I have always framed the practise in this manner, exhorting my first-year students to ask "why?" and to question everything that they read or are told. This liberatory yet highly individualistic practise arguably could be traced through the Enlightenment and back to Descartes, whose methodology of doubt required him to reject any premises that he himself had not rigorously and logically attained (Descartes 12). Likewise, I have hoped to produce students who would question authority, challenge their teachers, and think deeply about the world around them. To me, these principles seemed consistent with the overall goal of decolonizing the university classroom.

It was only when I first went to Pangnirtung, however, that I became aware that the critical practices that I had celebrated might not be universally applicable or appropriate. While several elders in the community are familiar with the learning styles of southern students and have adapted to their manner of doing things, younger Inuit also taught us about appropriate ways of learning from elders, and this did not involve peppering them with enthusiastic questions. Although this is the way in which southern students have learned to demonstrate interest, Inuit education models work differently. "Generally," write Alexina Kublu, Frédéric Laugrand, and Jarich Oosten, "children did not ask elders to instruct them, but the elders took the initiative in preparing and advising them whenever they thought it appropriate. In fact, the great respect in which elders were held often meant that young people were reluctant to pose questions to elders unless they were invited to do so" (Angmaalik et al. 7). Instead, young people were encouraged to learn primarily through observation and practise (MacGregor 46). When elders decide to offer advice—either directly or through storytelling—wise people listen. Emile Imaruittuq of Iglulik tells a story that he heard from Piugaattuk: "He said that when his father was on his deathbed, his mouth became swollen and enlarged. He said he had really swollen lips because whenever an elder tried to counsel him he would always talk back. He told people this so they would always respect older people" (Auplilaarjuk et al., *Law* 116). When asked why young people are no longer listening to elders, Lucassie Nutaraaluk of Iqaluit says, "*Nutaraaluk:* I think education is the root of this. The school children are being taught in English and are taught to ask questions" (Auplilaarjuk et al., *Law* 121).

These protocols, then, like the model followed by Angusugjuk, suggest that the kinds of reading practices that require students and scholars to subject the text to painstaking analysis, to rigorously question its commentators, and to reject the idea of authorial intention may be inappropriate in an Inuit context. However, in hearing this, one should not leap to the conclusion that Inuit tradition requires unthinking conformism and obedience, or—as Richard L. Norris asserts after reading David Olson—that "critical thinking (which makes thoughts the objects of reflection) is essentially synonymous with literacy, in that it is the way of thinking that evolved with the evolution of writing in order to deal with print" and that traditional Inuit were not cognitively capable of analysis (204). The reality is far more complex. The anthropologist Jean Briggs writes at length about the concept of *ihuma* (or *isuma*, in eastern dialects) as she experienced it amongst the Utkuhikhalingmiut of the Central Arctic. "*Isuma*," she writes, "refers to consciousness, thought, reason, memory, will—to cerebral processes in general—and the possession of *isuma* is a major criterion of maturity. Saying that a person has *isuma* is equivalent to saying that she or he exercises good judgment, reason, and emotional control at all times....The possession of *isuma* entitles a person to be *treated as an autonomous, that is, self-governing, individual whose decisions and behaviour should not be directed, in any ways,* outside the limits of the role requirements to which one is expected to conform" ("Expecting the Unexpected" 267, emphasis added).[43]

The social protocols built around this concept thus strike a delicate balance between respecting personal autonomy and heeding the advice of those in a position to offer it. As Briggs explains, "People who have *isuma* demonstrate this fact by conforming voluntarily, by obeying their 'leader' willingly when told to do a task, and, with increasing maturity, by foreseeing the needs and wishes of others and fulfilling them without being asked to do so. At the same time, they will strongly resist, by passive withdrawal or polite circumvention, any encroachment on their legitimate areas of privacy and self-determination" (Briggs, "Expecting the Unexpected" 267). The advice of elders, therefore, does not take a domineering tone; younger people are expected to listen attentively to elders' advice, but they also have to work actively to learn and understand it. When Ann Fienup-Riordan observed a Yup'ik culture camp in southwestern Alaska, she noted that "the youngsters were expected to be responsible for their own learning. According to Paul John, 'Another person can't learn for you, but we should try to learn ourselves from what we heard and try to be attentive as we learn.' As Theresa [Moses] said, 'We are in charge of our own lives'" (Riordan, "We Talk to You" 176).

The quality of *isuma*, as Briggs explains, can also be taken too far. "A person who has too much *ihuma* concentrates too much on one idea, one thought. In its most harmless form such concentration is viewed as 'inconsiderate.' More than one anthropologist who has worked with Eskimos, very possibly including myself, has been characterized by his hosts as *ihumaquqtuuq*, because he put such pressure on them with his continual visits, questions, more visits, and more questions, when the Eskimos would have preferred to work, talk, eat, or sleep, unbothered by the anthropologist" (*Never in Anger* 362).[44] For this reason, she says, "'Why?' is one of the rudest questions one can ask an Utkuhikhalingmiutaq [person of the Utkuhikhalik region]" ("Expecting the Unexpected" 267). Not only does it smack of an impertinent skepticism or an unwillingness to seek out understanding for oneself, but it infringes upon the autonomy of another person's private thoughts.

In the incident of the diving contest, Angusugjuk thus demonstrates an ideal learning experience. Rather than asking questions about what the "little black thing" might be, he makes the decision to follow his mother-in-law's advice. He thus exhibits faith in his elders and relations, but it is not a blind faith. Rather, he translates her words into his own action and experience; by diving down and fetching the seal, he sees for himself that her instructions were sound. That his "surprising" realization—that the thing he has fetched is a seal—does not come until the very end speaks to the importance of personal experience in knowledge acquisition; prior to diving down, he exhibits no understanding of his task or its object, but upon his return, he begins to see things clearly. In this way, he gains a new range of understanding—and a new vocabulary—that will enable him to function in this place; his mode of learning, furthermore, results in good social relationships and provides sustenance for his family.

The strategy that Angusugjuk models for readers of Inuit literature, then, may be challenging for some. Through the story, Kusugaq seems to advocate for a learning style that stresses compliance over criticism, and faith over doubt. While some may label this as "uncritical," a less-ethnocentric way might be to say that Kusugaq's story advocates a reading practise that results in *isuma*: the self-reliance, maturity, and intellectual competence that results from having listened carefully to one's elders. Again, the word used to describe the mother-in-law and her household is *isumataujut*: the ones in charge, or the ones with *isuma* (Spalding 5). Like any reader or listener, Angusugjuk struggles at times, and occasionally misses obvious things. The important point for students to take note of, though, is that even though Angusugjuk at times apparently lacks understanding, he does not let that interfere with his belief in the story; rather, he continues to track and dive for these mysteries, with faith that comprehension— or at least reward—will be forthcoming.

Kusugaq's audience, then, should perhaps learn this same kind of trust. For many readers, the story of Angusugjuk is full of "little black things"—references that go over our heads. Indeed, one of the things that can make classic tales somewhat intimidating to readers is the *strangeness* of their events. There is an episode in the "Kiviuq" story—an extremely long *unipkaaqtuaq*, which tells the tale of a man who travels far from his home—in which Kiviuq comes to the house of a strange old woman. In the version included by Penny Petrone in *Northern Voices: Inuit Writing in English*, the woman is Aissivang ("Spider"); in James Houston's film version of the tale, she is Igutsaqjuaq ("Big Bee [Woman]") (*Kiviuq*). Kiviuq approaches the house to see who is inside, peering in through a hole in the roof. In some versions, he spits on the woman to see what she will do. When she looks up to see where the leak is coming from (or to see why her light has disappeared, making sewing difficult), her eyelids block her vision. Quickly, she takes her *ulu* (women's knife) and slices off her eyelids, popping them into her cooking pot—or, in some versions, straight into her mouth. While this incident may seem discouragingly bizarre, it becomes easier when we realize that this strangeness is part of the story; Kiviuq himself is appalled at this sight, and knows immediately that the woman is dangerous. Far away from home, he is struck by the peculiarity of foreigners, and the reader shares in this sensation.

J. Edward Chamberlin says that "it is the *un*comfortability, the strangeness, that is crucial—the defamiliarization, the alienation, the incompleteness, the indeterminacy, the ungrammaticality—which remind us that the belief, and the knowledge, that we embrace (or that embrace us) are always accompanied by doubt, and that the literariness that we look for in a text is to be found in the strange ceremonies that certify beauty and truth and goodness" ("The Corn People" 68–9). This is not easy to accomplish—especially when academic readers have become adapted to scholarly practices that insist we be unfailingly critical: that we see through discursive constructs and flush out the latent ideologies in everything. Yet *panic* about non-understanding often leads us to make our worst critical decisions, as we search desperately for methodologies that will make quick and easy sense of the unruly text. For students, this kind of relief is our worst enemy—it means the end of struggle, the end of learning.

Angusugjuk is twice confronted with riddles, and both times he is rather delayed in solving them. Riddles, the story says, do not necessarily need to be solved. It is far more important to have faith in the stories, and in the people who tell them, as it is this belief that builds relationships of trust, of mutual responsibility and mutual respect. Audiences need to have faith, then, that although the rock may appear to be smooth, slippery, and unmanageable, there are finger holds in its surface—one simply has to take the time to find them. As readers—especially as readers of ancient tales—we have to listen carefully, pay attention to the signs, and, above all, listen to the *isumataujuit*—the people who know and who are at home in these unfamiliar places.

CONCLUSION: A NEW GENERATION OF UNIPKAAQTUAT

As mentioned above, Michael Arvaarluk Kusugak, Thomas Kusugaq's eldest son, has written a number of very successful books for younger audiences—and also has a reputation as a much-sought-after storyteller. The author of books like *A Promise is a Promise* (with Robert Munsch), *Northern Lights: The Soccer Trails*, and *Hide and Sneak*, Kusugak draws upon the stories of his childhood and adapts them for a mainstream audience. Indeed, unlike most other Inuit writers, Kusugak has a large fan base in southern Canada and around the world; four of Saturn's moons were even named after Inuit characters after a Canadian astronomer read one of his stories ("New Saturn Moons"). While Kusugak makes use of Inuktitut names and vocabulary, his books are written in English and are therefore uniquely accessible to non-Inuit. His first novel, *The Curse of the Shaman: A Marble Island Story*, was published in 2006 by publishing giant

HarperCollins. Within the span of one generation, then, the *unipkaaqtuat* told by Thomas Kusugaq have taken on the new and quite alien forms of children's books and young adult novel: forms that challenge critics to reimagine the shape and trajectory of the Inuit literary tradition.

Kusugak's novel *The Curse of the Shaman* tells the story of Paaliaq, a short-tempered but amiable *angakkuq*—shaman—who inadvertently curses the new-born son of his friend, Qabluittuq ("The-man-with-no-eyebrows"). This takes place in the time before the arrival of the *qallunaat*, when Inuit of the Aivi-lik region were still following the seasonal round, living on the abundant local resources. The novel's light-hearted but detailed account of life on the land emphasizes the strength and stability of Inuit families, in which children are cherished and also carefully taught about good behaviour. When The-man-with-no-eyebrows's son Wolverine is a young boy, he and his wife-to-be Breath listen to her grandmother tell the first episode in the story of Kiviuq, "the great-est man who ever lived" (62). In this story, the grandmother of a bullied orphan boy takes revenge on the community; all of the bullies are drowned in a storm, and only Kiviuq, who has the strength and persistence to continue to flip his kayak upright, survives. "Take heed, Wolverine and Breath," says the storytelling grandmother, "always be kind to orphans.... They have something very power-ful looking out for them" (73).

As in the story of Angusugjuk, this careful attention to the lessons contained in *unipkaaqtuat* serves Wolverine very well. As a young man, he finds a wounded young owl, and instead of killing it, he decides to adopt it; while this action does not fit perfectly with the directive to be kind to orphans, the general principle of generosity to those less fortunate seems to hold. A few years later, when Wolver-ine comes of age, Paaliaq's old curse comes into effect, carried out by the shaman's vindictive *tuurngaq*, or animal helping spirit, Mr. Siksik ("ground squirrel"). Wolverine thus gets stranded on Marble Island, unable to paddle back to the mainland because of mighty waves that appear suddenly at each attempt. Two factors save the young man from a life of total isolation or a watery grave. First, he recalls the story of Kiviuq and determines to become similarly adept at right-ing his kayak in bad weather—and at surviving the shamanistic storm. Secondly, Wolverine's rescued owl helpfully devours the ground squirrel helping spirit, thereby eliminating the source of the curse.

The Curse of the Shaman thus contains many of the same lessons as the *unip-kaaqtuat* told by the author's late father; readers will finish it with a clear sense of the importance of listening to elders and their advice. Stories do more than entertain, we learn; in the right circumstances, they will save your life. Through its cultural context and many references to *unipkaaqtuat*, furthermore, the novel maintains strong connections to Inuit tradition. Yet the novel's form—and indeed, even some aspects of its content—seem quite diametrically opposed to the conventions of the stories that inspired it.

For one thing, the novel, as a genre, requires a focus on the psychology of its characters that the *unipkaaqtuaq* tends not to include; as Anthony Burgess insisted in 1970: "The inferior novelist tends to be preoccupied with plot; to the superior novelist the convolutions of the human personality, under the stress of artfully selected experience, are the chief fascination." While *The Curse of the Shaman* would likely fall short of Burgess's rather ethnocentric criteria for aesthetic achievement, it does take pains to provide an insight into the inner reflections of its characters that is unlike anything to be found in the *unipkaaqtuat*. The shaman Paaliaq utters the curse that creates the major conflict in the novel, yet rather than constructing him as a stock villain, Kusugak invents a circumstance in which a reasonable person might do such a thing: Paaliaq, already on edge because of his infant daughter's crying, reacts in anger when The-man-with-no-eyebrows smiles at the shaman's short-temperedness—an embarrassing, childish trait. After Paaliaq brusquely refuses his guest's request to betroth their children, the author provides us with a glimpse into the shaman's mind: "He did not know why he had said 'No' but it was said, and the only thing to do was to stick with what he'd said. He thought what else he might add by way of explanation but something else came into his mouth and he said it before he had time to think about it. He said, 'As a matter of fact, when your son is of age to marry, he will never set foot on this land again!'" (24–25).

Paaliaq's pride—along with his helplessness to take back the words that he has uttered—render him sympathetic and relatable to his audience. Indeed, the idea that the shaman suffers from such a trifling character flaw humanizes what might otherwise be an intimidating figure. Likewise, Kusugak devotes pages to developing a rationale for the behaviour of Mr. Siksik, the helping spirit who carries out the curse despite the shaman's attempt to revoke it (26–27; 94–100). Although the story takes place in that mythical timeframe common to the *unipkaaqtuat*, its realistic mode seems to secularize many of its occurrences: Wolverine gains an animal helper, but simply as a pet, not a *tuurnngaq*; our young protagonist overcomes the curse-sent storm not through spiritual resources, but rather through physical training and determination; Ukpigjuaq the rescued owl kills the conniving ground squirrel spirit not because it has been sent to engage in shamanic combat, but simply because it is hungry. The novel thus demonstrates what it could have been like for people living in this world, and Kusugak thereby marks the way for readers unfamiliar with this culture and timeframe, requiring their sympathy and facilitating their understanding.

Traditional *unipkaaqtuat*, as seen above, are not so easily accessed by outsiders. Writing for a younger audience comprised largely of southerners, Michael Arvaarluk Kusugak sticks to the first episode of the Kiviuq story, excising later episodes with more controversial content, such as the time when Kiviuq murders his two adulterous wives, who had been having sex with a giant penis that they called forth out of a lake.[45] Kiviuq's motives in this ghastly event seem more or less clear—"*ninngaqtummarialugami*," says Thomas Kusugaq in his telling: "because he was really very annoyed" (53)—but the narration remains quite limited in its access to the full depth of Kiviuq's emotions. Again, *unipkaaqtuat* find this kind of detail unnecessary, partly because an insider audience often does not require this level of explication, being long familiar with the story's events, rather than shocked and therefore desperate to make logical sense of them. As Pelagie Owlijoot explains, "There is a moral to these legends that individuals have to figure out for themselves and gets them thinking. Traditionally, stories were told to amuse listeners, pass on ancestral history, provide lessons in moral conduct, communicate spirituality, and explain the existence of objects in nature. Inuit elders shared stories but did not provide descriptive details of characters or events. Rather, the Inuit way of telling stories was to lay the events out pragmatically. Without visual information or colourful storybooks, listeners were free to imagine the physical attributes of the characters and their surroundings" (13). *Unipkaaqtuat* thus demand more of their audience, requiring them to listen carefully and also allowing them the freedom to imagine the stories as they please—and to aquire the teachings that they need. Tellers therefore take greater risks when addressing outsiders, who may be poorly equipped to handle the wonderfully gruesome and explicit content of some *unipkaaqtuat*. Michael Arvaarluk Kusugak, cognizant of the many misrepresentations and misunderstandings of Inuit culture that continue to circulate in the South,[46] thus guides his readers much more carefully, disallowing the possibility that they might judge poorly or come to the wrong conclusion.

After all of these generic adaptations, some may wonder how "Inuit" *The Curse of the Shaman* is—or how "authentically" it acts as a vehicle for *unipkaaqtuat*. This has remained an issue for other Indigenous texts written in English and in genres with specific European origins; Kit Dobson writes that "Lee Maracle commented…in an interview that she wasn't sure that, for her, *Monkey Beach* qualified as a Haisla book because [Eden] Robinson wrote like a mainstream writer" (Dobson 56–7). Yet this notion—though undoubtedly expressing a sincere concern that traditional Indigenous genres also be utilized and celebrated—remains predicated on the idea that Indigenous traditions are authentic but ultimately static (Teuton, *Deep Waters* 10–11).[47]

Even for critics who accept that traditions can be adapted and still retain their Indigeneity, however, questions about *The Curse of the Shaman* may arise. I have wondered, for instance, why—if Kusugak wanted to "begin the process of introducing books to Inuit children that reflected their culture and history" (Schwartz 2)—did he not write the novel in Inuktitut? Or why did he not, at least, make the English version more challenging for readers, perhaps by offering less autoethnographic commentary and leaving more of his Inuktitut language untranslated? Why not retain the challenge and freedom of the *unikkaaqtuat* genre, which (as Owlijoot points out above) requires that its readers think carefully to come to conclusions about the moral of the story and also offers them the freedom of a range of interpretations? Why not resist the demands of the southern readership and the assimilative requirements of mainstream publishing? Why not challenge outsiders by making them work a little harder to access the authentic cultural information that they so desire?

But with the lessons that I have learned both from my experience in Inuit communities and from reading *unipkaaqtuat*, I would no longer ask these impolite questions. Although my training in the academy presses me to think critically about all of these things, I strive to remember the lessons of Angusugjuk, who had the wisdom to put his faith in those with greater knowledge than his. Instead of understanding *The Curse of the Shaman* as merely a colonized *unipkaaqtuaq*, then, we might attribute its author the agency that he deserves as an inheritor of his father's tradition and as an Inuk writer grappling with the challenges of the post-settlement era. In other words, Michael Arvaarluk Kusugak has made his decisions about the form in which to pass on the lessons of the *unipkaaqtuat* purposefully and strategically; as Michael D. Wilson writes, "Indigenous writers of contemporary fiction are generally less concerned with assimilation than they are about the power of appropriating and revising nonindigenous forms to create a literature of resistance" (qtd. in Teuton, *Deep Waters* xix).

The Curse of the Shaman should be understood, then, as a strategic extension of the *unipkaaqtuat* tradition, fulfilling the same function for contemporary Inuit youth as the Kiviuq tale did for Wolverine. Again, by filling in the details that will speak to a mainstream audience, Kusugak gains the capacity to guide his audience's conclusions; while this may be inconsistent with the workings of the *unikkaaqtuat*, it is a necessary adaptation in a time when the stories are being heard by those who—either because of geographic distance or linguistic/cultural interruptions—may not yet have the tools to make sense of them. As Joanne Schwartz writes: "[Michael Arvaarluk Kusugak] realized the tremendous need for Inuit stories, told by Inuit, to be part of the print world"—not only to counter the misinformation about Inuit life that had become prevalent in the south, but also to target a new generation of Inuit (2). Although some elders still tell *unipkaaqtuat* in their traditional forms, after all, the interference of southern media, educational systems, and other assimilative measures also means that some young Inuit may have never heard these stories—indeed, some may not even speak Inuktitut. *The Curse of the Shaman* provides them with an opportunity to learn about their history and to realize that the stories of their elders—even wearing new "skins"—can act as a source of great strength in times of adversity. Remembering Angusugjuk, then, readers might consider having faith in an authority like Michael Arvaarluk Kusugak; if we listen carefully and do as we are told, we may eventually surprise ourselves with how much we have learned.

THREE

"LET ME SING SLOWLY AND SEARCH FOR A SONG"
Inuit "Poetry" and the Legacy of Knud Rasmussen

These songs don't arrive like fragile orchids from the hot-houses of professional poets: they have flowered like rough, weather-beaten saxifrage which has taken root on rock. And they ought to matter to us.
—Knud Rasmussen, *Snehyttens Sange*

I put some words together,
I made a little song,
I took it home one evening,
mysteriously wrapped, disguised.
Underneath my bed it went:
nobody was going to share it,
nobody was going to taste it!
I wanted it for me! me! me!
Secret, undivided!
—"Song to a Miser," from Angmagssalik, East Greenland[1]

IN *THE JOURNALS OF KNUD RASMUSSEN*, the 2006 feature film by Igloolik Isuma Productions, the shaman Avva and his family arrive at Igloolik after a long and difficult journey.[2] Food supplies had been running low, and then had run out, and by the time Avva reaches the settlement, he and his people are starving. They are greeted outside the houses by a group of Inuit singing a hymn and wanting to shake hands in the *qallunaat* way. In residence at Igloolik, we learn, is Umik the Prophet, who welcomes the travellers, particularly when he sees that they are accompanied by Christians—namely, by Peter Freuchen and Therkel Mathiassen of the Fifth Thule Expedition.[3] Umik is leading a group of newly Christianized Inuit, and he invites Avva to join them: "We eat after we pray," he says: "the hunters bring their meat first to me and we all eat together after my sermon. Will you join us?" (329). "Maybe some day," Avva replies. His people are then faced with a choice: convert, and share in the feast, or keep the old ways, and continue to starve.

Avva and his family build their houses a short distance away. They are cold, sick, and weak from hunger. Freuchen and Mathiassen have given in; they have gone to pray—and to eat. Avva goes to visit an old friend, Anguliannuk, who (because Umik collects and then distributes the catch) has very little food to share:

ANGULIANNUK (WITH DEEP CONCERN) Old friend, you had a very difficult journey. (A HANGING SILENCE) Those songs. They are not so hard to learn....

AVVA Remember all the songs we used to sing when we were young and waiting for weather to change?

ANGULIANNUK (SMILING) Certainly! Our mouths never stopped flapping.

AVVA Hmmm, those were the days! I have no more room in my head to learn any new songs, my friend. (Kunuk and Cohn 335)

The conversion from the practise of *angakkuniq* (shamanism) to Christianity—from the singing of *ajaja* songs to the singing of hymns—forms the central conflict of *The Journals of Knud Rasmussen*. In the early 1920s, the era in which the film is set, the region that is now Nunavut was in the midst of a cultural shift. Although the Moravians had been in Labrador since the late eighteenth century, and although whalers, explorers, and Hudson's Bay Company traders had arrived intermittently throughout the nineteenth century, the first Christian mission was not established in Nunavut until 1894, when the Anglican Reverend Edmund J. Peck arrived at Uumanarjuaq (Blacklead Island), in Cumberland Sound (Laugrand, Oosten, and Trudel 3–9). A Roman Catholic mission was eventually built in Igloolik in 1931, but in the 1920s, Inuktitut Bibles and hymnbooks were already in circulation, and local proselytizers like Umik and his son Nuqallaq were already promoting Christianity (Blaisel, Laugrand, and Oosten 379–83).[4] One of their commandments, as recounted in the screenplay of *The Journals of Knud Rasmussen*, is that the converts should "sing only Jesoosie's songs. Do not sing the old songs that bring Satanasi to tempt Inuit through the drum, to burn forever in Hell" (Kunuk and Cohn 337). In other words, the arrival of Christianity meant the eventual banning of the activities of the *qaggiq* (the communal feasting house)—in particular, the singing of the old songs.

When Knud Rasmussen arrived at Repulse Bay (Naujaat) in 1921, he was pleased to find that the people there were, in his eyes, "still entirely primitive in their views and unaffected by outside influences" (Rasmussen, *Iglulik* 16).[5] He was particularly interested in finding those who would be willing to share with him "the ancient traditions of [their] tribe" (*Iglulik* 17). Mathiassen describes Rasmussen's "peculiar knack of quickly getting on terms of friendship and confidence with strange Eskimos" (*Report* 28); as the Padlermiut[6] leader Igjugarjuk put it, Rasmussen "was the first white man he had ever seen who was also an Eskimo" (Rasmussen, *Across Arctic America* 64). In fact, Rasmussen was born in Jakobshavn (Ilulissat), Greenland, and his mother was Inuk.[7] His fluency in Kalaallisut (the Greenlandic Inuit language) and his prior knowledge of Inuit traditions seems to have endeared him to elders like Avva, who related a number of their stories and songs. The result of the Fifth Thule Expedition, then, is an unparalleled collection of Inuit literary and critical traditions—a reservoir of the kind of material that would soon be obscured by the arrival of Christianity. Indeed, soon after the missionaries arrived in the Arctic, the term for *ajaja* or drum dance songs—*pisiit*—was itself converted; today, the primary signification of *pisiit* is "hymns."[8]

In Volume VII, No. 1 of the *Report of the Fifth Thule Expedition* (*Intellectual Culture of the Iglulik Eskimos*), Rasmussen gives a detailed description of the tradition of Inuit songs. "The great song festivals at which I have been present during the dark season," he writes, "are the most original and the prettiest kind of pastime I have ever witnessed. Every man and woman, sometimes also the children, will have his or her own songs, with appropriate melodies, which are sung in the qag·e, the great snow hut which is set up in every village where life and good spirits abound. Those taking part in a song festival are called qag·iʃut; the poem recited is called pisɛq, the melody of a song ivŋɛrut" (227).[9] In amongst the Inuktitut song terms, here, Rasmussen has casually placed another term of some significance: "poem" (*digt*, in the Danish). Like Franz Boas before him, Rasmussen identifies Inuit song making as *poetry* and often refers to the singers as poets.[10] The word "poem"—with its connotations of refinement and deliberate craftedness—demands quite casually a recognition of the sophistication of these compositions. As such, through his contributions to the *Report of the Fifth Thule Expedition* (the major source text for almost all future studies of Inuit tradition); Rasmussen can be understood as having created a canon of Inuit poetry.

Yet while Rasmussen emphasized the poetic nature of Inuit song, we might also suspect him of drawing upon the popular (and problematic) contemporary idea of the "primitive" human as an involuntary poet. Rasmussen notes that when he himself attempted to participate in the song festivals, "it was not easy to equal the natural primitive temperament in [the song's] power of finding simple and yet poetic forms of expression" (*Iglulik* 230). He goes on to note that "when one tries to talk to one of these poets on the subject of poetry as an art, he will of course not understand in the least what we civilised people mean by the term. He will not admit that there is any special art associated with such productions, but at the most may grant it is a gift, and even then a gift which everyone should possess in some degree" (*Iglulik* 233). Owen Barfield, in his 1927 *Poetic Diction*, surveys the idea of a long-distant "metaphorical period" in human history, when "myths, which represent the earliest meanings, were not the arbitrary creations of 'poets', but the natural expression of man's being and consciousness at the time" (102).[11] Though Barfield is somewhat skeptical of this hypothesis, he does dwell upon a perceived similarity between "primitive language and... the finest metaphors of poets" (86). Rasmussen's use of the term "poetry," then, may resonate disconcertingly with the idea that the expression of tribal peoples, because of some apparent difference in cognitive function, are naturally and unintentionally "poetic."

Rasmussen's actual discussion of the songs, however, would indicate quite the opposite: with an approach rare for an ethnographer of the 1920s, Rasmussen carefully depicts the individuality of each singer, and leaves no doubts about the very intentional artistry of their songs. Yet even if Rasmussen's poetic framing of the gathered texts did result in a broader recognition of the literary merits of Inuit song traditions, interpreting the song-poems is no simple matter. Not only do they make use of a specialized and often purposefully ambiguous vocabulary, but in the pages of Rasmussen's *Report*—and in the many other anthologies that followed—the songs are far removed from their original performance in the *qaggiq*. Indeed, as Sophie McCall argues, the process of reconceptualizing oral traditions as "poetry," which was again taken up in the latter half of the twentieth century by scholars like Jerome Rothenberg, Dell Hymes, and Dennis Tedlock, involves an inevitable excision of context (McCall, *First Person Plural* 18–27); indeed, this concern forms the basis of most critiques of the field of ethnopoetics.[12] As Laura J. Murray and Keren Rice claim: "Many native people fear the loss of control that comes with the reproduction of their words, on tape or on paper, because they have seen the dire legal effects of having their words misconstrued (or at least reconstrued with other people's interests in mind) in treaties and court decisions, and the crippling cultural effects of having their songs and histories reduced to quaint fairy tales or parables" (*Talking on the Page* xiii). As "poetry," then, Inuit songs are arguably removed from the tradition that produced them; "the 'Inuit voice,'" as McCall writes, "becomes monumentalized, static, transhistorical. It is not considered part of a dialogue but becomes showcased as an icon from the past" ("I Can Only Sing" 26). As the shaman Avva's conversation with his friend Anguliannuk suggests, songs are closely tied to the circumstances in which they are performed, and to alter them—or to give them up—could have major consequences.

Since Avva's time, the old songs have taken on a variety of different forms; some of these have remained closely connected to Inuit artists and communities, while others have wandered far from home. Yet the tendency to transform and to travel, I will argue, has been a part of Inuit song-tradition since long before the arrival of Europeans. This chapter will look, for example, at the tradition of *ikiaqtagait*—old songs that have had new words put to them—and at the ways in which these are used by contemporary Inuit artists, like the makers of *The Journals of Knud Rasmussen*. I will suggest that even within Inuit tradition, the old songs have undergone decontextualizations—and commodifications— that in many ways parallel (and certainly precede) their treatment in the south. Understood figuratively as "'objects'" of great craftsmanship and value, songs can be traded, borrowed, and recycled for a whole range of purposes; in particular, they can be used to establish (or strengthen) important resource-sharing relationships. The problem with understanding these songs as "'poetry,'" then, is not decontextulization, but rather the failure of outsiders to reciprocate for the resources that have been shared.

HUNTING SONGS

When Rasmussen arrived at the HBC trading post at Repulse Bay (5 December 1921), he had the good fortune to meet an elder named Ivaluardjuk, "one of the oldest members of his tribe" (*Iglulik* 17).[13] With his "long white beard and red, rheumy eyes, worn dim with [sic] over many blizzards," Ivaluardjuk comes across as a kind of Ancient Mariner; indeed, Rasmussen suspects that he may have a story to tell: "I discovered at once, in the course of our first talk, that Ivaluardjuk, though very careful about what he said, was remarkably well acquainted with the ancient traditions of his tribe. In order to draw him out a little, I narrated a few of the stories common in Greenland. These proved to be well-known here, and the surprise of the natives at finding a stranger from unknown lands able to relate old tales they fancied were exclusively their own, was such that in a short time the house was filled with inquisitive listeners. Thus I gained the old man's confidence, and we were soon discussing the folk-lore of his people as experts, the reserve he had shown at first being gradually discarded" (*Iglulik* 17). Having thus bartered for a story, Rasmussen listens as Ivaluardjuk recollects the old days "when all meat was juicy and tender, and no game too swift for a hunter" (17). "Now," Ivaluardjuk says, "I have only the old stories and songs to fall back upon" (17). With the encouragement of the gathered people, he agrees to sing one. The women begin "a monotonous air"—likely an *ajaja* refrain—and Ivaluardjuk sings:

Cold and mosquitoes,
These two pests
Come never together.
I lay me down on the ice,
Lay me down on the snow and ice,
Till my teeth fall chattering.
It is I,
Aja—aja—ja.

Memories are they,
From those days,
From those days,
Mosquitoes swarming
From those days,
The cold is bitter,
The mind grows dizzy
As I stretch my limbs
Out on the ice.
It is I,
Aja—aja—ja.

Ai! but songs
Call for strength
And I seek after words,
I, aja—aja—ja.

Ai! I seek and spy
Something to sing of
The caribou with the spreading antlers!

And strongly I threw
The spear with my throwing stick (sic!).[14]
And my weapon fixed the bull
In the hollow of the groin
And it quivered with the wound
Till it dropped
And was still.

Ai! but songs
Call for strength,
And I seek after words.
It is I,
Aja, aja—haja—haja. (*Iglulik* 18–9)

Here, in a trope common to songs performed at an assembly, the singer recalls a successful hunt. His quest for game, furthermore, is paired with the other central feature of this tradition: a reflection on the process—and the difficulties—of song making. Both are occupations that "call for strength," and both are heavy with the possibility of failure. The two come together in the fourth stanza ("Ai! I seek and spy / Something to sing of..."); as the hunter acquires his target, the singer—and the singer's audience—acquires the subject of the song.

But that was all many years ago. Now, in 1921, the elderly Ivaluardjuk is too weak to pursue caribou; now, he is a hunter of songs. "Memories are they / from those days," he sings: "the cold is bitter, / The mind grows dizzy / As I stretch my limbs / Out on the ice." Even in this recollection, the hunter's body is becoming still, supine, perhaps stiffening with the cold. His mind, however, "grows dizzy"—swarms, even, mosquito-like, as he seeks after the memory, and for the song to convey it. Now, when his limbs seem permanently stiff, and he can no longer leap up to hurl his spear, the songs are his prize—the sustenance that he brings to the community. Indeed, Rasmussen reports that "this utterance of an old man, who recognized that for him the joyous days of life were long since over and past, brought the noisy listeners to silence.... When sung, it produced an altogether extraordinary effect on those present" (19, 232). But the precise nature of this effect is rather mysterious. Rasmussen notes the silence and the settling of the crowd, he senses "piety and reverence," as if something sacred has occurred (19). But the exact significance of the song—one that the community knows well—is not known to him, and so neither does that meaning survive in the pages of *Intellectual Culture of the Iglulik Eskimos*.

Indeed, Ivaluardjuk's search for words, song, and memory is something that contemporary readers can sympathize with, even if they have never lain down on the ice as a herd of caribou passed by. Encountering Ivaluardjuk's song in the midst of Rasmussen's narrative is comparable to the rush of spotting the prey, but this particular *tuktu* is like a creature out of the world as it used to be—one who may be in the process of transformation, or whose form has not quite settled. Rasmussen himself warns us of this possibility, as he explains that he heard the song performed, and then wrote it down afterwards: "The ideas and expressions, and the general effect, of Eskimo songs are so unlike anything we are accustomed to in our own that it is not always possible to translate literally. The following is, however, as close a rendering of the original as can reasonably be given when endeavouring at the same time to reproduce something of the charm and the unconscious art displayed in the utterance of the Eskimo singer" (*Iglulik* 18).

"Cold and mosquitoes," then, is a song that has undergone many transformations. If we believe Ivaluardjuk, it came into being one day when he was out on a hunt, or perhaps it was soon after recollected in tranquility.[15] It would then have been sung in the *qaggiq*, likely many times, as it is now a piece that is well-known by all. Finally, it is sung for Rasmussen, who—like a good listener—does not attempt to write it down during the performance.[16] The version that appears on paper, then, is based entirely on a recollection. Rasmussen's memory was no doubt excellent, and he knew the language extremely well, but it is certain that major discrepancies exist between the published version and the one that was heard at the trading post in 1921. Rasmussen tells us, for instance, that the song began when Ivaluardjuk's wife "chanted in a clear voice a monotonous air, consisting of but a few notes constantly repeated" (*Iglulik* 18). Many lines of Inuit song poetry begin with the refrain *aja*; in the text of "Cold and Mosquitoes," however, that chorus appears only at the end of each stanza, rather than at the head of the line. Verses such as "aja—aja—ja" (8) or "Aja, aja—haja—haja" (38) may simply then be representative traces of the poem's original sung form, rather than precise records of its structure.

Many of the songs that Rasmussen includes in the *Report of the Fifth Thule Expedition* are given in Inuktitut as well in translation; unfortunately, Ivaluardjuk's own Inuktitut words did not make it into the published version. Instead, the song was translated from Rasmussen's Danish by William Worster and W.E. Calvert for the 1929 English-language volume *Intellectual Culture of the Iglulik Eskimos*. Rasmussen also included the song in his 1930 collection *Snehyttens Sange* ("Songs from the Snow-hut"); a German edition of this collection, *Schneehüttenlieder*, was produced by Aenne Schmücker in 1947. Calvert and

Worster's English translation of the song has perhaps become the most "canonical" version, in that it has been reprinted in Robin Gedalof's *Paper Stays Put: A Collection of Inuit Writing* (1980), John Robert Colombo's *Poems of the Inuit* (1981), and Penny Petrone's *Northern Voices*.[17] In 1973, Tom Lowenstein retranslated Ivaluardjuk's song, along with many others from *Snehyttens Sange*, for inclusion in his collection *Eskimo Poems from Canada and Greenland*. The poem that Lowenstein produced—based on Rasmussen's Danish—is called "A Hunting Memory," and it differs in subtle and significant ways from Calvert and Worster's (Lowenstein 25).[18] The most notable change is perhaps in the final stanza, which Lowenstein gives as follows:

> Aj! But songs
> require strength
> and I search
> for words.
> Here is the song.
> Here is the memory.
> It's only I who sings.
> Aja-aja-haja-haja! (Lowenstein 26)

Strangely, the stanza here contains three more lines than Calvert and Worster's 1929 version:

> Ai! but songs
> Call for strength,
> And I seek after words.
> It is I,
> Aja, aja—haja—haja. (Rasmussen, *Iglulik* 18–9)

In Lowenstein's translation, the simple refrain "It is I" has transformed into "Here is the song. / Here is the memory. / It's only I who sings." As it turns out, however, Lowenstein's version is closer to Rasmussen's Danish:

> Aj! Men sange bruger styrke og jeg søger efter ord.
> Her er sangen, her er mindet.
> Og det er kun mig, der synger. (Rasmussen, *Den store Slæderejse* 17)

> [But songs use strength and I search for words,
> Here is the song, here is the memory.
> And it is only I who sing.] [19]

The final line—omitted in Calvert and Worster's translation, but included in Lowenstein's—seems to provide some useful insight on the song's mysterious refrain. "It is I," sings Ivaluardjuk, as he recalls himself lying on the ice. "What is?" we might ask. Clearly, the subject of the sentence is something important, as the singer keeps coming back to it. The word "I" even becomes part of the sung refrain, as it blends into the first syllable: "aja—aja—ja."[20] Lowenstein's translation hints at an answer to this riddle: "It's *only I who sings*" (26, emphasis added). Rather than creating an inflated image of self, and a hyperbolic account of the deed (as is common in hunting songs), the singer finishes by admitting that it is *only* him, and only a song. This idea, in turn, might resonate with the fleeting and elusive nature of memory in the poem. Alternately, we may get a sense of the singer's isolation as an elder who remembers such things; there may be a kind of impotence suggested in the verse, as he is *only* singing, while others now hunt.[21] Whether or not this is an accurate representation of Ivaluardjuk's own feelings is uncertain, though Rasmussen himself was certainly caught up in, and convinced by, his masterful performance.

The songs that Rasmussen recorded from Ivaluardjuk, Avva, Orpingalik, Netsit, and others have been reprinted in numerous anthologies and collections, which vary widely in scope and quality.[22] Under the pretence of acknowledging the artistry of Inuit song traditions, many editors have gotten carried away by the inherent adaptability and ambiguity of Inuit songs. In 1973, for example, the American poet Edward Field published a book entitled *Eskimo Stories and Songs: Collected by Knud Rasmussen on the Fifth Thule Expedition*. In the late 1960s, Field had been commissioned to write "a children's book of translations of Eskimo poetry" for an elementary school social science curriculum (Johnson). Field drew his material from Volume VIII of the *Report of Fifth Thule Expedition* (*The Netsilik Eskimos: Social Life and Spiritual Culture*), with translations "retold from the literal English renderings" by Calvert and Worster (Field iv). The names of the individual singers are not included; rather, the source material is attributed to Rasmussen, who (Field writes) acquired it from "the Netsilik Eskimos, a remote tribe who live along the coast above the Arctic Circle" (Field xi). The volume is beautifully illustrated with prints by the Cape Dorset (Kinngait) artists Kiakshuk and Pudlo, who (unlike the singers) are credited for their work.[23] Field himself has mastered the genre of the "Eskimo poem"—a genre belonging entirely to the south. In his lively rendition of "Magic Words for Hunting Caribou," he writes:

You, you, caribou
yes you
long legs
yes you
long ears
you with the long neck hair—
From far off you're little as a louse:
Be my swan, fly to me, long horns waving
big bull
cari-bou-bou-bou. (59)

Field's homage to the hunting charm song contains traces of the original genre, with its use of epithets to refer to the game. But here, we see perhaps the reason why Field was unable (or unwilling) to credit these songs to their original authors: this poem is a combination of at least three magic songs that Rasmussen collected from the shamans Orpingalik, Inūtuk, and Nakasuk, and which were later published in *The Netsilik Eskimos*.[24] As Orpingalik sings:

kumᴀruᴀq niutɔ·q
You, louse-like, you, long legs
siuktɔ·q tiŋajo·k
You, long ears, you with the long neck hair,
ataunaŋa·t
Run not past below me.… (*Netsilik* 279)[25]

Clearly, Field has used poetic licence generously in his renditions. His "right" to do this could be a subject of much debate, particularly as the originals are "magic words," or shaman songs, which did not circulate freely (*Netsilik* 278). Field's "translations," however, have become quite popular, and *Eskimo Songs and Stories* has become a source text for several other artists. Jerome Rothenberg's *Shaking the Pumpkin*, for example, used Field's versions of the songs to represent "Eskimo" poetry (Rothenberg 41–4).[26] And in 1989, the composer Raymond Luedeke created a symphony for narrator and orchestra entitled *Tales of the Netsilik*, which also made use of Field's text.[27] At the beginning of the 2008 performance at Toronto's Roy Thomson Hall, the audience members were asked to imagine themselves in the Arctic, in an igloo—in the wild and dark world of the Netsiliks at the time when Rasmussen visited. Clearly, it is not the 1920s that are being evoked; rather, it is a kind of exotic, ahistorical space, into which

Rasmussen has been fortunate enough to stumble. Yet despite the attempt to conjure a sense of authentic "Eskimo-ness," Field's texts, and Luedeke's adaptations are only faint echoes of the original performances.

While there are some editors, like Lowenstein, who take care to include as much contextual information as possible in their collections of Inuit verse, many others, like Field, were content to erase the individual authorship of the singers. Edmund Carpenter attempts to justify this by claiming that "some [songs] were created spontaneously.... Others are age-old and belong to all. In neither do poets take care to be remembered as individuals, but simply disappear, as it were, behind their works; the poems, therefore, have been assigned to neither singers nor makers" (*Anerca* n.pag.).[28] The result, as Sophie McCall argues, is the creation of Indigenous song-texts as aestheticized fragments. "In many of these literary anthologies," she notes, "editors have retranslated, rearranged, and re-presented the songs without knowing the languages in which they first were performed. While some of the editors provide contextualizing information in headnotes or footnotes, the songs themselves are generally presented as freestanding lyric poems" (*First Person Plural* 184). Devoid of tedious specifics, the poems become representative of the human condition and are therefore universally appealing—or rather, they appeal—and are made accessible to—a white, mainstream audience.

While editors like Field and Carpenter attempt to situate Inuit song-texts within the realm of aesthetics, McCall reveals that this kind of celebration in fact carries a latent political motive: "the aesthetics of the ethnographic fragment," she argues, "ideologically reinforce the trope of 'vanishing primitive cultures'" ("I Can Only Sing" 21). Removed from their precise political and cultural contexts, the songs are recast as "the roots of a genuinely 'Canadian' literary tradition" and so become part of a nationalist project to harness the ideological power of the sublime Canadian North ("I Can Only Sing" 24–5). In other words, although the collections by Mary-Rousselière, Colombo, Lewis, and Carpenter may acknowledge the poetry of Inuit song-traditions, they simultaneously function to sustain popular (and stereotypical) understandings of the Arctic. Field, for example, introduces his work by reminding the reader that Inuit "live in one of the bleakest and most forbidding parts of the world, where winter lasts for ten months, where the temperature drops to 50 degrees below zero, where there are no trees, where the ocean freezes solid for seven months" (xii).[29] When people are perceived as being thus constantly locked in a struggle for survival, the significance of poetry—in all its frivolity and power—is even more extraordinary. As Edmund Carpenter puts it: "[t]he mystery is…that within this prison of ice and wind they are able to draw from themselves images powerful enough to deny their nothingness" (*Anerca* n. pag.). The 'Eskimo poet' here becomes a kind of existential icon—the human being crying out his "Song of Myself," in the face of impending annihilation.

While Rasmussen himself was no stranger to these kinds of romanticizations, he displayed a keen awareness of the importance of the songs' contexts, and he took care to preserve as much of them as possible. Unlike his contemporary Diamond Jenness (who recorded Inuinnait or "Copper Eskimo" songs in his station house and considered the performance antics of the singers to be a hindrance to his data collection), Rasmussen spoke the language fluently, attended *qaggiit*, and often wrote down the songs after the performance—perhaps to avoid spoiling the listening. Rather than simply publishing a catalogue of texts (again, as Jenness did), he weaves the songs into his narrative, providing pages and pages of detail about their singers, their performances, and the events that inspired them. But even this, he notes, does not seem to solve the problem of translation from performance to page. "There are many songs," he says, "which presuppose a thorough acquaintance with the events described or referred to, and would thus be untranslatable without commentaries that would altogether spoil the effect" (*Iglulik* 235). In the end, despite his understanding of the importance of context, he finds it impossible to adequately convey the magic of a song performed in the *qaggiq*. As he writes in *Snehyttens Sange*:

> when I remember the inexplicable way in which words, music and dance mingled into one great wave of feeling that lifted us up and for a moment made us forget everything else, I can understand more clearly than ever, *how difficult it is to take the songs of the Eskimos out of their own context.* For the words of the songs are only part of the whole intended effect. Read an opera libretto without music, staging and performers, and you have a comparison.... Whatever I did, I finally lacked all the things that gave the songs life in their country of origin. How could I recreate the sound of the drum—whether resonantly festive, noisy and defiant or softly lamenting—let alone the choruses which would rise and continue rising until the ecstasy suddenly beat them down into the hushed hissing of the spirit songs—those choruses which are to the song as breath which runs back and forth in the human throat? (qtd. in Lowenstein 107, 109; empasis added)

Rasmussen, then, finds himself caught in a difficult bind. To ignore the aesthetics of the song is to transform them into mere data and thereby to obscure the individuality and skill of their composers. Yet to convey the effect of the songs—to convince home audiences that he has witnessed a sophisticated artistic tradition in process—Rasmussen ultimately has to adapt the "poetry" that he records. At times, his very presence meant that the song was modified, as when Avva—singing one of his hunting songs—inserts a few explanatory passages for the benefit of his visitors (*Iglulik* 236). At other times, Rasmussen would ask the singers to fill in the blanks afterwards—to tell the story of the original event, which the rest of the community already knew.[30] In *Intellectual Culture of the Copper Eskimos*, he simply acknowledges that he is giving a "freer translation" in an attempt to convey the "wonderful poetry" of the songs sung to him by Netsit of the Inuinnait,[31] and he advises the reader that the literal translations will be available in another chapter.[32]

These kinds of interventions, as McCall argues, transform Inuit songs into lyric poems onto which southern fantasies about Inuit life can be projected (*First Person Plural* 22). The work of editing and translating that aims to convey their "spirit" to distant audiences, furthermore, has often altered them beyond recognition and stripped them of the "relations of address"—or social context—that give them meaning (*First Person Plural* 190). Knud Rasmussen—operating very much under the "salvage" model that McCall credits for the process of song collecting (*First Person Plural* 18–19)—therefore has much to answer for. Yet his participation in the creation of aestheticized fragments out of Inuit song tradition, I want to suggest, cannot be solely attributed to his ethnographic affiliation. In Innuinait (Copper Eskimo) territory, Rasmussen attended a song festival with a man named Netsit, who told him about the *iŋɛrʟrait pihe·*—the "songs of the departed ones" (*Copper* 162). "These songs are particularly popular," Rasmussen learned; "Sometimes they recall the name of the man who first sang it, but everything else about him has been forgotten beyond the fact that 'he once lived in our land'; only his song is remembered and sung in the dance-house" (162). As Rasmussen learned from the Arviligjuarmiut (Netsilik) shaman Orpingalik, magic songs—the songs used by shamans to create changes in the world—are "fragments that are supposed to have their strength in their mysteriousness or in the very manner in which the words are coupled together" (*Netsilik* 13). Like the songs of the departed, magic words have allegedly been stripped of their context, and their mysterious origins seem to add to their appeal—and to their potency.[33] The aesthetic of the fragment, this record suggests, was not alien to Inuit Nunaat. In the following section, I explore the ways in which the adaptation, fragmentation, and even appropriation of Indigenous songs—issues that have greatly preoccupied postcolonial scholars—may need to be reconfigured in an Inuit context.

EMILE IMARUITTUQ AND THE IKIAQTAGAIT (ADAPTED SONGS)

More than seventy-five years after the historic meeting between Knud Rasmussen and Ivaluardjuk, another Igloolik elder, Emile Imaruittuq, sings an *ajaja* song for a roomful of captivated listeners. This audience is also hoping to learn about Inuit traditions, but this time, the situation is slightly different: the performance takes place in a classroom of Inuit students at Nunavut Arctic College, and Imaruittuq has been flown in to Iqaluit as a visiting elder. The students have been asking him about *unikkaaqtuat*, traditional stories. Imaruittuq knows a few, but he tells the students that he is much better with *pisiit*, songs.[34] "Our ancestors used to create songs," he says, Sometimes the people who put the words to the song would like the tune. Sometimes they would make alterations to make the song suit themselves. This song was changed by one of my relatives, Maniq was her name. She made changes to this song that I am going to sing. This is Maniq's song. Because there were changes made to this *pisiq* [*taanna maniup pisia aaqigiaqsimakkanirmit* (Aupilaarjuk et al., *Maligatuqaliriniup* 208)], it is an *ikiaqtagaq*.

Maniup pisivininga ikiaqtaliavininga[:]
Maniq's song, with her changes[:]

[1]   aijaa ijajaajaajaa inngirajaalirlanga
Aijaa ijajaajaajaa, let me sing slowly
   inngirajaalirlanga pisiksaksiurlungalu
Let me sing slowly and search for a song
   ijajaajaajaa

[2]   aijaa ijajaajaajaa pisiksaninngiliqpunga
Aijaa ijajaajaajaa, I have not acquired a song
   pisiksaninngiliqpunga nunguusimangmatigut
I have not acquired a song because they have finished them on us
   ijajaajaajaa

[3]   aijaa ijajaajaajaa nunguusimavatigut
Aijaa ijajaajaajaa, they have finished them on us
   nunguusimavatigut sivullitta pisiksamik

They have finished them on us, our ancestors of any song
   ijajaajaajaa

[4]   **aijaa ijajaajaajaa maliktarigaluaqpit**
Aijaa ijajaajaajaa removing incoming snow
   maliktarigaluaqpit apivalliajuq manna
Are you removing incoming snow from this that is becoming snow
covered
   ijajaajaajaa

[5]   **aijaa ijajaajaajaa iqqaqtulirivara**
Aijaa ijajaajaajaa, I remember
   iqaqqtulirivarali ijjannguqturnira inna
I remember my difficulty in breathing
   ijajaajaajaa

[6]   **aijaa ijajaajaajaa nunguusimavatigut**
Aijaa ijajaajaajaa, they have finished them on us
   nunguusimavatigut sivullilitta pisiksamik
They have finished them on us, our ancestors of any song
   ijajaajaajaa

[7]   **aijaa ijajaajaajaa nungugiaqsinnarivuq**
Aijaa ijajaajaajaa, it is about to come to an end
   nungugiaqsinnarivuq tainiksaqanngimmata
It is about to come to an end because they have no title
   ijajaajaajaa

(Imaruittuq 203–4, emphasis in original)[35]

Rasmussen's rendition of "Cold and Mosquitoes" has its own share of riddles, but Imaruittuq's song—with its very literal translation—is clearly home to a different kind of ambiguity. Its narrative is much more difficult to discern and its referents are often mysterious. At the end of the performance, Imaruittuq says that he is "just singing part of the song. There is a lot more to it" (204). What we have here, then, is a fragment of sorts—a distilled version of a longer song, and of an event long past.

Not only has the song been shortened, but it has also been adapted, as Imaruittuq is careful to point out. Although he refers to it as "Maniq's song," he specifies that it is an *ikiaqtagaq*—a song that has had changes made to it (219).

In other words, although Maniq has had a hand in the song's creation, she is not its original (or sole) composer. Imaruittuq says that "*ikiaqtaaq* means, it's another person's song I am using but I am creating my own words" (201). *Ikiaqtaq*, as Peter Irniq explains it, literally refers to splitting; an *ikiaqtagaq* (with the passive ending -*gaq*), is something that has been split.[36] *Ikiaqtaq* is from *ikiaq*, which Spalding defines as "the in-between layer: insulation between two walls; inner shirt between underwear and jacket; the inner lining of a coat or garment" (19). In other words, the tune of the song (*qimik*) has been separated from its original words, and new words have been added (Imaruittuq 219). When later the students ask Imaruittuq if he has a *pisiq* (song) of his own, he responds, "I have an *ikiaqtagaq*" (211).[37] Here, he demonstrates the importance of acknowledging the song's history: namely, the identity of the song's composer (or adapter) and the fact that it is a borrowed tune. Irniq says the singer *must* acknowledge this, perhaps by saying "*pisiruna ikiaqtaq qanurlikiaq aturnialirivara*"—"how am I going to use this *ikiaqtaq*?"

Imaruittuq's song, like "Cold and Mosquitoes," is a text with a history. Imaruittuq calls it "*Maniup pisivininga ikiaqtaliavininga*" ("Maniq's song, with her changes"); she has added words to a borrowed tune. It is significant that Maniq is identified as being a relative of Imaruittuq; as Vascotto noted in a study of Kugaaruk (Pelly Bay) drum songs, song transmission tended to happen along kinship lines (212). As David Serkoak writes, "personal songs could also be given to another person. A song owner might give his song to show appreciation for help received in time of need, or to someone bearing the same name as himself" (79). Interestingly, this kind of transmission does not always require the recipient to maintain the song in its gifted form; rather, through the convention of *ikiaqtagaq*, adaptation is allowed. I suspect that Imaruittuq's rendition, while based on Maniq's words, may have undergone a few changes itself. In 1992, Imaruittuq recorded a song called "*Inngirajaalirlanga*" ("Let me sing slowly") for a song collection by Isuma; its lyrics are very similar, though by no means identical, to the song performed for the students at Nunavut Arctic College (*Unikkaat*).[38] In other words, there seems to have been further "splitting" of Maniq's song. And because Imaruittuq saw fit to record this *ikiaqtagaq*, I would like to take a closer look to determine what it—along with its singer—can tell us about the tradition that it belongs to.

The song begins with a trope that should now be familiar: "*Inngirajaalirlanga pisiksaksiurlungalu*"—"let me sing slowly and search for a song" (§1). For Rasmussen (and his translators), this idea was expressed as "songs / Call for strength / And I seek after words" (*Iglulik* 18). The idea of searching for "*pisiksaq*"—the material for a song—is an extremely common theme; the infix -*siuq*- (as in *pisik-saksiuq*-) here denotes "looking for," or "hunting," as in *natsiqsiuqtuq*—"he is hunting seals" (Harper, *Suffixes* 71).[39] Here, it opens up an immediate contradiction, as the speaker is—strangely—looking for a song *while singing*. The third line only confuses matters, as the singer claims that he "ha[s] not acquired a song," even though by this point, he is well into one. We get the sense, perhaps, that it takes more than singing to make a song; in the opening lines the singer tentatively tests the waters—singing *slowly*—seemingly uncertain whether he will find something to sing about, or whether a whole *pisiq* will be formed out of the raw musical matter.

These opening lines, then, are a trace of the process of composition, which then itself becomes a key subject of the song. As Tom Lowenstein observes, "the struggle to create form was…largely the poet's own responsibility: an imperative which was keenly and often crushingly felt, as is indicated by the frequent allusions to the difficulties of composition and a fear of failure—failure to perfect the song itself, and then to perform it in the feasting house without forgetting the words" (xvi). Lowenstein quotes Piuvkaq, an Utkuhikhalingmiut singer: "It's wonderful to make up songs: / but all too many of them fail" (45).[40] The precise nature of this failure is not made apparent. However, the conditions for success do seem to include a certain degree of restraint in the storytelling. There is little superfluous detail; rather, the singers convey great emotion, or an important event, with rare precision.[41] Part of this, no doubt, is enabled by the audience; as Rasmussen says of one of Avva's hunting songs, "it has been conveyed so often that Aua can make do with but the briefest reference in his text to the course of events" (*Iglulik* 238). The effect on the reader, however, is the impression that each word (or each post-base[42]) seems to have been chosen with great care, and must be of great significance.

In the case of Imaruittuq's "Let me sing slowly," there is a known story behind the song. Because many of the young listeners are not familiar with it, Imaruittuq fills in the blanks for them: "A lot of songs were stories…. The part about having difficulty breathing has a lot of meaning to it. At that time, there had been people buried in a blizzard. If they camped where snowdrifts tended to form, then they would be buried. So, they were cautioned to be aware of what would be covered in a blizzard. They were also told not to build an *iglu* under an *aluiqqaniq*, snow overhang. I have been told not to camp under an *aluiqqaniq* because it could collapse and bury the *iglu*. Then it becomes very difficult to breathe. My father too was buried in his *iglu* and it is very difficult to breathe. The air hole gets covered and you can't breathe. In the song, the word *maliktari-*

galuaqpit refers to keeping the air hole free of snow by removing the snow. In the song because she had difficulty removing the snow from the air hole she had difficulty breathing. That's the meaning of the song" (Imaruittuq 204–5).

This story—a cautionary tale—is conveyed in only four lines in the song: "... removing incoming snow / Are you removing incoming snow from this that is becoming snow covered[?] / I remember / I remember my difficulty in breathing" (§4–5). In many ways, this crisis functions like the sighting of the caribou in "Cold and Mosquitoes"; it is "something to sing of," or the subject of the song (*Iglulik* 18). But here, instead of the central theme of songmaking being partnered with the search for game, the process of composition is expressed in tandem with the work of digging out a buried snow house. This potentially dangerous scenario adds a new dimension to the opening words: "let me sing slowly," the speaker begins—sluggish, perhaps, in the heavy air. The search for a song—and the concern about not having acquired one—suddenly becomes a far more urgent occupation. As the Netsilingmiut shaman Orpingalik famously told Rasmussen, "I call this song ["My Breath"], for it is just as necessary for me to sing it as it is to breathe" (*Netsilik* 321).[43]

Again, for the students hearing the song at Nunavut Arctic College, this context may not be apparent; the reference to "removing incoming snow" may be—as it is for most southern readers—mysterious. The singers consulted in the pages of both the *Report of the Fifth Thule Expedition* and of the Interviewing Inuit Elders series suggest, however, that such confusion is not necessarily out of place. Imaruittuq explains that there are three kinds of traditional songs:

[1] *pisiit*, or *qilaujjarusiit*, which are *pisiit* sung with a drum...

[2] *iviutiit*, which were songs used to embarrass people, to make fun of them, to make fun of their weaknesses. They created songs to make fun of others.

[3] There are also *sakausiit*, songs used by *angakkuit* [shamans]. (Imaruittuq 202)

Rasmussen noted these categories as well, although he divided *pisiit* into two categories: songs of sentiment (or mood), and hunting songs (*Netsilik* 323).[44] *Iviutiit* he called "songs of derision"; these are the verses used in song duels between rivals, or less antagonistic "song cousins" (*Iglulik* 231; Lowenstein 107). At one point, Imaruittuq sings the students an *iviusiq*, and one of them asks: "what does the song mean? I didn't understand it at all" (Imaruittuq 208). "Probably because you were not meant to understand it," Imaruittuq says: "that's the way these songs were, these *iviutiit*" (208). In this case, the song might include a series of riddles that would obscure the insult—or heighten it, maybe, as the audience guessed its meaning.

In Imaruittuq's song, this tension between obfuscation and clarification plays out in each of the song's seven sections (each section is framed by the *ajaja* chorus, and repeats the same tune). The first lines of these sections each present a kind of riddle, or half-completed thought, which the second line then answers, or completes. "Let me sing slowly," begins the singer. The second line repeats this phrase, and then adds to its meaning: "Let me sing slowly and search for a song" (§1). The slowness of the singing here is explained by the action of the search; the singer is slowly feeling his way towards a song. "I have not acquired a song," he then sings—again, oddly, as he is now repeating the melody that he began with, thereby suggesting that he has indeed found a *pisiq*. His next line hints at an answer, but only barely: "I have not acquired a song because they finished them on us" (§2). In this way, the riddle of each section is never quite solved, as the answers set up further confusion, and carry the listeners along to the next question.

By the third section, we seem to be moving towards a kind of revelation; the mysterious phrase "*nunguusimavatigut*," "they have finished them on us," is clarified by a subject—"*sivulitta*," "our ancestors," or the ones who went first—and by an object—"*pisiksamik*," the "material for a song" (here qualified by the direct object marker -*mik*) (§3).[45] Something that is *nungusimajuq* can also be translated as "what is used up and remains so" (Schneider 224); the ancestors, in other words, have used up all the songs. Here, the singer seems to be revealing a central problem or cause for his sung reflections: he apparently is suffering from the anxiety of influence, as he laments the difficulty of creating an original piece. But just as we reach this crucial and revealing line, the song takes an unexpected turn, and a new riddle is introduced: "removing incoming snow / Are you removing incoming snow from this that is becoming snow covered[?]" (§4). In light of the opening verses of the song, this imagery is compelling; figuratively, the singer is being suffocated, or snowed under, by the immense canon of the ancestors' songs. Indeed, the reference to the snow house is flanked by the repeated verse "*nunguusimavatigut*" ("they have finished them on us") (§3, 6). Sweeping conclusions about the oppressive nature of tradition are likely inappropriate here; rather, we might understand that the singer—in accordance with conventions of modesty—is humbling himself before the task of trying to add to the great wealth of song.

For Maniq (the relative to whom Imaruittuq attributes the song), the solution to the problem of originality seems to have been to borrow a song; once again, this is an *ikiaqtagaq*—a song that has been adapted (Imaruittuq 203). As Imaruittuq explains it, "in this song, she said she was searching and searching for a song. She finally found a song which she made changes to. Because she wanted to make changes to the song, she asked the person who owned the song. He agreed. When she started to sing it, it had no title, for our ancestors had used up all the titles" (204). This last problem—the lack of a title—is only made apparent at the end of the song. "*Nungugiaqsinnarivuq*" ("it is about to come to an end") echoes the previous uses of the verb *nungu-*, to finish, or use up. Here, the song is about to be used up because, the singer explains, "*tainiksaqa-nngimmata*"—literally, "because they do not have a subject" (§7).[46] The need for *pisiksaq*, the material for the song, here becomes a lack of *tainiksaq*, the material for naming—a subject, or title.[47] Here, the singer again is humbly (and paradoxically) dismissive of the song; having failed to gain a title—and therefore, perhaps, a sense of wholeness or completion—the song has to come to an end. Like Imaruittuq's explanation, the last stanza picks up on the themes of the song, but leaves the audience with an appropriate sense of mystery. Yet despite the singer's claims that the song has not been found, and that it is incomplete, or that all the good ones have been used up, this song itself has gained a kind of canonicity, as Imaruittuq liked it enough to borrow it from Maniq, who in turn had borrowed a part of it from someone else.

The search for a song, like the lament for a title, are conventions; they come up again in Imaruittuq's own *ikiaqtagaq*, which he sings later on in the interview.[48] In other words, the song's sense of uncertainty, or of striving, is ironically something that the audience can find security in. As the elders point out, it is not always expected that the song will make perfect sense, or will reveal all of its mysteries. As Rasmussen learned from the Innuinaq (Copper) shaman Heq, "there are some songs that 'ordinary people do not have to understand. The wisdom in them is often concealed'" (Lowenstein xxi). The ones that conceal their wisdom most often tend to belong to the final category of songs—the *sakau-siit*, which Rasmussen called "magic words," or charms (Imaruittuq 202; *Iglulik* 157–68, *Netsilik* 278–93). As Rasmussen says, these "are not poems or songs in the same sense as the others" (qtd. in Lowenstein 108). Instead, as he explains in *Intellectual Culture of the Iglulik Eskimos*, "magic words, magic songs or magic prayers are *fragments of old songs*, handed down from earlier generations. They can be bought, at a high price, or communicated as a legacy by one who is dying; but no other person save the one who is to use them may hear them, otherwise they would lose their force" (157, emphasis added). These kinds of songs are often present in the *unikkaaqtuat* (the old stories), even though, as Rasmussen points out, the words themselves are often omitted (*Iglulik* 157). Rasmussen, however, was able to barter for many of them, and learned that "it is the usual thing that ordinary speech is not employed, but the special language of the shamans. Sometimes they make use of ancient words that have fallen into disuse in daily parlance, or vague and incomprehensible phrases, all intended to increase the effect and mysteriousness" (*Netsilik* 278).[49] Rasmussen made lists of this vocabulary, which is characterized by its use of epithet, as in the term "mamaicɔq" ("the ill-tasting one") to refer to the sea, or "hilauʌ·rtɔq" ("the one who has no breath"), meaning a corpse (*Copper* 110, 112).

Rasmussen came to believe that the Inuit song tradition grew out of this poetic, or magical, vocabulary. The word for drum, he points out, is *qilaut*, which "means literally 'that by means of which the spirits are called up'" (qtd. in Lowenstein 120–1).[50] The obscurity or opacity of the songs, then, has its origins in a spiritual aesthetic. The things that the singers do not explicitly say, but rather allude to, are the things that are conjured in the minds of the listeners as they work to solve the riddles. In the same way, the absence of a seal in a term like *qajuʌq*— "the one who gives soup"—is also its presence; the hunters call the animals by opening up a discourse in which they are not there (*Copper* 109). Likewise, in Imaruittuq's performance, it is the stated lack of a song—*pisiksaqninngiliqpunga*—that causes the song to emerge (§2). Again, this appears to be an aesthetic of omission—it is what is not said, or what must be filled in by the audience, that endows the words with an affective power.

Interestingly, Imaruittuq—though careful to reference Maniq's ownership of the song—does not seem concerned about its origins; indeed, the original composer of the song is never named, and the context of that performance seems to have been lost. While the knowledge of the damage that some ethnographers and editors have wrought may compel scholars to seek out the original recordings and their contexts as much as possible, this process—I would argue—also risks mimicking the search for authentic data that fuelled the early ethnographers themselves. In the process, we may miss the reality that adaptation and change have a place within Inuit song tradition. While the pages of the *Report of the Fifth Thule Expedition* can only ever provide us with a second- or third-hand understanding of the *pisiit* of Ivaluardjuk, Avva, Orpingalik, and Netsit, they do contain a remarkable collection of Rasmussen's own *ikiaqtagait*—his own adaptations of the songs. As Robin McGrath points out, "Rasmussen was not just an accomplished linguist, theologian and ethnographer, but was also an Inuit poet himself" ("Reassessing" 20). While he was in many ways an outsider, to deny his Inuit identity as a result of his appearance and upbringing seems archaic, particularly after such dismissals have been thoroughly critiqued by Indigenous scholars. While Rasmussen's work undeniably imported a number of strange concepts into the Canadian Arctic (in particular, the ideas that the culture was either "primitive" or "vanishing"), when viewed in another light, it might also function both as an adaptation and an extension of the usual process of transmitting songs and stories.

The issues that many scholars have raised about the appropriation or decontextualization of Indigenous songs are important ones; however, I would argue that we should also question the propriety of importing these concerns into Inuit territory. Etymologically, the word "appropriation" contains the idea of "rendering property," or assigning something particular ownership ("a'ppropre"). It should be obvious, however, that these Latinate notions of property and ownership differ drastically from their counterparts in Inuit language and culture. As elders Mariano Aupilaarjuk, Emile Imaruittuq, and Lucassie Nutaraaluk explain in *Perspectives on Traditional Law*, Inuit teachings have always contained strong warnings about stealing. However, the elders also differentiate between the taking of "hard objects"—such as a knife or a gun—and of "soft objects," such as meat. Aupilaarjuk explains that "the consequences for stealing hard objects were very severe as hard objects had annuaqquti, something that could cause death. If it was a soft object, if it was meat, and we stole it, it was not dangerous" (Aupilaarjuk et al., Law 30). Meat, after all, is meant to be shared; as Uqsuralik Ottokie explains, "We are told not to be stingy, even with the smallest piece of food. Don't keep it to yourself. If you are generous it comes back, and it will be a bigger amount" (Ekho and Ottokie 55). Likewise, if one informs someone that one has taken an object, or if one returns the object after having used it, it is not considered to be stolen (Aupilaarjuk et al., *Law* 139–142).[51]

The chief concern about outsiders like Rasmussen, then, is not so much that they might steal things; indeed, anxieties about appropriation actually seem far more common amongst the *qallunaat* themselves. Over the years, I have heard a number of southern students ask Pangnirtung elder Joanasie Qappik about the *inuksuk* that was used as the emblem of the 2010 Vancouver Olympics. The first time that the question was posed, I, too, expected that Qappik might express some degree of irritation about this wild adaptation of an important cultural symbol. On some occasions, he replied diplomatically that it was good that the south was showing interest in Inuit culture (and I have heard this opinion from a number of younger people, as well). Once or twice, he commented good-naturedly that the Vancouver *inuksuk* was clearly designed by people who didn't know much about *inuksuit*.[52] But this was said with amusement, rather than outrage. In other words, in cases of appropriation, the damage seems to be not so much inflicted on the *owners* as on the *thieves*, who may (like the Vancouver Olympic committee) wind up with a comically inappropriate symbol, or—where "hard" objects are concerned—with a more severe consequence.

Concerning "Song to a Miser," an *iviusiq* recorded in Angmagssalik, Greenland, Rasmussen gives the following context: "A man was once discovered to have been in the habit of fetching meat from his store during the night while other people were asleep. He ate his fill without letting his companions share the enjoyment. As soon as he had finished, he wrapped the remnants in a skin and hid them under the bed. One of his mates later took revenge by composing the following song…" (qtd. in Lowenstein 46). The resulting *iviusiq*, quoted in full in the epigraph to this chapter, depicts a man who composes a song but refuses to share it, hiding it under his bed so that no one else can "taste" it. Songs like this one—and like Ivaluardjuk's—are again endowed with a "soft" materiality that "feeds" the community (even if the words may be hard for some to swallow). Private enjoyment—and one can't help but think about the act of reading, here—is frowned upon. In *Snehyttens Sange*, furthermore, Rasmussen tells a story about an old man named Satdlagé, who—the story goes—never opened his mouth at a song festival. Finally, someone asked him why he never would contribute a song, when everyone else in the *qaggiq* was singing. Satdlagé told them the following tale:

> Once, when I was a young man, I wanted to compose a song about my village, and for a whole winter evening, I walked up and down in the moonlight, trying to fit words together which would go with a tune I was humming. I did find the words: excellent words which would convey to my friends the beauty of the mountains, and every delightful thing I saw when I went outside and opened my eyes. Pacing up and down on the frozen snow, I became so preoccupied with my thoughts that I quite forgot where I was. Suddenly I stop and lift my head. And look! In front of me, the mountain near our village rises higher and steeper than I have ever seen it. It was almost as if it was very slowly growing out of the earth and coming to lean over me: dangerous and threatening. It was then that I heard a voice coming from the air: "Little man!" it cried. "The echo of your words has reached me! Do you really think I can be contained in your song?" I was so frightened that I al-

most fell over backwards, and in the same moment, all the words I had
put together in my song fled from my mind, and I ran home as fast as I
could and hid in my hut. Even since then I have never attempted to put
words together. I had become afraid. (qtd. in Lowenstein 101)

Satdlagé describes a fear known well to both the folklorist and the literary critic.
How does one contain a thing of such great beauty? Is it foolish even to try?
Just as when the theft of "hard" objects causes a person's death, there is evi-
dently a larger system governing the appropriate sharing of resources—and it
will intervene when necessary. This, perhaps, sheds some light on the stance of
extreme humility adopted by so many composers of *pisiit*; rather than boast-
ing about having "captured" something of great power, they emphasize the in-
terminable effort (and often, the apparent impossibility) of finding or sharing
a song. Rasmussen, likewise, knows that he cannot preserve the awe-inspiring
experience of the *qaggiq* for the outside audience, and he is aware that his own
presence is changing the songs. But he is likewise sensitive to the dangers of jeal-
ously guarding the material that he has gathered, and perhaps for this reason,
he does not choose to remain silent. Rather, like Imaruittuq, he acknowledges
the known history of the song, and the fact that it has been adapted, and then
he sings it anyways.

The trouble with outside visitors, I would contend, is not the danger of thiev-
ery, but of hoarding. Southern conventions around resource-sharing differ drastically from Inuit protocols, and as a result, *qallunaat* are often viewed as being
petty, jealous, or stingy about their belongings. I would like to suggest, then, that
the problem is not that Rasmussen and his anthologizers took and published
Inuit songs, but rather that the *reciprocity* that such an act should engender may
still need to occur fully. The sharing of songs, like the sharing of food, often
happens along kinship lines and thereby affirms the relationship and mutual
responsibility of the participants. And even for those not held by the bonds of
kinship (like many outsiders), the rules of good behaviour dictate that resources
should still be shared (though sadly, not all *qallunaat* living in Inuit communities follow these conventions). Although it would be unwise to assume that
the protocols around song-sharing mimic the protocols around food-sharing
precisely, the near-ubiquitous comparison of songs to food-items (and of songmaking to hunting) within the song-texts themselves might suggest that songs
are likewise a "soft" item that might be more freely given and taken—and which
should not be hoarded. Having been nourished by these songs, however, Rasmussen, his anthologizers, and their southern audience are required to compen-

sate the communities that provided the sustenance. As is discussed in the final section, Rasmussen's *ikiaqtagait* are now making their way back up north, but the challenge remains for his readers to find their own ways of reciprocating.

IKIAQTAGAIT IN THE WORK OF IGLOOLIK ISUMA PRODUCTIONS

In *Intellectual Culture of the Iglulik Eskimos*, Rasmussen writes, "now that I have to describe, as far as I can, the performance as a whole, I can only say that the general feeling, the emotional atmosphere in a qag·e among men and women enlivened by song is something that cannot be conveyed save by actual experience. Some slight idea of it may perhaps be given some day, when the 'talking film' has attained a higher degree of technical perfection—if it gets there in time" (*Iglulik* 230). These words are strangely prophetic, as they seem to anticipate the event that has taken the Inuit literary scene by storm: the rise of the video storytelling of Igloolik Isuma Productions. Isuma, a film production company founded in 1985 by Zacharias Kunuk, Paul Apak Angilirq, and Pauloosie Qulitalik of Igloolik with the New York–born video artist Norman Cohn, began by producing short dramatized films like *Qaggiq (Gathering Place)* (1988), which recreated community life from the time before Inuit moved into permanent settlements. In 2001, Isuma released its first feature film, *Atanarjuat (The Fast Runner)*, which won the Camera d'Or at the Cannes Film Festival. The second feature film, *The Journals of Knud Rasmussen*, appeared in 2006, and brings this story full circle.

The Journals of Knud Rasmussen carries a somewhat misleading title; although the Fifth Thule Expedition provided much of the historical data used in the creation of this film, Rasmussen himself is a fairly minor character. Instead, the plot centres on the family of the shaman Avva and their eventual conversion to Christianity. In the scene with which this chapter opened, we can see how the issue of *siqqitirniq*—crossing over, or conversion—is represented by a conflict between two kinds of songs: the *pisiit* and *sakausiit* sung by Avva, and the hymns of Umik the Prophet—the former shaman who brought a version of Christianity to the Igloolik region in the winter of 1921–22 (Tungilik and Uyarasuk 2–3; Brody 47; Blaisel, Laugrand, and Oosten 379). At the end of the film, the members of Avva's group give in one by one to their hunger: they walk over to Umik's camp, where a group of Inuit are singing hymns before engaging in the *siqqitirniq* ritual—a kind of communion, in which the eating of the forbidden cuts of meat signifies the abandonment of shamanism (Tungilik and Uyarasuk 3). As the late writer Alootook Ipellie put it, "The psalm book now replaced / The sacred songs of shamans / ...It was not / 'Jajai-ja-jiijaaa' anymore / But— / 'Amen'" (58).

This encounter between Avva the shaman and Umik the Prophet, though inspired by historical events, is fictional. Avva did accompany Peter Freuchen and Therkel Mathiassen on the trip north from his camp at Port Elizabeth along the eastern coast of the Melville Peninsula, and Mathiassen does report a shortage of food, cold temperatures (between –40 and –50°C), and difficult terrain (Mathiassen 43–4). But when they reached the camp at Ignertoq on 18 March 1922—just over halfway through the trip—they met and were fed by the hunter Ilupâlik (44). They continued on to Pingerqalik—the last camp before Igloolik—where again they were given walrus meat, and at this point, Mathiassen reports, Avva left them and headed back south. He had wanted to turn back earlier, fearing for the lives of his dogs, but, as Mathiassen says, "he was persuaded to go on" (44). In any case, Avva never actually arrived at Igloolik with the Fifth Thule Expedition, and his conversion happened later on—at some point before Rasmussen returned from his inland trip to the Pâdlermiut (Caribou Eskimos), in January of 1923. Then, before Rasmussen headed out on his great journey westward to the Mackenzie Delta and Alaska, he stopped one more time at Avva's camp, where he reports that "above each hut waved a little white flag—a sign that the inmates had relinquished their old heathen faith and become Christians" (*Across Arctic America* 118). It was only at this point, *after* Avva had converted, that he spoke freely to Rasmussen about shamanism; in the film, the chronology is altered, and Rasmussen's two visits to Avva's household are collapsed into one.[53]

My interest here is not the historical accuracy or inaccuracy of the film, but rather, the way in which the conversion to Christianity is imagined by Isuma through a kind of song duel, as the *ajajas* sung by Avva and his family compete with the droning hymns of Umik's converts. Indeed, I imagine the film itself as a metaphorical *qaggiq* (a song house, or feast house) hosting a range of performances, many of them based on the adapted songs—and adapted stories—that Rasmussen gathered in the 1920s. Although Rasmussen passed away in 1933, and although his publications were aimed almost exclusively at an outside audience, the makers of *The Journals of Knud Rasmussen* have now found a way for him to compensate the community for the resources that were shared with him, as the material in *Intellectual Culture of the Iglulik Eskimos*, itself a Greenlandic Inuk adaptation of the original performances, is now reimagined by contemporary Iglulingmiut singers and storytellers. Figuratively, Rasmussen has been invited back into the *qaggiq*, a place where relationships are forged, tested, and ultimately, strengthened. While these performances do—as McCall points out—demonstrate an important recontextualization of Inuit intellectual material (*First Person Plural* 204), I believe that they also demonstrate the ways in which adaptation and song-sharing—even outside of the community—have longer term, relationship-building benefits that may only now be apparent.[54]

The Journals of Knud Rasmussen opens with a scene that takes place on board Captain George Comer's whaling ship, which is wintering in the ice off Repulse Bay. In the film, Comer himself is never seen, but the influence of the whalers is apparent: a young woman is experimenting with an accordion, and an older man is learning to write syllabics. As he spells his name out, sound by sound, we realize that this is none other than Evaluarjuk (Ivaluardjuk), singer of songs.[55] Indeed, it was one of his *ajaja* songs—recorded onto a gramophone—which accompanied the opening shot, in which the actors arrange themselves to pose in a black and white photograph. The film begins, then, with the theme of documentation, and it is instantly clear that we are no longer in the same world as *Atanarjuat*. Interestingly, the scratchy *ajaja* song of the opening sequence—which is recorded a few shots later by Evaluarjuk and Angutimarik—is actually a song that was used in Isuma's previous film: it is the love song performed by Atanarjuat and Puja. Here, that *qimik* (tune) is heard again, although the words have been changed. Now, it seems to have become an *ikiaqtagaq*, and like other aspects of Inuit culture, it is being recorded, for reasons that are presently unknown.

This scene turns out to be a kind of prelude, as ten years pass before the main action of the film begins. The events aboard Comer's ship are quickly echoed, however, in a scene that takes place at George Cleveland's HBC trading post at Repulse Bay in December of 1921. It is here that Ivaluardjuk meets Knud Rasmussen and the other members of the Fifth Thule Expedition. While Peter Freuchen drinks with Cleveland and his friends, Rasmussen talks quietly with Evaluarjuk, and tries to "draw him out a little" (*Iglulik* 17). The elder man obliges by inviting Rasmussen to visit the camp of his brother, the shaman Avva. When Rasmussen asks him why they are all living so far from Igloolik, Evaluarjuk doesn't answer, but two of the women, laughing, begin singing a hymn and shaking each other's hands. Their song anticipates the conflict that will later be revealed: it is in Igloolik that Umik the Prophet has begun his proselytization—characterized by hymn singing and handshakes—and Avva and his family are pointedly staying clear.

As if in counterpoint to this mock hymn, Evaluarjuk then begins singing a song of his own. In the film, we hear only three of its verses, but the longer version included in the published screenplay contains the following line: "*Aija, niglasuk qitturiatlu uimanartut takua*"—"cold and mosquitoes—they drive you crazy, those ones" (Kunuk and Cohn 365).[56] This is a version of the very same song that Rasmussen included in his *Report*; now translated from Danish and English back into Inuktitut for the film, it too is an *ikiaqtagaq* that has passed through a few more layers than usual. Here, at last, Ramussen's "sharing" of the songs via print dissemination results in some benifit for their community of origin, as the material he gathered can now be taken up by Iglulingmiut and adapted to their new purposes. Indeed, the film's reenactment of the song, furthermore, differs quite substantially from the description in the *Report of the Fifth Thule Expedition*. In *Intellectual Culture of the Iglulik Eskimos*, Rasmussen gradually leads the readers into the performance; he describes the journey from Danish Island to Repulse Bay, the appearance and character of Ivaluardjuk, the words that were spoken prior to the singing, and the effect of the song on the people assembled. In the film, however, the shots of Evaluarjuk's performance are interspersed with images of a travelling dog sled: the high-speed journey of Avva's large sled in the night, moving towards the first meeting with Rasmussen and his team (which occurs almost three months later). Evaluarjuk's song, in other words, transports the viewers out to Avva's territory—the symbolic stronghold of tradition. Much as it did for Rasmussen (and for Ivaluardjuk) in 1921, this song takes the audience far from the trading post and far from the hymns.

In Isuma's retelling, furthermore, the encounters between Rasmussen and Avva's family are presented through the *local* point of view. The meeting at the HBC trading post is in fact a flashback, as Evaluarjuk tells his family the story of his encounter with the Greenlanders. The encounter of the sleds in the night, furthermore, is shot from the perspective of Avva's sled; as we approach, we see the exotic bear-skin pants of the Greenlanders glowing in the dark. This might be compared to Rasmussen's description of the encounter: "We had had a long day's journey in the cold, and were now, in the fine starry night, just ready to set about building a snow hut, when suddenly, out of the darkness ahead, there appeared a long sledge with one of the wildest teams I have ever seen. Fifteen white dogs were racing along at full gallop with one of the big Hudson Bay sledges, at least 7 metres long, and six men on it. They sighted us, and came sweeping down right on top of us, and a little man with a big beard, his face covered with ice, leapt down and came running towards me.... His keen eyes rested on me, full of life and spirits, and he greeted me with a ringing: qujäŋnamik 'Thanks, thanks to the guests who have come.' This was Aua the shaman" (*Iglulik* 45).

In this filmic version of this encounter, Evaluarjuk's song is used as a kind of leitmotif to signify "tradition"; and the film is quite notably less concerned with recreating the original performance of the song. Like the magic words that Rasmussen recorded, the songs in Isuma films are performative; they have a task to carry out, and they get it done. Often, that task is symbolic, whether it be evoking a particular setting, a person, or an ideology. The beauty and strangeness of their language may be very much a part of their effectiveness, but they can also be understood via the action that they perform. McCall discusses this phenomenon in *Atanarjuat*, noting the way that the central song—the *pisiq* of the dead leader Kumaglak—functions as a kind of anthem for the community and is used in different ways each time it is performed (McCall 26–8). For McCall, this usage signifies an alternative to the decontextualized song fragments that appear in collections like Edward Field's. The film, she suggests, enacts a dramatic *re*contextualization of the Inuit song. "The song's power," as she puts it, "lies in its performance, and the relations of address cannot be separated from the song itself" (182).

The opening line of *Atanarjuat (The Fast Runner)*, "I can only sing this song to someone who understands it,"—which McCall takes as an assertion by Kumaglak that songs must stay within their communities—does not in fact refer to Kumaglak's "anthem" (*First Personal Plural* 182). Rather, the opening line is spoken by Tuurngarjuaq, the visiting stranger, and it refers to a different song (which is sung almost immediately after the line is spoken). Admittedly, this line does not appear in the published screenplay, and when it is spoken in the film we do not see the speaker; instead, there is a shot of the landscape, and a man with some dogs. But immediately after we hear it spoken, we move to the interior of the snowhouse, where Panikpak (Kumaglak's wife) says "*Atii*" ('Go ahead' or 'Let's hear it'), and Tuurngarjuaq sings. As such, I wonder whether the idea of Inuit performers "refus[ing] to sing" for fear that outsiders will misuse their songs may likewise be a misunderstanding (McCall, *First Person Plural* 189). While Inuit songs are shared according to specific protocols and along the lines of particular relationships, this does, on occasion, involve sharing songs with outsiders, as is evidenced by the decision of the singers to share their work with Rasmussen.

Tuurngarjuaq's statement—"I can only sing this song to someone who understands it"—is one, rather grim example of this. The opening scene presents a series of markers of his foreignness, which initially fosters light conversation (that is also tinged with rising competition between the two shamans). Kumaglak stands and slowly turns, showing off the design of his *atigi*, his caribou skin inner shirt: "Since your clothes are different," he says to the visitor, "have a look at mine." Recognizing his hosts' interest in and hesitation about people from other regions, Tuurngarjuaq offers to share a song. His introductory statement about the need for an audience with understanding, then, acts as an invitation for Kumaglak and

Panikpak to enter into some kind of relationship with him. With the word "*atii*" ("go ahead"), Panikpak acquiesces, and the stage is set for a friendly competition between the men. Unfortunately, Tuurngarjuaq has actually come to murder Kumaglak, and his insidious presence will haunt the community for years to come.[57] The word he uses in his opening line—"*inngirut*"—contains the idea of the song as a tool or instrument (literally, a "tool for singing"); here, Tuurngarjuaq seems to be using his light-hearted song to create trust in his audience—perhaps to mask his true purpose. While the scene, as a whole, does underline the danger of dealing with strangers, it also demonstrates the ways in which songs were occasionally taken out of context and repurposed—long before the *qallunaat* showed up.

As *inngirut*, a song gains an almost material presence as a trade good; just as shamans can use their abilities to help or harm people, the relationships created via the trading of songs reflects the intentions of the singers. In one of the pivotal scenes in *Atanarjuat*, the corrupt leader Saurriq sings his father's song in a show of power; it corresponds with his possession of the walrus-tooth necklace that the evil visiting shaman Tuurngarjuaq lifted from Kumaglak's body (McCall, "I Can Only Sing" 27). Lowenstein notes the material aspect of the songs as well; the idea that they are *crafted*, he says, "is implicit in [their] language. Words (like snow, or bones, or reindeer skin) are part of the material environment, and they have the sort of concrete property which can be woven, wrapped up, carved and put together, for either functional or aesthetic purposes" (xxii).[58] As is evident in "magic songs," and the stories used to describe them, words can have a very real, often transformative impact on the physical world.

Rasmussen understood well the trade value of songs, and he bargained for them throughout his journey. The idea of Rasmussen as a trader in intellectual culture is apparent in the film *The Journals of Knud Rasmussen* as well. When he and his team have arrived at Avva's camp and are sitting inside with their mugs of tea, the following exchange takes place:

RASMUSSEN: I came to hear songs and legends, if you will share them, and to learn about your beliefs.

AVVA: We believe happy people should not worry about hidden things. Our spirits are offended if we think too much.

RASMUSSEN: [thinks about this] Yes, I understand. Soon I am traveling west to meet the inland Inuit near Baker Lake. But my friends want to go to Igloolik, if you don't mind taking them.

[Avva does not respond]

NATAR: Father, I don't mind taking them. Maybe my brother-in-law [Taparte] will come too?

[Apak, Taparte's wife, gets up and leaves]

FREUCHEN: People...working...soon...trade...

AVVA: You want to trade.

FREUCHEN: Yes...trade.

AVVA: My family doesn't work for Whites. But everyone sees my son wants to help people who speak our language. [To Rasmussen] Sing us something in your language.[59]

Again, songs are here bound up in the barter economy. Rasmussen would like Avva to share his songs and to escort his friends up to Igloolik; Freuchen suggests that they have much to trade in return. Avva surprises them by asking for a deposit in kind: "sing us something in your language." Rasmussen (who had once hoped to have a career in opera) obliges by singing the opening lines of the famous aria "M'appari tutt'amor" from Friedrich von Flotow's Martha (Kunuk and Cohn 301).[60] Avva's reaction is difficult to read (truthfully, he does not seem overly impressed), but the performance seems be sufficient, and an agreement made. Freuchen and Mathiassen get an escort to Igloolik, and Rasmussen gets his songs and legends. In the Report of the Fifth Thule Expedition, we learn that he later reinvests them back into the song market; as he writes of his encounter with the Netsilingmiut shaman Orpingalik, "he gave me the words of several magic songs, I paying for them with some of those I had got from the Iglulingmiut. It was considered that these transactions were quite legitimate, for as they were made through the agency of a white man they could not, it was thought, offend the spirits" (Netsilik 13). There is some suggestion here that Rasmussen's status as an outsider may have increased the extent to which songs—magic songs, at least—were commodified. But on the whole, it appears that the decontextualization of songs is neither an appropriation nor wholly a qallunaat practice; indeed, it was condoned by the Inuit singers who agreed to share them, perhaps in order to create an alliance with a friendly stranger. Although "every magic word has its particular mission," and songs their particular task, part of their value is in the possibility of reuse or adaptation—paticularly when it leads to the forging of strategic alliances (Netsilik 13).

More importantly, when examining the ways in which Inuit songs have travelled and transformed, it is essential that we recall—and that we honour—the
agency of the singers who (in most cases) entered willingly into song-sharing
agreements with Rasmussen. While they may not have predicted the full extent
of the songs' dissemination, they were well aware of the power of their medium,
and they did not treat it lightly. In allowing Rasmussen to listen to and record
the songs—and in answering his questions about their significance—the singers
created a relationship of resource-sharing and partnership. Perhaps there was
immediate, short-term benefit to be derived (such as the trade that the filmic
Freuchen promises); perhaps the singers were interested in Rasmussen's Greenlandic song-items. Perhaps they recognized the ethnographer as distant kin and
thus felt obligated to him on some level. Or perhaps (depending on their perception of Rasmussen) they were pleased—like Joanasie Qappik—that *qallunaat*
were trying to educate themselves about Inuit traditions. Maybe some even knew
that their words, like "A Hunting Song," would one day come back to their communities of origin. In any case, I believe that like the original singers, we should
have faith in the robustness of these songs—and in the larger principles that correct their misuse by disciplining both those who steal and those who hoard.

Likewise, the task of current viewers may be to find ways of honouring the
resource-sharing relationships that Rasmussen entered into—and which Isuma has rekindled in the twenty-first century. Although Isuma's work is geared
largely toward local, Inuktitut-speaking viewers, their work also functions—as
Arnold Krupat points out—as a medium for Inuit stories and songs to reach a
global audience ("Atanarjuat" 608–609). Indeed, Isuma's films can be accessed
for free via their internet video portal, IsumaTV; a virtual *qaggiq*, this site also
hosts predominantly Indigenous filmmakers from around the world who are
likewise looking to share their work. With this generous distribution in mind,
then, how can audience members reciprocate—or prevent the flow of resources
from travelling only in one direction? One possibility might be to make use of
IsumaTV's donation options, which invite viewers to contribute what they can
to Isuma's ongoing projects. Another might be to recognize—as Shari Huhndorf
points out—that Isuma's filmmaking is closely linked to Inuit political sovereignty (*Mapping* 74–78): something that international audiences may likewise
have the power to bolster through political action (or even through something
as simple as the consumption of seal products). One important first step, however, may be to de-emphasize prominent concerns about the decontextualization of cultural material; these anxieties, though at times productive, ironically
shut down the possibility of equitable relationships for fear of reinforcing the

errors of the nation's colonial history (and present reality). A more productive and empowering approach might be to think about viewing Isuma's work in terms of reciprocity—and trusting that the filmmakers know what they are doing when they make their work widely accessible. Like the offer of food, this resource should not be refused or handled squeamishly; rather, visitors to the *qaggiq* must learn to accept the gift—and the responsibilities that come with it.

In the final scene of *The Journals of Knud Rasmussen*, after Avva's son and daughter have both "crossed over" to Umik, Avva walks out on the land, far from the houses and the sound of the hymns. In the old days, this is where he might have gone to sing magic words, which "may be uttered under the open sky, but only in places where there are no tracks in the snow" (Rasmussen, *Copper* 113). Now, he summons his spirit helpers, but only to banish them. "I am grateful for all the help you have given me in my life," he cries, "but now I have to send my spirit helpers away. Now I will follow the road of Jesus and you have to leave me." Weeping desperately, the spirits walk away, out into the distance.[61] This scene is another *ikiaqtagaq*—an adaptation. The version that Rasmussen heard was less final: Avva is reported to have told him, "but now…I am a Christian, and so I have sent away all my helping spirits; *sent them up to my sister in Baffin Land*" (*Across Arctic America* 127, emphasis added). In the film version, that sense of continuance is not obviously included—unless of course we count the existence of the film itself, and the appearance, after eighty-six years, of Avva's helping spirits on camera. I would argue that both versions of this event are accounts of adaptation; both are stories of survival. Like those spirit helpers, the old songs are increasingly being put to new purposes, whether they are performed in the context of a college classroom, or as part of the soundtrack to a film, or whether they inspire contemporary Inuit poets and musicians.[62] And although many of these songs are now *ikiaqtagait*, Isuma demonstrates that it is this kind of adaptation that keeps the songs in the service of the community—even if that means sending them away from time to time.

FOUR

"I CAN TELL YOU THE STORY AS I HEARD IT"

Life Stories and the Inuit Qaujimajatuqangit Land Bridge

Kisutuinnarmik apirijaujunnaqpunga qaujimajannik [I can be asked what I know.] *Uqarunnaqpunga kisiani qaujimajannik* [I state only what I know.]

—Saullu Nakasuk, *Interviewing Inuit Elders*

WHEN THE IMPLEMENTATION OF THE NUNAVUT ACT created two distinct territories out of the former NWT, the new territory of Nunavut inherited a public government structure that closely mirrored the administration that has already been in place. "The Nunavut 'package...'" as Jack Hicks and Graham White write, "was designed to both accommodate Inuit self-government aspirations yet fit comfortably within established traditions of mainstream Canadian governance" (31). Given that the vast majority of the territory's inhabitants were also beneficiaries of the Nunavut Land Claims Agreement, though, it was clear that some adaptations were going to be necessary (Wenzel 240). In other words, Nunavut needed to "Inuitize" its way of doing things ("First Annual Report" 20).

The topic of traditional knowledge and its role in developing policy had already been on the table for a number of years, and in 1998, the Nunavut Social Development Council (NSDC) hosted a conference on the subject in Igloolik. What resulted was the idea of *Inuit Qaujimajatuqangit* (IQ), or "what Inuit have known for a very long time": a concept perhaps best understood as "The Inuit way of doing things: the past, present and future knowledge, experience and values of Inuit Society" ("First Annual Report 7).[1] Shortly thereafter, the Government of Nunavut created an Inuit Qaujimajatuqangit Task Force, co-chaired by Louis Tapardjuk and Simon Awa, with Sandra Inutiq, John Ningark, and elders Elisapee Ootoova and Mariano Aupilardjuk. The 1999 adoption of the Bathurst

Mandate—"the primary statement by the Nunavut Government about Inuit Qa-ujimajatuqangit as a guiding directive for governance in Nunavut," confirmed the new territory's commitment to "develop[ing] an open, responsive and ac-countable government" within the "context" of IQ (Wenzel 241, "Simplicity and Unity").

In its first report, the IQ Task Force identified a crucial problem with the at-tempts to incorporate IQ into the workings of government. "The problem," the report said, "can be expressed in the following question:

Should the Nunavut Government try to incorporate the Inuit Culture into itself,

or...

Should the Nunavut Government incorporate itself into the Inuit Cul-ture? ("First Annual Report" 7, emphasis in original).

They go on to make the point that the public government with which Nunavut had been endowed was not a culturally neutral space; rather, it came with a particular set of practices and ideologies that actually resisted the integration of IQ (5). Indeed, those with the greatest expertise in IQ—usually unilingual elders who had grown up on the land—could find no place within the governance of the new territory, which functioned primarily in English, according to an alien set of principles (11). Instead of attempting to insert decontextualized fragments of Inuit practise into an imposed, foreign system, then, the Nunavut Govern-ment must instead incorporate itself into the larger Inuit system that has long predated it in the territory (9).

In exploring the relationship between *Inuit Qaujimajatuqangit* and literary studies, then, we must ask the same kinds of questions. This book has taken as its premise the idea that Inuit literary texts and traditions readily adopt "new skins"—new labels, systems, or frameworks—when strategically useful. In the *unikkaaqtuat*, however, the donning (or sometimes shedding) of skins is almost always a temporary measure; as the Task Force wrote, "The decision to borrow a pre-existing model of public government allowed Nunavut leaders to begin ad-dressing needs immediately and it also 'bought them some time' to transform the borrowed model into an Inuit model of government" (10). While the use of bor-rowed forms may have bought Inuit texts some time—or perhaps, some space—there will come a moment when their usefulness may need to be reevaluated. Inevitably, the man in bears' clothing makes a break for home, and Kiviuq's goose-wife puts on her feathers and leaves for the south. In other words, the characters revert to their original forms and to the traditions that they were born into.

Such a framework should not be understood as essentialist or anti-adaptive. The Task Force aims, rather, to ensure that Inuit have control over the kinds of adaptations that take place and the results that emerge, rather than remaining subject to a foreign system that continually undermines local tradition. *Inuit Qaujimajatuqangit* itself is adaptive; one of its core principles is *Qanuqtuurniq (or Qanuqtuurunnarniq)*, "The concept of being resourceful [and/or innovative] to solve problems" or the "ability to improvise with what is at hand" ("First Annual Report" 8; Arnakak, "Incorporation" 39). As Jaypetee Arnakak writes, "There is no single defining factor of being Inuit, but this comes close. Inuit culture is qanuqtuurniq" (Arnakak, "What is IQ?"). IQ, furthermore, "is intended to include not only Inuit traditional knowledge, but also the contemporary values of Nunavut's communities (Arnakak, "Incorporation" 34)[2], and rather than existing in a static and totalized form, it continues to be shaped by the input and experience of elders and leaders.

Realistically, though, how might the Government of Nunavut adapt its relationship with IQ to allow the latter the security and prominence that it deserves? Likewise, how can a literary criticism most ethically integrate itself into Inuit tradition? The Task Force lays out a number of steps toward the building of new strategy. For the purposes of adapting their advice to my current task, I focus primarily on the first one: the development of an oral history program. "We are quickly losing our elders—the last generation of elders that grew up on the land. This is the last generation that can teach us the values and principles of IQ that have guided our people for centuries. It is essential that we capture this knowledge for future generations" ("First Annual Report" 21). As a concept, IQ is shaped largely through consultation with elders, who function as the authorities on the Inuit way of doing things. Again, the result is a diverse and dynamic body of knowledge, which the Government of Nunavut has—for practical reasons—attempted to distill into a set of general principles.[3] While these principles, as the Task Force points out, may be difficult to put into practise in a meaningful way ("First Annual Report" 7), consultation with elders becomes a concrete method for policy makers to attempt to correct the imbalances that exist in the current system.

In the years since the Task Force's report was released, the Department of Culture, Language, Elders and Youth (CLEY) has regularly hosted an Inuit Qaujimajatuqangit Katimajiit—a meeting of IQ experts who advise the government on its implementation. It also runs a program called Inuit Societal Values Initiatives and was behind the 2011 opening of Piqqusilirivvik, the Inuit cultural learning facility in Clyde River. The territory has also taken seriously the need to record elders' knowledge; this has resulted in a number of oral histories and elders' lifestories.

In this final chapter, I explore the possibility of similarly integrating literary criticism into *Inuit Qaujimajatuqangit*. After all, while elders' narratives are often explored for principles that will guide policy, administration, and everyday life, they also have a great deal to say about stories and storytelling; indeed, I argue that they contain crucial information about Inuit literary concepts that challenge the prevailing theories of the southern academy. While these ideas inevitably involve interpretation on my part—like the directive of the Task Force to "translate the wisdom of the elders into the realities of day-to-day government operations" (20)—they also work towards the creation of a conceptual "land bridge" between radically different knowledge systems (14).

ORAL HISTORY AND LIFE STORIES

Julie Cruikshank points out that "recording a life history is usually a social activity. It is the collaborative product of an encounter between two people, often from different cultural backgrounds, and incorporates the consciousness of an investigator as well as that of a subject" (*Life Lived* x). Indigenous autobiography, in other words, is in many ways an ethnographic genre. Just as writers of autobiographical texts enter into what Philippe Lejeune refers to as a "pact" to represent themselves truthfully, Indigenous memoirs are expected to provide accurate witness to the reality of Indigenous life.[4] In addition to *unikkaaqtuat* and songs, Rasmussen collected a variety of autobiographical narratives during the Fifth Thule Expedition.[5] In 1922, for instance, when Rasmussen visited Igloolik, Avva recounted the story of how he had gained his powers; Penny Petrone then includes this memoir in the "Personal Narratives" section of her anthology *Northern Voices: Inuit Writing in English* (120–5). Although Rasmussen was probably less interested in his informants' personal development and articulation of self than in gathering evidence with which to form hypotheses about Inuit culture and beliefs, this document exemplifies an autobiographical tradition that extends well into contemporary Inuit literature.

Versions of alphabetic and syllabic writing were introduced in the Arctic by European missionaries, and like other useful technologies (such as rifles and radio) the people had no qualms about making these ones their own.[6] McGrath explains, furthermore, that "the ability to read and write was necessary for Bible study, so missionaries provided paper, and natives were encouraged to write out their life stories to practise these newly acquired reading and writing skills. Keeping diaries was also encouraged as a way of ensuring that the Sabbath was identified and observed as a day of prayer and reflection, and these diaries frequently took on the form of autobiographies or were later used in their composition.... Of 783 works published by Inuit prior to 1981, more than one quarter can be identified as being primarily reminiscent or autobiographical" ("Circumventing" 223–4).[7] Early diaries include the 1880 writings of Abraham Ulrikab, a Labrador Inuk who travelled to Europe with his family in order to participate in Carl Hagenbeck's ethnographic display at the Hamburg zoo.[8] Back in Labrador, memoirs soon began to follow diaries, and in 1893, seventy-four-year-old Lydia Campbell began writing her *Sketches of Labrador Life*, which was first published in the St. John's *Evening Telegram* (McGrath, *Canadian* 84). In 1940, a Labrador woman named Anauta (Lizzie Ford Blackmore), who was working in the United States as a performer/lecturer, published an autobiography entitled *Land of the Good Shadows: The Life Story of Anauta, an Eskimo Woman*.[9] And in 1964, Lydia Campbell's great-grandniece Elizabeth Goudie wrote a memoir that was later published under the title *Woman of Labrador*.

In other parts of the Canadian Arctic, many other memoirs and personal reminiscences were also appearing; many were serialized in northern publications like *North, Inuktitut, Inuit Today, Inukshuk*, and *Nunatsiaq News*, and never appeared as independent monographs. Robin McGrath's thorough research in the 1980s documents hundreds of texts of this kind. Her doctoral thesis, *Canadian Inuit Literature: The Development of a Tradition* provides an excellent overview of the texts available at the time, as does her 1979 *Canadian Inuit Literature: An Annotated Bibliography*. In 1980, she published selections of contemporary Inuit writing in a small anthology entitled *Paper Stays Put: A Collection of Inuit Writing*, beautifully illustrated by the late Alootook Ipellie.[10] Penny Petrone's larger 1988 anthology *Northern Voices: Inuit Writing in English* also excerpts an extremely wide range of material, and includes a section entitled "'When All Meat Was Juicy and Tender': Personal Narratives, Letters, and Transitional Literature" (101–98).

For both Robin McGrath and Penny Petrone, life writing is a "transitional" genre—an early stage in a literature's "development" (Petrone 105). As McGrath explains:

> There are a number of reasons why autobiography is one of the first forms of written literature to emerge in a newly literate society. First, one of the most obvious subjects for a new writer to attempt is that which he or she knows best—the self; second, the contact that promotes literacy constitutes a major disruptive force in the lives of pre-literate people, and autobiographies seem to thrive during times of political, technological, or environmental upheaval; and finally, autobiography has a pre-determined chronological structure, a limited subject matter, and generally requires little research or invention, but at the same time it is flexible enough to accommodate the inclusion of oral songs and stories, religious or spiritual speculation, political opinion, or history. ("Circumventing" 223)

McGrath's terminology ("newly literate"; "pre-literate") tends unfortunately to evoke now-discredited ideas of social evolution, and there is a sense that literary traditions, too, have a predetermined developmental path. Soon, it is suggested, Inuit writers will no longer have to rely on the "easy" genre of the memoir and can instead progress toward the production of more "sophisticated" genres, like the novel. The idea seems to be that in order for a text (or a tradition) to be fully literary, it must be predominantly "invented," or fictional. A literary text, here, is not defined as one in which form matters as much as content; rather, it is understood to be directly related to narrative creativity or inventiveness.

Theories of autobiography, however, have revealed the ways in which subjects recreate themselves as literary characters and endow their life stories with narrative conventions; indeed, McGrath herself notes that "Inuit men writing about themselves frequently use some or all of the elements of the narratives of the two major epic heroes, Kaujjarjuk and Kiviok" ("Circumventing" 224).[11] In particular, she observes that the structure of I, Nuligak—the memoir of an Inuvialuit man whom the whalers called Bob Cockney—follows the structure of the tale of Kaujjarjuk, the maligned orphan.[12] Maurice Métayer, the Oblate priest who edited and translated Nuligak's text, also noted this resemblance: "The Eskimo legends of the fatherless little orphan are continually recalled," he says (Nuligak 9). McGrath goes on to argue that the Cape Dorset photographer Peter Pitseolak—author of the 1975 life story People from our Side—"is more like the hot-tempered Kivviok," and that "the episodic structure of the work mirrors the circular journey pattern of the Kiviok myth" ("Oral Influences" 162; "Circumventing" 224). Depending on a critic's biases and point of view, this could be viewed either as sophisticated literary allusion or—for those mired in the literary evolution schema—as mere narrative imitation by an author who lacked the creativity to construct his own.

Making a strong argument for the aesthetic sophistication of Indigenous autobiographical texts, Sam McKegney notes in his discussion of Anthony Apakark Thrasher's autobiography *Thrasher: Skid Row Eskimo* that "few residential school survival narratives have found their way to publication *as literature.*... [They] are mainly invoked as testimonial evidence and discussed in distinctly non-literary terms" (59, emphasis added). Here, McKegney draws attention to an important challenge in the study of life writing: the testimonial quality of the genre, which results in an overwhelming interest in the historical and ethnographic data contained in autobiographical texts. In *Fictions in Autobiography: Studies in the Art of Self-Invention*, Paul John Eakin writes that "most readers naturally assume that all autobiographies are based on the verifiable facts of a life history, and it is this referential dimension, imperfectly understood, that has checked the development of *a poetics of autobiography*" (3, emphasis added). While autobiography and oral history provide historical perspectives, cultural information, and life lessons that are of undeniable value, most literary critics would likely now agree that questions of language and literary form are *inseparable* from the historical and political qualities of texts. To pay close attention to them, furthermore, recognizes the individuality and autonomy of storytellers, rather than understanding them as involuntary cultural ambassadors—and their tales as ethnographic artifacts. For this reason, McKegney carefully notes the ways in which the formal aspects of Anthony Apakark Thrasher's text reflect its situation: "rather than mapping a path from institutionalized oppression to intellectual and spiritual emancipation, Thrasher's writing remains mired in un-freedom, powerfully symbolized by the cage from which he writes" (61). He argues that *Skid Row Eskimo* is "in many ways antithetical to the *Bildungsroman* structures of other survival narratives" and of the autobiographical genre more generally (61).

Reading Indigenous autobiographies as literary texts, then, has an important strategic function: it aims to liberate Indigenous authors from ethnocentric assumptions regarding their choice of genre and from ethnographic readings that diminish readerly appreciation of their skill. Keeping in mind the directive adapted from the IQ Task Force—that literary criticism be integrated into IQ, rather than vice versa—however, I would like to raise some questions about literary readings in this context. While they undeniably have their uses, to what extent do they risk imposing the priorities of southern academics onto Inuit texts? Are literary readings—with their emphasis on aesthetics and their uncertainty about didacticism—supported by Inuit practice? Does the *Inuit Qaujimajatuqangit* regarding stories and storytelling include the aesthetic appreciation of elders' life stories? Asking these questions, I hope, can act as one way of ensuring that IQ retains its deserved prominence in these discussions.

Over the last thirty or so years, the readership of Inuit literature has drastically changed, as Inuit growing up in the settlements have become interested in what life was like before the massive government interventions of the 1950s and '60s. The pragmatic, ethnographic aspects of life writing or life telling have in fact been harnessed by Nunavummiut, as Frédéric Laugrand argues, "to better affirm the continuity of their ancestral values, as if history had never displaced them" [pour affirmer encore mieux la continuité de leurs valeurs ancestrales, comme si l'histoire ne les avait jamais bousculées] ("Écrire" 111). The primary sources for these ancestral values are the memories of Inuit elders, and as a result, the years of political organizing that resulted in the creation of Nunavut were also marked by a renewed interest in the collection of oral traditions (Laugrand, "Écrire" 98). Christianization, tuberculosis, residential schools, community relocation, and the influence of television have all interfered with the transmission of Inuit knowledge, but the life narratives of elders can help to compensate for these interruptions. As a result, institutions and communities across the Arctic have established oral history or oral traditions projects, and some of these have resulted in published volumes. As Laugrand says, "the Inuit were now becoming the principal actors in a movement destined to validate and safeguard their traditions" ("Écrire" 98). [Les Inuit devenaient maintenant les acteurs principaux d'un mouvement destiné à valoriser et sauvegarder leurs traditions.]

In 1976, a small collection entitled *Stories from Pangnirtung*—the result of a series of locally initiated interviews with eleven elders—was published by Hurtig, with illustrations by renowned Iglulingmiutaq artist Germaine Arnaktauyok (Akulujuk et al.). In 1989, Hattie Mannik began interviewing members of the Baker Lake Elders group, and in 1998, she published *Inuit Nunamiut: Inland Inuit*, a collection of elders' memories and reflections. This project was funded by various governmental offices and organizations, such as the Government of the Northwest Territories Department of Culture and Communications' Oral Traditions and Cultural Enhancement programs, the Department of Indian and Northern Affairs, Inuit Tapirisat of Canada, and the Nunavut Research Institute (NRI). In 1998, NRI and the Royal Ontario Museum published *The Arctic Sky: Inuit*

Astronomy, Star Lore, and Legend—the product of John MacDonald's work with the Igloolik Oral History Project. And in 2004, McGill-Queen's University Press published *Uqalurait: An Oral History of Nunavut*—the result of more than ten years of work by David Webster, Suzanne Evaloardjuk, Peter Irniq, Uriash Puqiqnak, David Serkoak, John Bennett, Susan Rowley, and dozens of Nunavut elders.

Many more oral histories have been collected but have yet to find their way into print. The Angmarlik Interpretive Centre in Pangnirtung, for instance, has a number of taped interviews with elders (many of whom are now deceased); some of these have been translated into English, but they have not yet been transcribed in Inuktitut.[13] The archives of the Igloolik Oral History Project, meanwhile, contain a great deal of unpublished material;[14] part of this collection is also housed at the Northwest Territories Archives in Yellowknife, along with the Ulukhaqtuurmiut (Holman Region) History Project, the Inuit Broadcasting Corporation Elders Project, and many others. The Baker Lake Hunters and Trappers Organization and Inuit Heritage Centre have also sponsored a number of other oral history and land-use studies; the resulting reports contain incredibly detailed maps, stories, and legends about Utkuhikhalingmiut and Akilinirmiut territory.[15] These are only a few examples of the existing cultural organizations and archives.

Projects of this kind fulfill an important cultural function; as the editors of the first volume of Nunavut Arctic College Interviewing Inuit Elders series put it, "in a rapidly changing society, the preservation of the knowledge of the Inuit elders is of great value to the cultural identity of modern Inuit" (Angmaalik et al. 1). Frédéric Laugrand reminds us, however, that oral history projects have a political dimension as well ("Écrire" 102). In the case of land use and occupancy projects—such as the 1976 ITC-commissioned *Inuit Land Use and Occupancy Project* led by Milton Freeman,[16] or the 1977 *Our Footprints Are Everywhere: Inuit Land Use and Occupancy in Labrador*—oral histories are tied directly to land claims. Laugrand expands upon this, arguing that in accordance with the political movements of the 1970s and '80s, oral traditions have also been used to create a sense of a collective social memory—"a discursive move deemed necessary in an era when the dominant ideology was defined by the denial of cultural differences" [une prise de parole jugée nécessaire à une époque où l'idéologie dominante consiste précisément à nier les différences culturelles] ("Écrire" 102). Beyond the creation of a collective memory, the act of remembering and of telling stories about the past might itself be thought of as a deeply political act. Elders' testimonies give Inuit a venue in which to tell (or read) their own version of history, and they bring a particular reality to the history of Arctic administration, as Inuit talk about the experience of residential school, of the deaths of their dogs, of life in the settlements, or of relatives who disappeared into medical ships and never returned. In this context, oral histories become acts of resistance, or of healing. Inuit also have the opportunity to remember, or to conjure, the time before the rapid cultural changes of the late-twentieth century; auto-ethnographic narratives about the ways of the *inummariit*—the "*real* Inuit"—are radical and empowering, particularly in the hands and ears of Inuit youth.

None of these political factors, however, would cancel out the possibility of literary readings; literary scholars would simply extend the conversation by exploring the *ways* in which elders' stories created these effects through the use careful (and often beautiful) language. In order to understand whether these kinds of readings impose upon IQ, however, we will need to take a closer look at what elders have to say about Inuit storytelling.

WHAT INUIT HAVE KNOWN FOR A VERY LONG TIME—ABOUT STORYTELLING

When I first went to Pangnirtung and had the opportunity to participate in interviews with elders, I was initially surprised by the elders' readiness to state that they did not know the answer to a question. In the academic world that I had come from, authority figures hardly ever admitted to not knowing anything. But these elders, I soon learned, were following a strict protocol about appropriate kinds of speech, or storytelling. Many of them began their interviews with some variation of this statement: "I am only going to tell you what I know from experience." During the oral history courses that eventually resulted in Nunavut Arctic College's Interviewing Inuit Elders series,[17] instructors Alexina Kublu, Frédéric Laugrand, and Jarich Oosten also noted that the commitment to speaking only from experience was a consistent feature of elders' narratives. During an interview with Saullu Nakasuk and Pauloosie Angmarlik from Pangnirtung, Julia Shaimaiyuk asked:

> Sometimes when you are telling about something, I hear you saying, "I can't talk about what I haven't experienced." Did you get told…?
>
> Saullu: Yes.
>
> Julia: One is not to talk about something without having experienced it?
>
> Saullu: Yes. One is not to talk about something just from hearsay [*unik-kaaqtuqariaqanngittuq tusatuinnaqtaminirmik*], because it is too easy to speak a falsehood [*sallusarainnarmat*]. It is not desirable to tell un-

truths [*Uqaruminaqpanngilaq sulinngittunik*]. (Angmaalik et al., *Pigia-rutit* 5)

The phrase used for "what I haven't experienced," here, is *qaujisimanngitan-nik*, which uses the same root as the term for "traditional knowledge," *qaujima-jatuqangit* (or *qaujimanituqangit*). *Qauji-* refers to knowing; the addition of the infix *–sima-* "describes a state acquired through a completed action" (Harper, "Suffixes" 70): something that is already known by the speaker, or in this case, not known (and therefore not something that the speaker can comfortably provide information about). As the translators make clear, however, "knowledge" refers specifically to something that the speaker knows *from personal experience*, as opposed to the kind of "knowledge" attained at the university, which continues to be primarily derived from secondhand sources, like teachers or books. In the Inuit context, something that the speaker has only heard about—*tusatuin-naqtaminirmik*—does not count as something that is "known."

Throughout the Interviewing Inuit Elders series, students raise topics that the elders may not have personal experience with; at times, they explain that they cannot answer: "Nobody ever really told me the full story so I can't pass it on to you," says Lucassie Nutaraaluk of Iqaluit;[18] "I don't want to guess, since nobody has ever really told me the whole story" (Aupilaarjuk et al., *Law* 185). Again, these kinds of responses challenge the process of gathering oral history, requiring the students to constantly revise the questions that they had prepared. As the editors of the series explain, the interview was already "by no means a normal situation: as elders are held in great respect, students were not accustomed to subjecting them to long lists of questions" (Angmaalik et al. 3).[19] The unfamiliar context of the classroom, however, created a space in which this breach of conduct could be acceptable, and the elders encouraged the students to question them (Angmaalik et al. 3–7). As Mittimatalik (Pond Inlet) elder Elisapee Ootoova put it, "you shouldn't be wary of asking us any questions *as we are not at home*" (Angmaalik et al. 4; emphasis added). Likewise, on occasion, the elders respond to questions by stating that they have "only heard" about the topic from another person, but then decide to share a few details—though always with the qualification that the knowledge is second-hand. "I can tell you the story as I heard it," Nutaraaluk says (Aupilaarjuk et al., *Law* 183).

As Kublu, Laugrand, and Oosten explain, these protocols lead to a body of knowledge that is dynamic and variable (Angmaalik et al. 9–10). "Each elder had his own knowledge and experience and was prepared to acknowledge the value of different opinions and experiences related by others," the editors write

(Angmaalik et al. 10). Laugrand has written elsewhere that the idea of establishing a communal Inuit identity and cultural history is unappealing to many elders: "for them, such a project risks the formation of inaccurate generalizations that would not be compatible with the desire to respect the diversity of local experience, traditions, and histories" ("Écrire" 100). [Pour eux, une telle opération risque d'aboutir à des généralisations abusives et peu compatibles avec leur souci de respecter la diversité des expériences, des traditions et des histoires locales.] As Nutaraaluk says when asked to tell the story of Sedna, "I'll tell you the story as I heard it. I think our stories vary from community to community even though they are the same *unikkaqtuat*. I want you to know there are variations" (Aupilaarjuk et al., *Law* 188). This diversity, however, provides a real challenge for southern scholars, who are often eager to reconcile differences, iron out inconsistencies, and work toward the development of theories. Richard Dauenhauer and Nora Marks Dauenhauer explain that they "prefer to offer details of ordinary lives, and report what actually happened to identifiable people, in contrast to making generalized abstractions about 'the culture' or how 'they' used to do things 'in the old days'" (*Haa Kusteeyí* xi). Likewise, the critical discourse of Inuit elders is geared toward the telling of individual truths, rather than the discovery of Truths, as the latter will—ironically—almost always be too general to be accurate. The genre of the life history, however, is an effective way of ensuring that the knowledge shared remains grounded in the context of individual experience.

The term for "life stories" used in the Interviewing Inuit Elders series is *inuusirmingnik unikkaat*: stories from *inuusiq*, "one's life; one's experience" (Spalding 27). Interestingly, the elders made a distinction between this type of storytelling and others, such as the *unikkaaqtuat*, or traditional tales. At one point, a student asked Hervé Paniaq of Iglulik,

Were you told unikkaaqtuat [when you were a child]?

Paniaq: Just any old story?[20]

Can you tell us a story that you have heard?

Paniaq: Yes, are we also here for that?

The reason why we are here is to leave words behind for our descendants.

Paniaq: There is one person [Alexina Kublu[21]] who can tell a story now. She taped one today and two the other day. If we start story-telling now, the day is going to be too short. (Angmaalik et al. 52–3)

Paniaq's reluctance to tell an *unikkaaqtuaq* in the middle of his life-narrative strikes me as significant. During my first summer in Pangnirtung, the program coordinators invited a number of local elders—including Evie Anilniliak, Joanasie Qappik, Jaco Ishulutaq, Inuusiq Nashalik, and Jamesie Mike—to come and speak to the students; they also hired an interpreter, Marie Uviluq from Igloolik, to facilitate these lessons. Uviluq made it very clear to us that she was not a "translator"—she was not there to simply repeat what was said, and therefore to efface herself in the process. Rather, she *moderated* the discussions, and was very strict in instructing us about the appropriate protocols to use when addressing the elders. Often, instead of translating, she would tell the students that their question was not appropriate, or did not make sense, and that we should think of a different one. One of the most common corrections that the students received was about changing the subject—if the elders had come to talk about climate change, then we should ask questions about climate change. I gradually became aware of our tendency to propel a discussion haphazardly from one topic to another; in our view, anything loosely associated with the theme was fair game. Once, during a visit by Jamesie Mike and Inuusiq Nashalik, we were allowed to change the subject, but we had to first establish that we were doing so, and only with the elders' approval.

This experience leads me to speculate that when the Nunavut Arctic College students asked Hervé Paniaq to tell an *unikkaaqtuaq* during his interview, he was surprised by what he perceived as a change in topic. "Are we also here for that?" he asked (Angmaalik et al. 52). But what is the distinction between the two genres? As I detailed in Chapter 2, an *unikkaaqtuaq* is literally "a story that goes on for a very long time," but it typically refers to tales that have been handed down over generations, which is why it is often translated as "myth." The term "myth," however, fails to capture the nuances of the genre of *unikkaaqtuat*. The Nunavut Arctic College students asked the elders about the factuality of these long stories:

Were the stories about animals turning into humans true? [*Taimaqai takkua inuruuqqaningit sulimmata?*]

Imaruittuq: They were probably true. That's why there are stories about this. [*Sulingmata kisiani taimauvaktuq.*]

Nutaraaluk: They have to be true. [*Taimaak kisiani sulimmata…*] All animals could turn into people, according to what we were told. They turned into people a long time ago before there was Christianity. (Aupilaarjuk et al., *Law* 196; *Maligatuqaliriniup* 203)

Similarly, in Volume 3, *Childrearing Practices*, a student asks Uqsuralik Ottokie from Kinngait, "Are unikkaaqtuat, the old stories, beneficial to children?" (Ekho and Ottokie 114). She answers: "The unikkaaqtuat are beneficial to children. *At one time these stories were true, but because they are so old they just became stories.* They are very useful for children. There are all sorts of stories that can be told to children. Most times, children start settling down when you tell a story. Most of the stories that we heard were true and they have a definite benefit for children" (114, emphasis added).

The stories are true, the elders suggest—or, they used to be true, but then the world changed its rules. That said, the extent to which the veracity of the old stories is confirmed varies from teller to teller. Again, we should be wary of generalizing statements like "the elders believe these myths to be true"; it is important to keep in mind that an *unikkaaqtuaq* may be what J. Edward Chamberlin refers to as "a ceremony of belief…not a chronicle of events" (*If This Is Your Land* 179). After all, the elders often mention the entertainment value of the *unikkaaqtuat*, whether in putting children to sleep—or scaring them. As Imaruittuq says, "the *unikkaaqtuaq* of the ptarmigan myth made children squeamish about baby lemmings. It was for pure entertainment" (Aupilaarjuk et al., *Law* 179).[22] They sometimes address the possibility that the storytellers were bending the truth; Naqi Ekho, who was born in Uumanarjuaq (Blacklead Island), discusses the stories that she was told about *inugarulliit* (little people), saying, "maybe we were being fooled, but on the other hand, maybe it was true" (Ekho and Ottokie 117).

The difference between *inuusirmingnik unikkaat* and *unikkaaqtuat*, then, cannot be reduced to a distinction between the historical and the mythical.[23] A number of scholars have pointed out, meanwhile, that the factuality of stories is more of a southern concern.[24] As Ann Fienup-Riordan writes, "legends and historical accounts are considered equally reliable sources or information, simply referring to different time periods—the distant past and recent times. As such, legends and historical accounts exist along a continuum and are not mutually exclusive" (xx). Imaruittuq says that "Kiviuq used to be an *unikkaaq* but since it is so old we call it an *unikkaaqtuaq* today" (Aupilaarjuk et al., *Law* 179). The distinction here is temporal—once the story became old enough, it switched genres. However, the switch might also be related to a sense of distance from the original teller or from the experience of the original events. Having been passed from person to person, the story passes deep into the realm of hearsay, and as such its connection to personal experience is lost.

The telling of an *unikkaaqtuaq*, then, seems difficult to reconcile with earlier assertions about the importance of speaking from personal experience. How

does this protocol work with Inuit oral tradition, which necessarily involves relating events that one has "only heard about"? This, perhaps, is ultimately why
unikkaaqtuat form a separate genre from life stories; when one tells an *unikkaaqtuaq*, it is necessary and acceptable to speak of things beyond one's experience. "I can tell you what I have heard," the elders say. They might also add
the suffix *-guuq*, used for reporting discourse; in the Siglit dialect of Tuktoyaktuk and Sachs Harbour they insert the postbase *-niq-*, which indicates hearsay
(Harper, *Suffixes* 18; Lowe 124).[25] *Unikkaaqtuat*, therefore, are not only long stories that are set in the past; they are stories that require (or allow) storytellers to
deviate from the strict relaying of their own, personal experience.

When Robin McGrath referred to life stories as the preferred genre of "new-
ly-literate people," she alluded to the reality that the Western tradition has, since
the Enlightenment, demonstrated a preference for what T.S. Eliot called "the
individual talent"—for innovation and invention—over tradition. Again, in order to gather autobiography into the esteemed category of literature, critics have
stressed its invented or crafted nature. I wonder, however, how elders would
react to the idea that their life stories are literary texts. Again, the English term
"literature" does not translate very easily into Inuktitut; a literal translation—
titirarniq, or "writing"—has the same limited scope as the source language, as it
does not include the ancient traditions of story and song. Are aesthetics—concepts of artfulness, crafting, or form—a consideration when elders are passing
on what they know from experience? Again, are literary readings of *inuusirmingnik unikkaat* justified within the framework of IQ?

While I am wary of generalizations, it is worth noting—as we work to construct a "land bridge" between IQ and literary studies—that the moments in
which the elders in Interviewing Inuit Elders draw attention to their ability as
storytellers, or to the form or aesthetics of stories, occur overwhelmingly in rela-
tion to the *unikkaaqtuat*. When the students are interviewing the Igloolik elder
Emile Imaruittuq, they ask him to tell the story of Kaugjagjuk, the orphan. "I can
tell you the story of Kaugjagjuk," he says, "but I am not a very good story teller"
(Aupilaarjuk et al., *Law* 186).[26] They then ask him if he has heard about Ailaq
and Papik (188).[27] "I've heard about them," Imaruittuq say, "but I'm a very bad
story teller. As I keep telling you, I'm terrible at telling stories" (Aupilaarjuk et al.
Law 188). In the first volume of the same series, we hear something similar from
Alexina Kublu—now the Languages Commissioner of Nunavut—before she tells
the *unikkaaqtuat* that she heard from her father, Michel Kupaaq Piugattuk: "I
am not what in Inuktitut is considered to be an 'uqamminiq,' someone who is
linguistically nimble," she says (Angmaalik et al. 151). There is a strong sense, it

seems, of the way in which *unikkaaqtuat* are supposed to be told, and these issues are far less prominent in the context of *inuusirmingnik unikkaat*, or life stories.

One exception to this occurs when Nutaraaluk is asked to talk about *akitsirarvik*—a place where traditional trials were held. Nutaraaluk says that he is not able to talk about it, as he has not heard the full story, and then adds, "I long for my uncle Paujungi because he used to be an excellent story teller and had a lot of knowledge.... I am not a very good story teller" (Aupilaarjuk et al., *Law* 185). Interestingly, Nutaraaluk's expression of concern about his storytelling abilities is not in response to a request for an *unikkaaqtuaq*; rather, he is being asked to speak about something that he has heard about, but not experienced. Aesthetics, this would suggest, are especially important in relating secondhand or reported speech. The reasons behind this are not stated, though we might speculate that it has to do with the departure from speaking from experience. When telling an *inuusirmingnik unikkaaq*, a storyteller has complete authority, but when telling an *unikkaaqtuaq*, the teller performs in the context a relationship with the person who told her/him the story—and with all other past tellers. Perhaps the caveats indicate a fear of not doing justice to the tradition, or perhaps they constitute a rhetorical gesture: an expression of humility.

The purpose here is not to derive a general theory of Inuit "literature" or literariness; given the variety of ways in which elders and other Inuktitut speakers define and talk about genres of storytelling, this would likely only lead to the kinds of inaccurate generalizations that Kublu, Laugrand, and Oosten warn about: "all [Inuit] knowledge is social by nature," they remind us, "and the idea of objectified true knowledge holds little attraction or fascination" (9). I would like to propose, however, that incidents of reported speech (whether brief or as long as an *unikkaaqtuaq*) open up the possibility for aesthetic considerations of storytelling—at least, within the framework in which the elders who participated in Interviewing Inuit Elders are working. In a way, then, this may serve as the same kind of conceptual "land bridge" that the IQ Task Force has been seeking for the Government of Nunavut. While elders are more likely to refer to their life stories are direct representations of their own experience (rather than as carefully crafted works of aesthetic value) for the listeners or readers of these stories, the words spoken immediately fall under the category of something that one has "heard about." As a result, listeners become responsible for the *form* of the *unikkaat*, since the stories conveyed not only the elders' experience—they convey it in a good way.

LIFE AMONG THE QALLUNAAT AS A "LITERARY" TEXT

This discussion of genre and of Inuit literary criticism will, I hope, assist students and scholars in thinking about the many Inuit autobiographies and oral histories in existence. I would like to look briefly at one that exemplifies the ways in which Inuit authors draw upon and adapt traditional genres—and contribute to the process of Inuit literary criticism. Minnie Aodla Freeman, author of *Life Among the Qallunaat*, is of the same generation as some of the elders interviewed by Nunavut Arctic College; because of the location of her childhood home in the James Bay area, however, the *qallunaat* world had a greater impact on her early life. Her book—written in English—draws upon some southern conventions of autobiographical writing; however, it might also be meaningfully understood within the tradition of *inuusirmingnik unikkaat*, or speaking from experience.[28] Like the elders in the Interviewing Inuit Elders series, however, Freeman at times crosses over into other genres. In these instances, she, too, demonstrates a comparable concern for aesthetics that contributes further to an understanding of Inuit notions of "literariness" and literary criticism.

Life Among the Qallunaat was published in 1978; it tells the story of Freeman's childhood in the James Bay region and of her eventual 1957 journey to Ottawa, when she was twenty years old, to work for the Department of Northern Affairs. This is where the book begins: with Minnie[29] newly arrived in the nation's capital, negotiating the unfamiliar landscape of the big city. One-third of the way through the book, Freeman changes gears in order to tell us about her early childhood, when she made the seasonal rounds with her people—the Cape Hope Islanders, led by her maternal grandfather, Weetaltuk.[30] Their homeland is by far the southernmost region of what is now Nunavut, and as a result, Minnie's family often comes into contact with Cree people, with Hudson's Bay Company traders, and with French clergy. Minnie is intermittently subjected to the assimilating institutions of the south, as she attends residential school, works at the hospital in Fort George, and spends time as a tuberculosis patient in Hamilton. Eventually, the narrative comes full circle: she accepts a job in Ottawa and heads south for a true immersion in *qallunaat* culture. We learn that although she goes home occasionally to visit, Minnie stays in the South, having married a *qallunaaq*—the anthropologist Milton Freeman.

Life Among the Qallunaat was not Freeman's first rendition of her story. In 1971 she wrote a play, *Survival in the South*, which was performed at the National Arts Centre in Ottawa (McGrath, *Canadian* 91). Robin McGrath later included it in her collection of Inuit writing, *Paper Stays Put* (Gedalof 100–2).

The main character is called Minnie Aodla, but the story is to some extent fictionalized; rather than recounting specific moments in Freeman's experience, it constructs a representative story of arrival—and confusion—in the South:

NARRATOR...

(Cue for red light, traffic stops)

Why have we stopped?

(Cue for green light, traffic starts)

Oh, so many things to see, so many stores...so many people walking fast and looking so sad...look at the height of that house. (Gedalof, *Paper* 104)

Here we have the trope—also found in Anthony Apakark Thrasher's *Skid Row Eskimo*—of the Inuk lost in the city, overwhelmed by cars and the rules of traffic. As such, *Survival in the South* seems to frame Minnie's experience in a way that fits the expectations of southern audiences. While *Life Among the Qallunaat* also contains many accounts of the very real alienation that Minnie experienced in the South, it intersperses these experiences with witty and poignant reflections about the cultural differences that strike Minnie during her travels.

McGrath likewise understands Freeman as a kind of cultural critic, but she refers to *Life Among the Qallunaat* as "in many way a ruthless indictment of white culture.... There is a strong sense of the anger, bitterness, and isolation experienced by young Inuit in residential schools and in the South, and Freeman is direct in her description of the sexual harassment native girls suffered at the hands of white teachers and employers" ("Circumventing" 228–9). For McGrath, this perceived critique functions as a safe alternative to the autobiographical cataloguing of either personal achievements or complaints, practices which—she argues—Inuit women writers avoid ("Circumventing" 226, 224). Dale Blake, however—who interviewed Inuit autobiographers like Freeman during her dissertation research—allows Freeman the opportunity to express her own intentions; she tells Blake that her book "has never had any intention... to be political at all," and Blake takes her at her word (qtd. in Blake 147). Heather Henderson, meanwhile, notes that "Freeman's deceptively simple style belies her narrative sophistication and concern with language. For how, indeed, could a translator...be other than sensitive to the power of words?" (61). Indeed, Freeman's vivid, humorous, and poignant reflections provide ample material for readers with ears attuned to the ways in which good stories are told. I would like to look at two examples, here, in which Freeman departs from the genre of *inuusirmingnik unikkaat*—and therefore moves (like the elders interviewed at Nunavut Arctic College) into the realm of Inuit literary criticism.

In a section entitled "School Is Not the Only Place of Education," Freeman talks about the winter in which her grandmother told her many stories. She writes: "Some of my ancestors were very good storytellers and the stories were passed on verbally from generation to generation as we did not have a way of writing. Everything had to be told from memory, just as we always memorized the landscapes of our hunting areas. Each generation had to carry them in their heads and tell them year in and year out" (109). Freeman offers an example of a brief story about a stingy man who transforms into an *inuppak*—a fearsome giant. But the focus of the section is not an *unikkaaqtuaq* at all; it is an *unikkausinnguaq*—an invented story (though Freeman does not use this term). "Sometimes," she says, "someone would invent a new [story]. Here is my contribution to this tradition, a story that I invented, but a story that is not very delightful to pass on to my children" (109). She then tells a tale about a young husband and wife, Nakuk and Maviak, who are excited to have a new son. Nakuk imagines that his son will be a great hunter of muskox and so names him Malittak ("he is followed"), explaining that "maybe the muskox would follow the birth of their son and the herds would be many again" (110). Nakuk plans a feast to celebrate Malittak's birth, and a ceremony to help bring the herd back. But no sooner has the ceremony been completed that the community sees an unfamiliar boat approaching, and Nakuk goes down to talk to two *qallunaat* strangers. He returns with disconcerting news: "The two officials from the *qallunaat* world have asked us not to hunt muskox for the next fifty years" (111). The community begins to grieve, but the story does not end on a sad note; in a split second, Nakuk adapts, and begins telling a new story about his son's life: "We are very fortunate that our son will never have to know how to hunt muskox, for he is fresh and will have the strength to be a great seal, polar bear, whale and narwhale [sic] hunter. Yes, he is very fortunate, for this we will name him Arlu—Killerwhale—the most feared and relentless hunter of the seas" (112).

Like the stories that Freeman tells about her own life, this one is a kind of parable, and it deals with the theme of storytelling directly. The *unikkausinnguaq* opens with Nakuk narrating the course of his son's life; he creates a kind of prophecy in which the son's birth is synonymous with the return of order to the world and the reestablishment of the old ways (109–10). The community uses different kinds of ceremony to make this happen, and the story is a key part of it. Then comes the almost cinematic intrusion of the *qallunaat*, who boss people around in their characteristic way and threaten to shatter the community's ties to its traditions. But this story is not a tragic tale of vanishing; its protagonists do not helplessly disperse or abandon their lifestyle. Instead, they demonstrate the way in which stories can be adapted, or invented, and can put a community back together. Nakuk refuses to be victimized; rather, he quickly re-narrates the government ban on the muskox hunt: it is his son's destiny to hunt other game—and of that, he suggests, there is plenty. With a new story, Nakuk can maintain his family's link to tradition and close the breach that the *qallunaat* policies have created.

Freeman's tale is thus an invented story about an invented story, and it therefore comments on the process and purpose of storytelling of this kind. Again, it is during the departures from *inuusirmingnik unikkaat* that literary concerns become highlighted; stories like these, I contend, serve as instructive moments of literary criticism. In reading this tale, I always wonder at the acquiescence of the people after they receive word that the muskox are not to be hunted. Nakuk and his community work hard from the beginning of the story to ensure their continued livelihood based on the muskox herds; why, then, do they give up as soon as the *qallunaat* have laid down the hunting ban? This says something about the authority that *qallunaat* wielded; Freeman's subsequent story of her grandfather's futile attempt to prevent her from being sent back to residential school sheds some light on this: "he always gave in to what he called authority," she explains, "for the sake of keeping peace and to prevent bad feelings" (112). Nakuk's resistance, however, may be detected in the telling of the new narrative about his young son; rather than construing his obedience as a passive and victimizing condition, he regains control over his and his son's identity by inventing a story. Likewise, Freeman's invention of the larger tale evokes her family's own experience with colonial policy and cultural change and thus adds an element of subtle critique. The story's juxtaposition in the text with the tale of the *inuppak*—the man whose greed transformed him into a dangerous monster—seems to resonate with the subsequent representation of the *qallunaat*, who likewise restrict the community's access to the resources that they are entitled to. In telling this story, Freeman emphasizes its newness. Like her character, Nakuk, she is creating a narrative with a particular purpose; in this way, paradoxically, the new story locates itself via its subject matter within a long-established system of knowledge making and adaptation: "Here is my contribution to this tradition, a story that I invented" (109). In this way, Freeman's story serves a didactic purpose: it reminds readers of the usefulness, potency, and flexibility of storytelling. As the IQ Task Force recommends, it enables Inuit control of the nature of required adaptation; it finds continuance in times of great change.

The students and elders in *Interviewing Inuit Elders* are similarly concerned with the moral of stories. When the students ask Imaruittuq about the story of Ailaq and Papik, they say that "the reason that we are asking specifically about them is because it is a story with a message for people's lives" (Aupilaarjuk et al., *Law* 187). Although literary scholars may be wary of reducing stories to their morals (thereby glossing over their nuances[31]), it is also important to accept this very pragmatic side of storytelling—and the emphasis that elders place on it. As Imaruittuq says, stories "made each one of us think, made us think hard.... storytelling can be very beneficial. For example, hunters will exchange stories about where the dangerous parts of the ice are, how they survived a blizzard, et cetera. These stories are very useful in our lives" (Aupilaarjuk et al., *Law* 179). In an interview with Dale Blake, Freeman said that "her main purpose in writing *Life Among the Qallunaat* was to keep memories from dying out: 'We need to put it on paper for our future children, for Inuit by Inuit'" (Blake 147).

Freeman also remembers a time when she was travelling with her family and a terrible storm blew up (97). It was so bad that they could not even make camp, and they had to crowd together in a makeshift tent held down by overturned sleds. The next morning, however, the sky was clear and beautiful—it "was just like *pinguartuk*, like fantasy," Freeman says (97). They saw their destination, Charlton Island, right ahead of them. Freeman recounts, "we passed an old cabin which stood up amongst the trees. Grandmother said, 'You used to live there when you were a baby.' *She did not actually say it like that; instead she remarked that my little foot marks were up there near the cabin*" (98, emphasis added).

Note, here, Freeman's attention to language, and the way in which she divides the story into content and form: "here's what my grandmother said, and now here's how she said it." The purpose of the grandmother's story is in its content—it indicates that a homecoming is occurring, as the family returns to the place where Minnie was a baby, and it is made especially meaningful after the long, difficult night of the storm. In a way, this might be a metaphor for the entire book, as Freeman imaginatively finds her way back to her origins, or tracks her own footprints. But Freeman, in relaying her grandmother's comment, is also aware of the necessity to pass on the *way* in which the story was told—here, through a beautifully poetic metonymy: "my little foot marks were up there near the cabin" (98). Her grandmother was telling a fiction; she was speaking figuratively, we can assume, as Minnie's baby footprints are not actually still visible in the snow. As reported speech, this statement's form remains prominent in Freeman's mind; as a result, this becomes a literary moment—one that sets the tone for Freeman's own literary project, which pays homage to the storytelling traditions and innovations of her people. Again, Freeman reminds us of the power of elders' stories to guide younger Inuit, as this one connects Freeman to her homeland—and reminds her of the value of her own rememberings, which can thus be locked into memory by the art of a good storyteller.

There are but two examples of an Inuk author's critical commentary on the role and the nature of storytelling; if we pay attention, most Inuit texts—whether oral or written, in Inuktitut or English—abound with these moments. Inuit literary criticism, it is safe to say, is not new territory. If we know where—and how—to look, we can see that it is tracked through with the foot marks of elders and students, writers and storytellers. And by reading the life stories and oral histories being produced in Inuit Nunaat for the teachings they contain about literary theory and practice, students and scholars will discover that *Inuit Qaujimajatuqangit* includes literary knowledge. Now, the evidence of Inuit aesthetic concerns—such as when elders profess an apparent lack of skill in storytelling, or when authors like Freeman remain attentive to the way in which stories are told—does not render literary analysis (as practised in southern academies) unproblematic. Analysis, like critical thinking, has its own cultural origins and ideologies; like the rigorous questioning of elders, it may often strike Inuit audiences as inappropriate, or at the very least, foreign. "Literary criticism," like the other "skins" that I have used to dress Inuit texts, may thus fit imperfectly. The IQ Task Force, aware of these slippages (which it conceives of in spatial terms), imagines that "in time, perhaps, as people move back and forth, the cultural chasm will disappear, the Nunavut Government will merge into the Inuit Culture, and the bridge will no longer be necessary" (15). This day is not yet at hand in Nunavut, and likewise, the southern academy has far to travel before meaningful dialogue and collaboration with IQ can reliably occur. But in the meantime, the literary knowledge that can be harvested from elders' stories may form a "land bridge," both for southerners seeking a better understanding of the north and for Inuit interested in harnessing the potential of the academic world—as did the elders at Nunavut Arctic College.

One can't help but wonder, however, what the prophesied day will look like when the "bridge"—or the "skin"—is no longer necessary. What might a truly Indigenous "academy" look like in Nunavut? The Clyde River Piqqusilirivvik—with its emphasis on acquiring and documenting traditional knowledge, land-based skills, and Inuktitut language—acts as one example, as do the various community and college programs that get Inuit students out of classrooms, into elders' living rooms, and out on the land. Likewise, the resources being created by Inuit scholars and experts—especially those spoken and written in

Inuktitut—presage an academic practice that will shrug off the dominance of southern modes of thinking. In some ways, then, Indigenization is happening already, but in other regards, there is a long way to go. I look forward to the day when Inuit Studies conferences are held exclusively in Inuit Nunaat, when the majority of speakers are Inuit, and when *qallunaat* allies are following (not leading) the conversation—in Inuktitut. That day might seem far away, and the path that leads there may be difficult to locate.

Luckily, though, the stories are there to guide us.

INUUQATIGIITTIARNIQ
Living Together in a Good Way

THE PROTOCOL ABOUT SPEAKING FROM EXPERIENCE is a hard one to keep in this line of work. When I have long conversations with students and colleagues—particularly in the context of graduate examination settings—I am often struck by the realization that within an Inuit framework, none of us really "knows" what we're talking about. Rather, our debates are furnished almost exclusively with content gathered from the writing of others, which itself likely derives predominantly from books. Protocols in Native Studies and some other disciplines—though certainly not English—do encourage time spent "in the field," where scholars may gain some first-hand knowledge. In speaking about it, though, they are required to put a limit on their articulation of personal experiences, utilizing the safer and more professional modes of discourse that—despite the interventions of postmodernism—in many cases remain "objective." While some scholars tell stories, not all of them get away with it, and there are risks in breaking out of the modes of speech that have traditionally been a source of strength and safety for academics.

Students and scholars of Indigenous literatures thus face a real challenge in writing contributions like this one, as they attempt to honour the very diverse audiences to whom they are responsible. Ethics and current protocols require that we keep community concerns in the foreground and that our language be inclusive to non-academic readers. Realistically, though, our work is primarily read by other academics, with their own strict—and often intimidating—standards and expectations. The protocol of anonymity in peer review, for instance, while ensuring rigour and protecting the publishing process from unfair bias, also gives us permission to be truly nasty to one another. So while I am aware that my readership here is primarily academic, I would like to share some final, personal reflections that may also be of interest to a northern audience. While I don't mean to erect an insurmountable binary between Inuit communities and the academy—I certainly know students and scholars who work in both realms—their cultures remain markedly different. As I have suggested throughout this book, this difference provides an opportunity—in the spirit of *qanuqtuurniq*—for both Inuit and academic traditions to find ways of adapting to their changing situations.

When the *Inuit Qaujimajatuqangit* Task Force called for the building of a "land bridge" between Inuit culture and the Government of Nunavut, it foretold that this bridge would be "founded on the bedrock of primary relationships within Inuit Culture...[:]

a) The relationship of a people to their land, and by extension to their culture;

b) The relationship to one's family;

c) The relationship of the individual to his or her own inner Spirit;

d) The relationship to one's social grouping (to one's community or organization) or the relationship between social groupings" ("First Annual Report" 5, 8).

As readers of Inuit literature—beings who currently occupy a parallel land bridge—how can we prioritize these relationships? How can we embody *Inuuqatigiittiarniq*, the principle of living together in a good way, through elements like "respecting others, relationships and caring for people" ("Guiding Principles")? What does literature—and writing about literature—have to do with these principles? While the IQ Task Force suggests that adaptations need to happen on both sides, my reflections here draw primarily on my experience of my own, primary environment: the southern institution within which I am privileged to work. Speaking plainly, I would like both academic and northern readers to know how the reading of Inuit literature—and the experience of Inuit ways—continue to shape and challenge my work, and my life, in the south.

RELATIONSHIP TO LAND

The IQ Task Force calls the relationship to land "the *primordial* relationship (the first relationship and the one from which the others flow)" ("First Annual Report," emphasis in original). In 2011, the Pangnirtung Summer Program camped for one week at a place called Itillikuluk—the "little crossing over" place—near the northern limits of Cumberland Sound. One of our elders, Joanasie Qappik, had suggested the spot, and even in the days before we left, we had great fun poring over maps of the Sound, listening to stories about his many travels in the area. Out in the boat, Joanasie pointed out many, many places, the names of which record the extensive and dynamic history of the region. Sometimes, when we were out looking for seals or beluga, he would ask the *qallunaat* which way Pangnirtung was from our location (our guesses must have been amusing). He was teaching us to pay attention to our surroundings and to try to acquire at least a basic literacy of the extensive land-text through which we were moving.

Very near Itillikuluk is a special site called the Blind Man's Walk, and on the way back to camp one day, the small fleet of boats carrying our entire camp stopped there, just off shore. Visible on the cliff face is a steep and rocky pathway, very striking in the right light. I was excited to hear its name, thinking that it must refer to Aningaat, the blind brother whose sight was restored by the loons. But our interpreter, Henry Mike, informed me that that was a different story. Once the group was gathered, our knuckles grazing against the hulls of the boats as we held them together, Joanasie spoke to us about that place. He pointed out the path where the blind man had walked, and then concluded with something that stands out in my memory as wonderfully baffling: we had heard the story, he said, and this is where it happened. Like me, the students seemed mystified—what was the story?—but I was proud of them: they didn't question our elder, but simply observed the place and then settled down to return to camp. For me, and perhaps for them, this was a good reminder of the literacy that we lacked in that place—of the stories that I hadn't heard but that were layered into the landscape all around me. Joanasie Qappik is a true expert in this field.

Experiences like these act as a reminder of the ways in which Inuit literary traditions are deeply rooted in geography. Again, the state of *silatujuq*—having wisdom—aligns itself practically with a close understanding of one's *sila*, one's environment. This is something that we need to keep in mind when reading and listening to Inuit literature, but it is not easily achieved from the remoteness of a library or southern classroom. Even universities, however, are situated in their own nuanced and highly significant geographies. As Daniel Heath Justice points out, they are all on Indigenous land ("Seeing (and Reading) Red" 102). That sense of not knowing—or of the many stories yet to be heard and of the critical knowledge that they contain—encourages me to gain a better understanding of the territory that I am a guest in: the Treaty 6 lands in which I am fortunate to make my home, and which have their own protocols, histories, and knowledge systems. What it means to be a part of that relationship—to have responsibilities as well as benefits that flow from this place—is something that I think about daily, and I am grateful to those friends and mentors who have shared their thoughts on this with me.[1]

RELATIONSHIP TO FAMILY

Pijitsirniq "(or the concept of service)," the Task Force says, "expresses the obligation and responsibility to the family and its survival—and by extension to other members of the community ("First Annual Report" 16). In writing this book, I have thought always about the family that has welcomed me in Pangnirtung. How, as a "scholar" in the south, can I also be a good *arnaliaq* (godmother) and *panik* (daughter)? How does my work—and how does this book—repay the generosity of the people who have taught me so much? When I have the privilege of being in Pang, I can show my appreciation by cooking, cleaning, bringing groceries, making tea, listening, joking, playing with babies, and sometimes, just by sitting quietly. But how can I honour what they have given me while I am far away, doing things like this? Peter Kulchyski always reminds the Summer School students to try to be helpful to Inuit whom they meet in the south; this is one small way of matching the hospitality that we are always shown in Pangnirtung. But aside from that, and aside from phone calls and care packages, I am still trying to find ways in which my work as a literary scholar can truly constitute *pijitsirniq*. Rather than citing these connections as an attempted marker of legitimacy, I raise them here with a sense of responsibility and reciprocity—one that I think seriously about without being able to boast of answers.

In the meantime, my *ataata* (father), my *angusiaq* (godson), and his mother, Karen, have also encouraged me (perhaps without knowing it) to think about my responsibilities to my own family. When I begin my courses at the university, I now like to ask my students about the places they come from and where they are going. How many, I always ask, grew up in the same hometown as their parents and grandparents? How many will return there? The answer is not very many. Like mine, many of my students' families are scattered across the continent (and sometimes, across the globe), and their busy lives can make it difficult to maintain those ties closely. The university demands a great deal from us, and many of us have forgotten—through work and through other elements of our cultures—that our relations should mean something to us. My time in Pangnirtung has encouraged me to try to heal the disconnects in my own familial relationships, to discover and to remember my responsibilities, and to show respect to my own family, as different as it is from the one in Pang.

RELATIONSHIP TO ONE'S "INNER SPIRIT"

Though the connotations of "inner spirit" will mean very different things to different people, the IQ Task Force explains this in the following way: "As the child grows into an adult in the family context, he or she must develop a strong sense of inner worth and personal identity. This sense of identity and inner spirit is fostered through [*Pilimmaksarniq*]—the concept of skill and knowledge acquisition through learning, doing and practice" ("First Annual Report" 16). During our trips out on the land, the Pangnirtung Summer School has been fortunate to work with women like Evie Anilniliak, Tinah Nowdlak, Ooleepa Ishulutaq, Alukie Metuq, Margaret Nakashuk, and the late Towkie Etuangat, who have been willing to teach the students about working with sealskin. Over the years, I have learned to scrape, stomp, wash, dry, stretch, soften, and sew—always with a good deal of help—*qisik* (sealskin) into *pualuk* (mittens). It has provided a wonderful opportunity to attempt to learn *inuktitut*—to learn in the Inuit way— by watching carefully and then trying it yourself. Marie Uviluq once told me that when she was a girl, sewing was always difficult because she couldn't see what she was doing. "Why couldn't you see?" I asked. "Tears," she replied. Sewing in and around Pangnirtung is a wonderful way to join a community—and also to subject oneself to a peer review process more rigorous than anything that the academy has conceived, as women all over town inspect the quality of your stitches. But the sense of self-worth that I gain from creating even a very imperfect pair of *pualuk* is something that I have yet to garner from any of my peer-reviewed publications.

Gaining even the foundations of skills like sewing, or making *palaugaq* (bannock), created a major shift in perspective for me. As a graduate student, and now, as a faculty member, I have been immersed in a culture in which one is expected to work at one's job constantly. Activities like making things or socializing, I once firmly believed, simply took up time when you could have been writing your dissertation or furthering your career—and this was something to be frowned upon. It has taken me several years and the help of dear friends to recover from this strange state, and to realize how unbalanced and damaging it is. I now try to encourage my students to think about balance in their own lives, and to not give in to the pressure to study all the time—especially not at the expense of other parts of their selves and of their own core relationships. And I continue to try to learn to do other things—activities that bring me closer to my environment, my family, my community, and myself.

RELATIONSHIP TO ONE'S COMMUNITY

In 2011, the Pangnirtung Summer School lost two dear friends within the space of a week. Towkie Etuangat and Noah Metuq are greatly missed by their families and by all of the students who had the pleasure of knowing them. In the difficult days that followed, we saw the community rally around these families and our friend, Moe Evic, told the students they, too, needed to go pay their respects. So we visited, we baked, we did dishes, we cleaned, we set up and put away hundreds of chairs. We grieved for our friends. Fundraising auctions sprang up to bring in relatives who live in other communities. We saw a community in action, and I understood this as an example of *Piliriqatigiingiq* or "working together for a common goal" ("First Annual Report" 16). Along with the concept of "*Aajiiqatigiingniq* (or the concept of consensus decision-making)," this is the way in which the IQ Task Force explains relationship to one's community (16). The intricacies of community decision-making are something that I have little experience with, but I have witnessed the ways in which people in Pangnirtung work together and help each other out. There never seems to be a question of "whose job it is"; rather, if you're there, and you see something that needs doing, you do it. If someone needs help, you help them without hesitation. As the late Thomas Kimeksun Thrasher told me and Sam McKegney in Tuktoyaktuk, "If someone you see needs a shirt, take yours off and give it to him. And if you have plenty of soup and he has nothing, give it to him. You can get yours later because you're healthy. Never let someone wish for anything."[2]

Working together and helping out: the academy has its own terms for this: "collaboration" (or maybe "interdisciplinarity") and "service." These are things that faculty members are expected to do, and at my institution, they are translated as much as possible into quantifiable work-units, which are then measured against the contributions of other faculty for the distribution of a finite amount of money via yearly salary increments. As such, new faculty members are encouraged to be strategic about where they place their energies, avoiding tasks that "do not amount to much" on their CVs. For women, the danger of overextension and underrecognition seems to be greater, as cultural pressures urge us to be pleasing, helpful, and compliant. Working within this system, I often wonder how to think about my efforts outside of their monetary value (in terms of salary increments) or their role in moving me toward tenure. How, as a pre-tenure faculty member, can I prioritize the principles of *inuuqatigiittiarniq*? How can I be a good member of my community—and a good human being—in this place? How do I make time for students, for community work and relationship building, and for political action that my institution will not accredit? My time in Pangnirtung has taught me that I simply have to act in ways that I feel good about and responsible for, rather than only in ways that are profitable or prudent; gender politics and overwork aside, the alternatives—isolation, competition, and stinginess—are not appealing.

I frame these stories not as examples of achievement that should be imitated, but rather as ongoing struggles that I face as I walk the IQ "land bridge." In attempting to adapt Inuit principles to my academic life, I'll admit to not being very worried about appropriation, since most of my teachers do not seem to consider attempts at good behaviour appropriative. Like my Inuktitut conversation attempts, they might often be humorous, awkward, or unsuccessful, but the effort generally seems acceptable. There are many scholars out there who embody the ways in which academic work can honour Indigenous knowledge and serve the interests of communities, and I am grateful for their example. To the elders and community members who have taken time to answer questions and, more importantly, who model the application of these IQ principles in their own lives, I am indebted. To the authors, storytellers, and performers who inspire me with their knowledge, creativity, and skill, and to the upcoming writers and scholars who will astonish us all, thank you for the work that you do. I will continue to try to learn from your examples.

Qujannamiik!

APPENDICES

APPENDIX A:

Six Versions of Ivaluardjuk's Song
I. Rasmussen's Danish (1921)
II. Trans. W. E. Calvert and W. Worster (1929)
III. Trans. Tom Lowenstein (1973)
IV. Trans. Aenne Schmücker (1947)
V. Ivaluardjuk's song in *The Journals of Knud Rasmussen* (Inuktitut)
VI. Ivaluardjuk's song in *The Journals of Knud Rasmussen* (English)

I. RASMUSSEN'S DANISH:
Myg og kulde, disse plager følges aldrig ad.
Her jeg lægger mig på isen, lægger mig på sne og iss, så min kæbe klaprer.
Det er mig, aja - aja - ja.

Er det minder fra de tider,
fra de tider, myggen sværmer,
fra de tider, kulden lammer, der får tanken til at svimle,
mens jeg strækker mine Lemmer ud på isen -
Det er mig, aja - aja - ja.

Aj! men sange
bruger Styrke,
og jeg søger
efter ord.

Aj! Jeg spejder og ser, hvad jeg nu vil synge om: Renen med de brede takker!

Og jeg slyngede med styrke spydet med mit kastetræ.
Og mit våben tøjred' tyren midt i bækkenbenets hulning,
og den skælvede for vunden, til den segned' og blev stille.

Aj! Men sange bruger styrke og jeg søger efter ord.
Her er sangen, her er mindet.
Og det er kun mig, der synger. (Rasmussen, *Den store Slæderejse* 17)

II. TRANS. W. E. CALVERT AND W. WORSTER (1929)

Cold and mosquitoes,
These two pests
Come never together.
I lay me down on the ice,
Lay me down on the snow and ice,
Till my teeth fall chattering.
It is I,
Aja-aja-ja.

Memories are they,
From those days,
From those days,
Mosquitoes swarming
From those days,
The cold is bitter,
The mind grows dizzy
As I stretch my limbs
Out on the ice.
It is I,
Aja-aja-ja.

Ai! but songs
Call for strength
And I seek after words,
I, aja-aja-ja.

Ai! I seek and spy
Something to sing of
The caribou with the spreading antlers!

And strongly I threw
The spear with my throwing stick (sic!).
And my weapon fixed the bull

III. TRANS. TOM LOWENSTEIN (1973) "A HUNTING MEMORY"

Cold and mosquitoes
are torments
that never come together.
I lie down on the ice,
I lie down on the ice and snow
so my jaws chatter.
This is I!
Aja-aja-ja.

Is it memories
of the seasons,
of the seasons,
(mosquitoes swarming)
of the seasons
(ice paralysing)
make the mind swoon,
as I stretch my limbs out
on the ice?
This is I!
Aja-aja-ja.

Aj! But songs
require strength,
and I search
for words. Yes, I!
Aja-aja-ja.

Aj! I raise my head and see
the subject of my song :
the broad-antlered reindeer!

Powerfully I hurled
the spear and throwing-pole,

In the hollow of the groin
And it quivered with the wound
Till it dropped
And was still.

Ai! but songs
Call for strength,
And I seek after words.
It is I,
Aja, aja—haja—haja.
(Rasmussen, *Iglulik* 18–19)

my weapon tethering the bull
right in the middle of the loin
He trembled, and he fell.
And then lay still.

Aj! But songs
require strength,
and I search
for words.
Here is the song.
Here is the memory.
It's only I who sings.
Aja-aja-haja-haja!
(Lowenstein 25–26)

© Tom Lowenstein (1973).

IV. TRANS. AENNE SCHMÜCKER (1947)
"JAGDERINNERUNG"

Mücke und Kälte
diese Plagen,
kommen nie zugleich.
Hier lege ich aufs Eis mich,
lege mich auf Schnee und Eis,
bis die Zähne klappern.
Das bin ich.

Aja—aja—ja.

Kommt Erinnerung
an die Zeiten,
an die Zeiten,
da die Mücke schwärmt,
an die Zeiten,
da die Kälte lähmt,
die Gedanken traurig macht,
wenn ich meine Glieder strecke

auf das Eis hin?
Das bin ich.

Aja—aja—ja.

Ach! Mein Sang
bedarf der Stärke,
und ich suche
nach dem Wort,
ich…aja—aja—ja.

Ach, ich erspähe und ich sehe,
wovon ich nun singen will:
Renntier mit den breiten Schaufeln!
Und ich schleuderte in Stärke
mit dem Wurfholz meinen Speer.
Und die Waffe traf den Bock
mitten in des Beckens Höhle.
Und er bebte ob der Wunde,
bis er hinsank
und ward still.
Ach! Mein Sang
bedarf der Stärke,
und ich suche nach dem Wort.
Ja, ein Lied ist's,
ein Gedenken,
und der singt,
das bin nur ich.

Aja—aja—haja—haja! (Rasmussen, *Schneehüttenlieder* 39–40)

V. IVALUARDJUK'S SONG IN THE JOURNALS OF KNUD RASMUSSEN (INUKTITUT)

Ivaluarjuk (ingisivuq)

aija, kialikianguna taimaituta atuaqatapik
halalalalalalaja halalalalalalaja

aija, inuataliuna ilisarinniarpagu
irsinal&arajarpuq
halalalalalaja halalalalalalaja

aija, angutiqatimalu kunigumajima; pinasuarusingit
ipjuajanginakit salausukpaktunga
halalalalalaja halalalalalalaja

aija, salausukpatunga akuliaqatami
halalalalalalalaja, halalalalalaja, halalalalalaja

aija, salausukpakpin sutuinamut ima
halalalalalalalaja, halalalalalaja, halalalalalalaja,

aijia, niglasuk qikturiatlu uimanartut takua
halalalalalalaja, halalalalalalaja,

aija, isurillalunga sikumi aputlirmi aglirulalirninu
halalalalalalaja, halalalalalalaja,

aija, tainiksarsivunga nagjuligalungmi
halalalalalaja, halalalalalalaja, halalalalalaja,

aija, ak&igarmullima tartuna&apara nagjulijuarmanna
halalalalalaja, halalalalalalaja, halalalalalaja,

aija, isumaksasiurpunga tainiksaningima qinajujarpunga
halalalalalaja, halalalalalalaja, halalalalalaja
(Kunuk and Cohn 364–365; my transcription)

VI. IVALUARDJUK'S SONG IN THE JOURNALS OF KNUD RASMUSSEN (ENGLISH)

This version closely resembles (but is not an exact copy of) the version found in Calvert and Worster's English translation of Rasmussen's *Intellectual Culture of the Iglulik Eskimos.*

EVALUARJUK *Cold and mosquitoes, These two pests never come together. I lay down on the ice, Lay down on the snow and ice, Until my teeth fall chattering. It is I, Aja—aja—ja. Memories from those days, From those days, Mosquitoes swarming, The cold is bitter, The mind grows dizzy, As I stretch my limbs, Out on the ice. It is I, Aja—aja—ja. Ai! But songs call for strength, And I seek after words, I, aja—aja—ja. Ai! I seek and spy, Something to sing of, The caribou with spreading antlers!*

EVALUARJUK *And strongly I threw, The spear with my throwing stick. And my weapon fixed the bull, In the hollow of the groin, And it quivered with the wound, Until it dropped and was still. Ai! But songs call for strength, And I seek after words. It is I. Aja, aja—aja—ajaja.* (Robinson 297)

APPENDIX B:

Songs by Imaruittuq
I. Lyrics to "Inngirajaalirlanga" ("Let Me Sing Slowly")
II. Imaruittuq's Own Song

I. LYRICS TO "INNGIRAJAALIRLANGA" ("LET ME SING SLOWLY").

Performed by Immaroitok (Imaruittuq) and Qamaniq (singers) and Saturqsi (drum). This song, recorded on Isuma's CD *Unikkaat Sivunittinnit: Messages From the Past*, bears a strong resemblance to the song by Maniq that Imaruittuq performed at Nunavut Arctic College (Aupilaarjuk et al., *Law* 203–204). There are some changes to the lyrics, however, and some of the lines appear in Imaruittuq's own song (Aupilaarjuk et al., *Law* 211–212). Parts of stanzas 4, 5, and 9 are different from the Nunavut Arctic College versions, and I translate them here.

1. aijaa ijajaajaajaa inngirajaalirlanga
Aijaa ijajaajaajaa, let me sing slowly
inngirajaalirlanga pisiksaksiurlungalu ijajaajaajaa
Let me sing slowly and search for a song ijajaajaajaa

2 aijaa ijajaajaajaa pisiksaninngiliqpunga
Aijaa ijajaajaajaa, I have not acquired a song
nunguusimangvatigut sivullitta pisiksamik ijajaajaajaa
They have finished them on us, our ancestors of any song ijajaajaajaa

3 aijaa ijajaajaajaa nunguusimavatigut
Aijaa ijajaajaajaa, they have finished them on us
nunguusimangvatigut sivullitta pisiksamik ijajaajaajaa
They have finished them on us, our ancestors of any song ijajaajaajaa

4. aijaa ijajaajaajaa tainiksaqajjaanngila
Aijaa ijajaajaajaa it does not have a title
tainiksaqajjaanngila pisiq una ikiaqtaq ijajaajaajaa
It does not have a title this song which has had words put to it

5. aijaa ijajaajaajaa tainiksaqajjaanngila
Aijaa ijajaajaajaa it does not have a title
tainiksaqajaanngila nirjutillu naliannit ijajaajaajaa
It does not have a title even of any animal

6. aijaa ijajaajaajaa maliktarigaluaqpit

Aijaa ijajaajaajaa removing incoming snow

maliktarigaluaqpit apivalliajuq manna ijajaajaajaa

Are you removing incoming snow from this that is becoming snow covered ijajaa-jaajaa

7. aijaa ijajaajaajaa iqqaqtulirivara

Aijaa ijajaajaajaa, I remember

iqaqqtulirivarali ijjannguqturnira inna ijajaajaajaa

I remember my difficulty in breathing ijajaajaajaa

8. aijaa ijajaajaajaa nunguusimavatigut

Aijaa ijajaajaajaa, they have finished them on us

nunguusimangvatigut sivullitta pisiksamik ijajaajaajaa

They have finished them on us, our ancestors of any song ijajaajaajaa

9. aijaa ijajaajaajaa nungugiaqsinnarivuq

Aijaa ijajaajaajaa, it is about to come to an end

nungugiaqsinnarivuq tainiksaqajjaanngimang ijajaajaajaa

it is about to come to an end because it has no title. (Unikkaat; my transcription)

© Igloolik Isuma Productions (1992). Reproduced with permission.

II. IMARUITTUQ'S OWN SONG

Do you have a pisiq of your own?

Imaruittuq: I have an *ikiaqtagaq*. I can certainly sing part of it. It's quite long. I'm probably not going to remember how it all goes.

aajaa samaajaajaajaajaa inngiqtalaurlanga

Aajaa samaajaajaajaajaa let me sing

inngiqtalaurlanga pisiksaqsiurlungalu

Let me sing and search for a song to be mine

samaajaajajaajaa aajaa

aajaa samaajaajaajaajaa nagvaa&&arniarnanga

Aajaa samaajaajaajaajaa, searching but not finding

nagvaa&&arniarnanga qimiksamik nakiqtumik

Searching but not finding a tune which has accurate speed

samaajaajajaajaa aajaa

aajaa samaajaajaajaajaa nagvaaraluaqpunga
Aajaa samaajaajaajaajaa I have found one though

nagvaaraluaqpunga ikiaqtaksanniglu imma
I have found one though to probably put my words to
samaajaajajaajaa aajaa

aajaa samaajaajaajaajaa tainiksanigunnanngilaq
Aajaa samaajaajaajaajaa it is unable to acquire a title

tainiksanigunnanngilaq pisiq una ikiaqtaq
It is unable to acquire a title, this song which has had words put to it
samaajaajajaajaa aajaa

aajaa samaajaajaajaajaa tainiksanigunnjjanngilaq
Aajaa samaajaajaajaajaa it is quite unable to acquire a title

tainiksanigunnjjanngilaq nirjutillu naliinnit
It is quite unable to acquire a title even of any animal
samaajaajajaajaa aajaa

aajaa samaajaajaajaajaa iksivauja&&aqtunga
Aajaa samaajaajaajaajaa I sit doing nothing

iksivauja&&aqtunga iglukallangniglu imma
I sit doing nothing in probably numerous houses
samaajaajajaajaa aajaa

aajaa samaajaajaajaajaa pijatuariliriga
Aajaa samaajaajaajaajaa the only thing that I now do

pijatuariliriga niriuttaujarniq una
The only thing that I do now is wait for the arrival of someone
samaajaajajaajaa aajaa

aajaa samaajaajaajaajaa inngiqtalaurlanga
Aajaa samaajaajaajaajaa let me sing

inngiqtalaurlanga pisiksaqsiurlungalu
Let me sing and search for a song to be mine
samaajaajajaajaa aajaa

aajaa samaajaajaajaajaa nirittauja&&aqtunga
Aajaa samaajaajaajaajaa I await the arrival of someone

nirittauja&&aqtunga tikitau&&arniarnianga
I await the arrival of someone despite no one coming home to me
samaajaajajaajaa aajaa

aajaa samaajaajaajaajaa qinuisaaraluaqpiit
Aajaa samaajaajaajaajaa I am being patient

qinuisaaraluaqpiit ajurnaqsivakkillunilu
I am being patient though at times it becomes hard to do
samaajaajajaajaa aajaa

aajaa samaajaajaajaajaa siaqqalau&&aqtunga
Aajaa samaajaajaajaajaa the times that I have been without

siaqqalau&&aqtunga kiinaujaqanngimut
The times that I have been without for the lack of money
samaajaajajaajaa aajaa

aajaa samaajaajaajaajaa unangmijjavanngilakka
Aajaa samaajaajaajaajaa I have no desire to emulate

unangmijjavanngilakka angutilli parnajuktut
I have no desire to emulate men who are getting ready
samaajaajajaajaa aajaa

aajaa samaajaajaajaajaa parna&&arniarnanga
Aajaa samaajaajaajaajaa I'm not bothering to get ready

parna&&arniarnanga parnagaksaqannginnama umiamik
I'm not bothering to get ready because I have no boat to get ready
samaajaajajaajaa aajaa

aajaa samaajaajaajaajaa sujuruluuvillikiaq
Aajaa samaajaajaajaajaa what is the matter with me

sujuruluuvillikiaq ajulua&&aqtungali
What is the matter with me that I am so incapable
samaajaajajaajaa aajaa

aajaa samaajaajaajaajaa nungugiaqsinnarivuq
Aajaa samaajaajaajaajaa it is about to end

nungugiaqsinnarivuq tainiksaqanngimulli
It is about to end for lack of a title
samaajaajajaajaa aajaa (Imaruittuq 211–214)

© Nunavut Arctic College (2000). Reproduced with permission.

GLOSSARY

ajaja	a sung refrain used in many songs
angakkuq (pl. angakkuit)	shaman
ikiaqtagaq (pl. ikiaqtagait)	a "split" song; a song which has had new words put to it
Inuit Nunaat	the Inuit homeland, or traditional territory
Inuit Qaujimajatuqangit (IQ) or Qaujimanituqangit	"what Inuit have known for a very long time"; Inuit traditional knowledge
inuk (pl. inuit)	person
inuktitut	"in the way of Inuit"; a term for Inuit language
inummarik (pl. inummariit)	a *real* Inuk
inuuqatigiittiarniq	healthy communities; living well together
inuusirmingnik unikkaat	life stories; stories from life experience
Inuvialuit	Inuit of the Western Canadian Arctic
isuma (or ihuma)	thought; reason; intelligence
isumataq (pl. isumatait)	leader
iviusiq (pl. iviutiit)	a song used to embarrass someone, as in a song-duel
-miut	an ending meaning "people of" (a place)
natsiq (or nattiq)	ringed seal
nuna	land
pisiksaq	material for a song
pisiq (pl. pisiit)	personal song; hymn
qaggiq (pl. qaggiit)	song-house, or feasting house
qallunaaq (pl. qallunaat)	white person, Southerner
qanuqtuurniq	resourcefulness; adaptibility
qimik	tune; melody
qujannamiik	thank you
sakausiq (pl. sakausiit)	song used by shamans; magic song
sila	environment; climate, weather; wisdom
silattuqsarvik	college; a place to become wise
tagvani (or tavvani)	here
tainiq	the subject of a song
taunani	down there; toward the sea

Thule	a term for the ancestors of modern Inuit; also a former trading station (and now a village, Uummannaq, in Greenland), from which Rasmussen's expeditions take their name
tuniit (sing. tuniq)	the people who preceded the Thule Inuit; Dorset
unikkaaq (pl. unikkaat)	story; something which is narrated
unikkaaqtuaq (unikkaaqtuat)	"traditional" or classic story; myth; story that goes on for a long time
unikkausiq (pl. unikkausiit)	a story told in a particular way; sometimes also understood as a myth, or classic (canonical) tale
unikkausinnguaq	"an imitation of an unikkausiq"; possibly a fictional story
-vut	singular ending meaning "our"

NOTES

INTRODUCTION

1   An Inuit Knowledge and Climate Change (IKCC) project description describes this as follows: "Numerous Elders, geographically distributed across Nunavut, observed that the positions of the sun, moon, and stars had shifted and concluded that the 'earth had tilted'. The IKCC team considered these observations seriously and interviewed scientists to see if scientific evidence existed on this topic. Waldemar Lehn, an expert in atmospheric refraction, indicated that climate change is likely warming the upper atmosphere and this air is colliding with cold surface temperatures to create an 'inversion' ideal for refraction. According to Lehn, when these inversions occur they can bend light, similar to a prism, and this can change the position of the sun, moon and stars, especially near the surface of the earth. Indeed, Elders' observations of a 'tilted earth' are likely evidence of a warming world, which is altering the 'visual landscape' of the Arctic. Peer reviewed publications on this topic are forthcoming" ("Igloolik (IKCC)").

2   *Inuktitut* magazine is published by Inuit Tapiriit Kanatami (ITK), Canada's national Inuit organization. Nungak's article was originally published in *Windspeaker* 22, 1 (2004): 21, 26.

3   The suffix –vik can, depending on context, indicate either a time or a place. See "Grammar» -vik (affix)."

4   For more on the concept of *sila*, see d'Anglure, *Être et renaître inuit* (84–105).

5   Audra Simpson's discussion of tradition was drawn from her presentation at the 2012 Native American and Indigenous Studies Association.

6   The 109 stories recorded by Métayer were eventually published in 1973 in a three-volume French/Inuinnaqtun collection—*Unipkat: Tradition Esquimaude de Coppermine, Territoires-du-Nord-Ouest, Canada*—by the Centre for Northern Studies of the Université Laval. A selection of these stories was later included in Métayer's much smaller but better-known collection *Tales from the Igloo* (*Contes de mon iglou*). The story paraphrased here is Texte 17, "Visite au village des ours grizzly" (Métayer, *Unipkat* Vol. 1 124–132). In *Tales from the Igloo*, the story appears as "The Orphan and the Bears" (Métayer 25–31).

7   For the story of Kiviuq and his fox wife, see (for one example) the version told by Thomas Kusugaq (Spalding, *Eight Inuit Myths* 51–66).

8   For the story of Kiviuq's encounter with the wolf mother and daughter, see "The Wolf Women and Kiviuq's Homecoming" in the online resource "Kiviuq's Journey."

9   I take the idea of "peoplehood" from Tom Holm, J. Diane Pearson, and Ben Chavis's article "Peoplehood: A Model for the Extension of Sovereignty in American Indian Studies."

10   Thomas Kusugaq's story of Aningaat can be found in *Eight Inuit Myths* (33–50).

CHAPTER ONE

1   For a discussion of the "two Nunavuts" created by these dual agreements, see Wenzel, "From TEK to IQ" (239–240).

2   As Philip Lauritzen mentions in *Oil and Amulets: Inuit: A People United at the Top of the World*, Inuit representatives from the Chukotka region in Siberia did not attend the first ICC meeting (23). However, they are now full members of the ICC (Simon, *Inuit: One Future* 14).

3   Inuit Tapirisat of Canada was the previous name of Canada's national Inuit organization, Inuit Tapiriit Kanatami ("Inuit are united in Canada").

4   While "Inuit" is often rendered in English as "people," or "human beings," the subtleties of its many connotations beg a more precise translation, which Rachel A. Qitsualik gives as "The Living Ones Who Are Here" ("Is It 'Eskimo' or 'Inuit'?"). For a longer discussion of the term, see Therrien (145–166).

5   *-miut* is a suffix meaning "people of." While traditional ethnonyms like Nattilingmiut or Aivilingmiut are still in use, they have now been supplemented by *-miut* terms for particular communities (e.g., Iqalungmiut—the people of Iqaluit), or for new regional designations (e.g., Nunavummiut—the people of Nunavut). Note that these are now geographic rather than ethnic markers: the term Nunavummiut can include all residents of Nunavut, including the 15% who are non-Inuit.

6   For the history of Inuit political activism in the twentieth century, see Mary Simon's *Inuit: One Future, One Arctic* (13–44), Peter Kulchyski's *Like the Sound of a Drum: Aboriginal Cultural Politics in Denendeh and Nunavut* and *Kiumajut* (250–254) *(Talking Back): Game Management and Inuit Rights 1900–70* (co-authored with Frank James Tester; 165–272), and Marybelle Mitchell's *From Talking Chiefs to a Native Corporate Elite: The Birth of Class and Nationalism among the Canadian Inuit* (341–385).

7   The term "imagined community" is taken from Benedict Anderson's book *Imagined Communities*, which explores the ways in which nations are imagined—and thus invented and sustained—by their members (6).

8   Ideas of social and cultural evolution "continue to lurk within the terminology we use to describe those who do not possess what we call writing or who cannot read written texts. Their unwritten past is 'prehistory,' and they are 'preliterate'" (Chamberlin, "From Hand to Mouth" 139).

9   *Tirigusuusiit, piqujait*, and *maligait* can be very loosely translated as "ritual rules" (elsewhere called taboos), "customs" or "customary laws," and "rules" (literally, "things that are followed"), and they give a sense of the precision with which pre-colonial Inuit society was governed (Aupilaarjuk et al., *Law* 1–3).

10   As Holm, Pearson, and Chavis explain, the adoption of outsiders has not been uncommon in Indigenous societies, and "race, to Native Americans, was not a factor of group identity or peoplehood" (16). Discourses of blood and racial purity were to come later; in the traditional models, peoplehood also was determined by imagination.

11   The brother and sister stories are a series of tales that culminate in the creation of the sun and moon. See "Aningagiik: Brother and Sister Legends" in Kublu 162–181.

12   *Ijirait* are also called *tarriaksuit* or *tarriassuit* (shadow people) in South/East Baffin (Aupilaarjuk, *Cosmology* 51–54). See also Bennett and Rowley 159.

13   *Iqqiliit* is a rather disparaging term meaning "louse eggs" (Spalding, *Dictionary* 30). *Allait* is from *alla*, stranger (Schneider 19). Like *Iqqiliit*, the term can also denote "Indians" more generally.

14   *Qallunaat* appear in the Sedna/Nuliajuk story: they are said to be descendants of the puppies that Nuliajuk had with her dog-husband, who were set afloat in a *kamik* (boot). In some versions, the rest of the puppies were sent overland to become the *Iqqiliit*, or Indians (Aupilaarjuk et al., *Law* 189).

15   The Tununirmiut are a North Baffin Inuit group, in the Pond Inlet (Mittimatalik) area. The Nattilingmiut, or Netsilingmiut (people of the place where there are seals), are from the area around Taloyoak in the Kitikmeot region of Nunavut (*Uqalurait* 340).

16   The term for the first people has a variety of spellings, and appears in the plural as Tuniit, Tunit, Tunnit, Tunrit, Tornit, Tornrin, or even Tungi, and in the singular as Tuniq, Tunik, Tuneq, or Tunerk. Accounts that emphasize the large size of the Tuniit sometimes refer to them as Tunitjuat or Tunijjuat.

17   While Mathiassen believed that the Tuniit were the Thule people (190), Guy Mary-Rousselière suggested—and contemporary archaeologists agree—that the legends in fact refer to the Thule's predecessors: the Dorset people ("The Tunit" 17, 19). See also Sutherland 6.

18   The Thule Inuit are also known as the *Taissumanialungmiut*—"literally, the people of a very long time ago" (Brody, "Land Occupancy" 189).

19   The word for "thumb" is also an Inuk name, which is usually spelled Kublu, or Kullu.

20   See Chamberlin (*The Harrowing of Eden*) and Berkhofer (*The White Man's Indian*) for a detailed study of colonial representations of Indigenous peoples, or as Berkhofer puts it, the "invention" of "the idea of the Indian" (3).

21   The original reads: "*Angirraruvit unipkaarniaraluaq&uni avituarangni taimalu puiguq&uguluguuq. Nauguuq iqqaumannanngittualuit tamatkua silaup inugni. inummariugaluittauq taimanna ivaptut iliktut pisuktut. Taimanna qatipluginnguuq puigurnaqtualuit. Tagvaguuq itqaramiup uqqaumaliramiuk unipkaasigiarami, imanna katilauqtamanik quviasuk&uni katisilaurami unipkaasigiaramiuguuq tagvaguuq qiasialuk&uni*" (Patiq 40, my transcription from syllabics).

22   Tuniit are often depicted fleeing; Patiq goes on to tell a story of a Tuniq who ran away to avoid meeting Inuit (40).

23   According to Simeonie Quppapik, *inuksuk* means "that which acts in the capacity of a human," either by conveying messages about the landscape or by assisting with the hunting of caribou (qtd. in Hallendy 22). Inuksuit that take the shape of humans are called *inunnguat* (in imitation of a person).

24   Interestingly, the format that Qitsualik uses in providing translations varies widely. On page 38, when she writes "oh, how he and the others had brought in *tuugaaliit*, those small, dark whales with the spiralled tusks!" she privileges the Inuktitut by withholding the English term (narwhals). On page 46, meanwhile, she provides a literal and immediate translation: "the boy's name turned out to be Siku ('ice')."

25   For an example of the autoethnographic tendencies in "Skraeling," see page 43, when the boy Siku grabs Kannujaq by the wrist: "[n]o one had ever dared behave so aggressively toward him. Among his own kind, physical aggression occurred only between the most dire enemies—and never openly. Otherwise, it was a symptom of madness."

26   Therrien explains the *inua* as being the "owner" of a person (or animal, as per the usage in Nunavik) (147).

27   Igloolik Isuma Productions is the film production company behind *Atanarjuat (The Fast Runner)* and *The Journals of Knud Rasmussen*.

28   Linda Hutcheon refers to the totalizing potential of literary history in "Interventionist Literary Histories" (404–405).

29   In Inuktitut, the word *ivaluk* can mean both "sinew" and "thread."

CHAPTER TWO

1   The story of the blind boy is "Aningaat" (33–50); the one about the hunter is "Nassiqsuittuarjuk" (23–32); and the quick-tempered hero can be found in "Kiviuq" (51–66) in Spalding, *Eight Inuit Myths*. Kiviuq is also spelled Kiviu, Kivioq, Kiv(v)iok, or Keeveeok.

2   On overzealous editing of Inuit stories, see McGrath, "Editing Inuit Literature: Leaving the Teeth in the Gently Smiling Jaws." The tastes of casual southern readers are probably

better suited to collections like Maurice Métayer's 1973 *Contes de mon iglou,* which features bite-sized legends in translation accompanied by vibrant illustrations.

3   *Aivilingmiutitut* is the language of the Aivilingmiut (people of the Aivilik region—the 'place with walruses' near Repulse Bay).

4   The first line of the morphemic translation is "Angusugjuk / they say good hunter / was he / really / very away / in a state of being / while / he they say / arriving home / he doorway / his own / in dog / small / very seeing / because he grabbing / he / it going in / he" (Spalding 1).

5   The boundary between the fields of literature and linguistics, as Robert Bringhurst has pointed out, is at times somewhat indeterminate. See *The Tree of Meaning* 211.

6   Owen Barfield mentions the (now outdated) association between the "primitive" and the poetic—the idea that "the 'infancy of society' [was peopled with] an exalted race of amateur poets" (73).

7   Spalding's dictionary (*Inuktitut: A Multi-Dialectical Outline Dictionary [with an Aivilingmiutaq Base]*) was also compiled with the assistance of Thomas Kusugàq.

8   Although Spalding had moved away from Inuit subject matter, in his thesis, he did seem to maintain his interest in myth. The first line of his dissertation declares that "Wordsworth is a mythopoeic or mythmaking poet" ("Wordsworth" ii). He goes on to explain that "in working through Wordsworth's spiritual odyssey, I discovered that he had lived through or acted out at least three ancient pastoral myths…" (vii). He argues further that Wordsworth may not have done this consciously, but rather out of "psychological necessity…by struggling and journeying in the realm of [his] own spirit" (vii–viii). A comparison of Spalding's treatments of Kusugaq and of Wordsworth might be interesting, if somewhat obscure.

9   On the didacticism of the *unipkaaqtuat,* Spalding says: "Above all, these myths are lessons in humanity to all of us, instructing us to be more courageous, more compassionate and wiser, less prone to jealousy, anger, and greed, more social and helpful" (*Eight Inuit Myths* vi).

10 The problem of reading Indigenous cultural production for its ethnographic or testimonial value rather than for its aesthetic merit reaches beyond scholarship of oral traditions; it has also governed many readings of Indigenous written literatures and interpretations of other kinds of cultural productions. As Ted Chamberlin asserts, "these texts deserve an attention that acknowledges their aesthetic and intellectual character, their beauties and inseparably—their truths, instead of reducing them to evidence in a cultural, historical, political, or psychological casebook" (Chamberlin, "The Corn People" 72).

11 The pronunciation and spelling difference between *unipkaaqtuat* and *unikkaaqtuat* is regional; some eastern dialects "assimilate" double consonants, rendering -pk- into -kk-, -bl- into -ll-, etc.

12 Unless indicated otherwise, all quotes from Peter Irniq are from personal correspondence. Irniq is an Inuk cultural teacher and the former Commissioner of Nunavut.

13 My thanks to Saila Michael, who taught me about the word *unikkaaqtuq.* Michael, who is from Iqaluit via Coral Harbour, has taught Inuktitut at York University and also (with Alana Johns) at the University of Toronto. All quotes by Michael are from personal communication.

14 This quote from Louis-Jacques Dorais is from personal correspondence.

15 Womack critiques the scholarly tendency to view contemporary Indigenous writing as inauthentic or tainted in *Red on Red* (63–67). See also Weaver, *That the People Might Live* (x).

16 For misguided views that posit orality as a developmental stage preceding literacy, see Ong (4–15) or Goody (148–166).

17 For a range of perspectives on the issue of rendering oral traditions into print form, see Murray and Rice's *Talking on the Page: Editing Aboriginal Texts.*

18 The collectively edited volume *Reasoning Together: The Native Critics Collective*—which gathers together work by prominent Indigenous scholars like Womack, Daniel Heath Justice, Lisa Brooks, Robert Warrior, and Christopher B. Teuton—contains a range of essays that turn to classic tales for critical inspiration. The directive to "describe an ethical Native literary criticism" involved for many of the contributors a return to the foundations of Indigenous intellectual traditions: the oral traditions (95). Daniel Heath Justice's essay "'Go Away, Water!': Kinship Criticism and the Decolonization Imperative," begins with a telling of the story of Water Spider, who was able to fetch fire for the animals (147). Once she had managed to secure the fire in a silk-woven bowl, Justice says, "Water Spider could have hidden this rare and wondrous warmth from the others.... But she honored her kinship obligations and brought Fire to share with all the Animals in the Middle World" (147). Justice employs this symbolic moment to discuss the importance of practising kinship principles in Indigenous criticism—in other words, the importance of enacting a criticism that is concerned with its impact on and relationship with community. Kinship, Justice reveals, is far more meaningful to Indigenous communities than is the discourse of race and identity. Here, an idea exemplified in a classic story is taken as a guiding principle for Indigenous scholarship.

19 For a longer discussion of the ways in which community stories offer literary critical guidance, see Christopher B. Teuton's *Deep Waters* (xi–xv; 1–7).

20 Spalding refers to Kusugak as his "informant" once, in the book's dedication (Spalding ix).

21 *Nassilingmiut* is also spelled "Netsilingmiut" (people of the place of the seal). *Nassilik* literally means "it has seals," and –miut is the ending meaning "people."

22 The people of the Repulse Bay region are predominantly Aivilingmiut (see note 3).

23 At the time of Kukik's death, Jack Anawak, a member of the Legislative Assembly of Nunavut, spoke of her to the House as "one of the leaders and the pillar of the community [in both Naujaat and Rankin Inlet]" (Anawak).

24 Angusugjuk's name can be translated as "Great Man." Angu(t) = man; -sugjuk = superlative (Spalding 1).

25 "Nothing but a skull" is a translation of *Niaquinnarmiguuq* (5). *Niaquq* = head; *-innaq-* = exclusiveness (just/only); *mi* = (likely the direct object marker *-mik*); *guuq* = 'it is said.' I refer to Spalding's dictionary, and Kenn Harper's *Suffixes of the Eskimo Dialects of Cumberland Peninsula and North Baffin Island*. Thanks also to Alana Johns for help with the parsing.

26 Spalding's translation says "parents," but the original is *anaanakkukka*, which he parses as "mother / association of / [my (pl)]" (5, emphasis added). An alternate translation might be "people related to my mother," or "my mother's household." Indeed, the mother turns out to be a key figure; we never hear about the father. Thanks to Alana Johns.

27 "Chiefs" is Spalding's translation of "isumataq" (5); he also uese "boss" (5; 12). The root of the word *isumataq, isuma,* refers to "thought" or "intelligence." Spalding's dictionary says that this is the usual Aivilingmiutitut term for a camp leader.

28 The word for "jellyfish" used here is *nuvak'iq* (blobs of phlegm) (6, Spalding's translation). The challenge is actually phrased *nuvak'iqsiuqatigijumavaa* (does he want him for a jellyfish hunting-partner?).

29 This is not *quinangnaqtuq*—"it tickles" (literally, "it makes you pee"); instead, the phrase used here is *uimanaqtualuungmata*, which Spalding parses as "excitement / causes / that

which / very / are / because they" (6). The root is *uima*, as in *uimajuq*—"he is excited; loses his head or loses control of himself" (Spalding dictionary 179). Meanwhile, the *Inuktitut Living Dictionary* notes another connetation of *uimajuq*: "he acts rapidly," or "to hurry."

30   Titirarti (literally, "writer," or clerk) was Spalding's Inuktitut name (Irniq, "Mourning").

31   Interestingly, during the seal-hunt contest, the Giant Bear hunts in the manner of a man: poised with a spear over a breathing hole (10). This could derive from the close correlation between humans and bears, who are often depicted in the *unikkaaqtuat* as living parallel lives.

32   For more on tracking as reading, see J. Edward Chamberlin's "Hunting, Tracking, and Reading" (67; 70–71).

33   I am rephrasing Spalding's morphemic translation, which runs "much to his surprise floe edge / on the lying on her back /she" (2).

34   As Robert Bringhurst explains: "When we hear stories one at a time, we're still in a sense trapped in the bus with the tourists. A single story might reseed itself, like a tree—a monoecious tree, like a pine or a spruce. (Other stories, I think, are dioecious, like willows: they need another companionable story with which to mate.) But even an orchard of trees, all the same species, is not the same as a forest. A coherence system of storytelling is like a system of science and mathematics. And like a forest, it is more than the sum of its parts. So long as it remains alive, a literature is a system of storytelling, not just a collection of stories or myths" (*Tree of Meaning* 28).

35   The story of the fox wife also appears as "Fox in Human Form" in Mark Kalluak's *How Kabloonat Became and Other Inuit Legends* (62–67), in James Houston's *Kiviuq* film, and in Kira Van Deusen's *Kiviuq: An Inuit Hero and His Siberian Cousins* (234–257).

36   In the version told by Samson Quinangnaq (recorded by James Houston for the film), Kiviuq takes the goose's socks. As Quinangnaq explains: "The story is that in those days, birds wore socks on their feet." In other versions, it is the feathery skins which are stolen by the hero. See "Kiviuq's Journey."

37   My rephrasing of Spalding's "away down there / in land / has / it so relative / s / my away down there / in / are / now / they. So house / from next / very / from going out / ones who / have / will / because it polar bear / fierce / is." Note that in Spalding's literary translation this speech is reported, but in the original it is direct.

38   Inuktitut has an extremely detailed system of indicating directions (Nagy 75).

39   For further reading about Kaujjarjuk, see Petrone, "Revenge of the Orphan Boy" (17) or *Akirnimut Unipkkaaqtuat: Stories of Revenge* (12–16).

40   For the story of Aningaat, see "Lumaajuuq, the Story of the Blind Boy," *Inuit Unikkaaqtuangit: Inuit Legends Vol. 2* or "Aningagiik: Brother and Sister Legends" in Kublu 162–181.

41   Epithets are common in hunting songs and stories. As McGrath points out, hunting songs often "used the language of incantation in which a seal is 'blubbery one'" ("Oral" 165).

42   "Much to his surprise, they say, that little black thing turned out to be a seal" is my rephrasing of Spalding's morphemic translation.

43   For more on *ihuma*, see also Briggs, *Never in Anger* (358–366).

44   Briggs explains that elders, as well as anthropologists, can be in danger of the condition of excessive *ihuma*; because elders have such powerful minds, they may begin to brood or become unhappy, particularly if they are ill, housebound, or isolated (*Never in Anger* 363).

45   For further discussion of the challenges of interpreting the "Penis in the Lake" episode, see Van Deusen 202–223.

46   As Joanne Schwartz writes, "Kusugak's impulse to write served a two-fold purpose. One was to reclaim the stories and to supersede the tellings of white writers. To achieve this, Kusugak writes in English so he is able to reach a wide audience and one that until recently had not heard an authentic voice from the North" (2).

47   As Christopher B. Teuton writes, "But no matter how many examples are given of Native Americans writing in support of their nations, communities, and traditional ways of life, orality continues to be invoked as a marker of authenticity. Ironically, this formulation has become part of Native American studies through the reification of oral tradition. The source of this notion of authenticity exists in the oral-literature dynamic, which has yet to be completely destabilized in Native American literary studies. Just as the primitive was constructed as a lens through which the West could understand and define itself, the oral culture has been constructed so that Western, literate society would have an evolutionary marker with which to measure its historical progression" (10–11).

CHAPTER THREE

1   "Song to a Miser" can be found in Lowenstein 46.

2   Although Rasmussen uses the spelling "Aua," "Avva" is more correct. See Joanna Awa, "The Story of a Name."

3   The Fifth Thule Expedition (1921–24), led by the Greenlandic anthropologist Knud Rasmussen, aimed to document the culture of the "Central Eskimos" of the Canadian Arctic and Alaska. Peter Freuchen, a cartographer and biologist, was Rasmussen's long-time expedition partner; Therkel Mathiassen was a cartographer and archaeologist (Mathiassen, *Report on the Expedition* 7–12).

4   Proselytizers like Umik were interpreting Christianity, however, without the approval of the Church. For further details of the activities of Umik and other Inuit religious leaders, see Blaisel, Laugrand, and Oosten's article "Shamans and Leaders: Parousial Movements Among the Inuit of Northeast Canada." Umik and his son Nuqallaq had come to Iglulik from Pond Inlet, where Nuqallaq had killed the trader Robert Janes after Janes became a threat to the community. Nuqallaq was later tried, and convicted, in the first government-run murder trial in what would become Nunavut. This story forms the basis of Shelagh Grant's *Arctic Justice: On Trial for Murder, Pond Inlet, 1923*.

5   Like other ethnographers of the era, Rasmussen cultivated an exaggerated sense of the pristine nature of local traditions. The Netsilingmiut, Aivilingmiut and Amitturmiut Inuit of the region traded regularly at the Hudson's Bay Company post in Repulse Bay and had been in contact with *qallunaat* for over a hundred years.

6   The Padlermiut, or Paallirmiut ("Willow-people"), are part of a larger group than the Expedition called "Caribou Eskimos": people living in the Kivalliq region just west of Hudson Bay.

7   "It was my privilege, as one born in Greenland, and speaking the Eskimo language as my native tongue, to know these people in an intimate way. My life's course led inevitably toward Arctic exploration, for my father, a missionary among the Eskimos, married one who was proud of some portion of Eskimo blood. From the very nature of things, I was endowed with attributes for Polar work which outlanders have to acquire through painful experience. My playmates were native Greenlanders; from the earliest boyhood I played and worked with the hunters, so that even the hardships of the most strenuous sledge-trips became pleasant routine for me" (Rasmussen, *Across Arctic America* xxxii).

8   The singular of *pisiit* is *pisiq*. In the Kivalliq region, it is often spelt *pihiq*.

9   qag·iʃut (*or qaggijut*) means "they are assembled," or "the ones who are assembled" (Schneider 277). *Qimik* is another term for "melody"; the one given here, ivŋɛrut (or *inngiruti*), means literally "a tool for singing" (Imaruittuq 219).

10   Franz Boas, who visited Cumberland Sound in 1883–1884, writes that "[a]mong the arts of the Eskimo poetry and music are by far the most prominent" (240).

11   Barfield refers, for example, to Macauley, who "assert[s] that half-civilized nations are poetic *simply because* they perceive without abstracting, and absolutely regardless of *what* they perceive" (84).

12   The Muskogee scholar Craig Womack, for instance, writes that he is "concerned about what happens to the political intent of the stories when they are separated from their tribal contexts" (*Red on Red* 62).

13   Ivaluardjuk was Amitturmiut, belonging to the people of the Melville Peninsula, who were known to Rasmussen as the Iglulingmiut (the people of Iglulik). Ethnonyms such as Iglulik, Netsilik, and Copper are anthropological in origin; I have attempted to give the more precise designations, courtesy of Bennett and Rowley's *Uqalurait: An Oral History of Nunavut* (458–464).

14   This (sic!) disclaimer appears in Calvert and Worster's text. I am uncertain as to what it refers to.

15   Lowenstein notes that "in most cases [of song-composition], a quasi-Worsdworthian process took place, in which the poet retired into the solitude of nature, and struggled to fit words to the tune he had previously composed" (xx).

16   Rasmussen expresses his regret that he was not able to make any recordings of the songs, as the phonograph was "out of order" (*Iglulik* 230).

17   The first three lines of the song also appear in *Uqalurait: An Oral History of Nunavut* (215). Father Guy Marie-Rousselière's 1961 *Beyond the High Hills: A Book of Eskimo Poems* includes Ivaluardjuk's preamble to the song ("those days…when all meat was juicy and tender") but does not acknowledge his authorship (29).

18   Several different translations of this song are included in Appendix A.

19   Thanks to Professor Marianne Stenbaek for the translation of the Danish.

20   Although this sound feature is not present in the case of the Danish refrain "*Det er mig*," it was likely at work in the original, which could have used the word "*uvanga*."

21   As Chamberlin writes: "[o]ne of our oldest conflicts is between *those who dream about things and those who do things*, between those who sing songs and tell tales and those who raise meat, grow vegetables and cook supper. Doodlers and doers. The useless and the useful" (*If This Is Your Land* 28, emphasis added).

22   Beyond the previously-mentioned anthologies by Robin Gedalof (McGrath), Tom Lowenstein, and Penny Petrone, collections that draw upon Rasmussen's work include Edmund Carpenter's *Anerca* (1959), Jerome Rothenberg's *Technicians of the Sacred* (1968) and *Shaking the Pumpkin: Traditional Poetry of the Indian North Americas* (1991), Richard Lewis' *I Breathe a New Song: Poems of the Eskimo* (1971), James Houston's *Songs of the Dream People: Chants and Images from the Indians and Eskimos of North America* (1972), Charles Hoffman's *Drum Dance: Legends, Ceremonies, Dances and Songs of the Eskimos* (1974), Daniel David Moses and Terry Goldie's *An Anthology of Canadian Native Literature in English* (1991), and Neil Philip's *Songs Are Thoughts: Poems of the Inuit* (1995).

23   This disparity in Field's acknowledgement of the singers versus the artists may speak to the southern recognition of Inuit as sculptors and printmakers, but seldom as writers and storytellers. Both artists were members of the West Baffin Eskimo Cooperative. Kiakshuk was born in Nunavik in 1886, and died in Cape Dorset in 1966. Pudlo Pudlat was born in 1916 near Kimmirut and died in 1992 in Cape Dorset.

24   The songs that Field combines in "Magic Words for Hunting Caribou" are by Orpingalik (Rasmussen, *Netsilik* 15; 279–280); Inūtuk (*Netsilik* 280–281); and Nakasuk (*Netsilik* 286). Rasmussen titled them all "Magic words to bring luck on a caribou hunt."

25 Even Rasmussen's translation of Orpingalik's is not word-for-word; he has added much of what is implied—in particular, the vocative tone of the verses: "You, louse-like," he says, instead of the more literal translation of *kumaruaq*: "big louse" (from *kumak*, "louse" and *–ruaq* "largeness"). Schneider translates *kumaruaq* as "tiny insect (paper spider, or any tiny insect)" (151).

26 To Rothenberg's credit, he also consults Rasmussen's *Netsilik Eskimos* in compiling *Shaking the Pumpkin*, and he re-inserts the names of the original singers where possible.

27 Although the program notes simply attribute the stories to Rasmussen, the section titles (Earth and the People, Magic Words, Day and Night: How They Came To Be, The Things in the Sky, Sun, and Moon, Thunder and Lightning, How We Know About Animals, Hunter, Heaven and Hell) are a clear indicator that Field's *Eskimo Songs and Stories* was the source text. Perhaps appropriately, Field's own authorship has here been obscured. My sincere thanks to Linda Hutcheon for drawing my attention to this performance.

28 In a related gesture to the perceived vastness and homogeneity of the Arctic, editors and publishers have also had a tendency to print tiny rectangles of text on enormous white pages, possibly with a few igloos or bears drawn in the corner (see Colombo and Carpenter).

29 This popular sense of the "harshness" of the Arctic environment is almost ubiquitous in southern descriptions. As Marshall Sahlins writes: "Having equipped the hunter with bourgeois impulses and paleolithic tools, we judge his situation hopeless in advance" (4). These characterizations differ markedly from Inuit conceptions of their environment and lifestyle, which, though realistic about the challenges of cold temperatures and occasional food shortages, often emphasize the beauty and bounty of the land. Inuit writers or lecturers do occasionally invoke the discourse of Arctic "harshness," usually to emphasize the ingenuity of Inuit traditional knowledge.

30 In *Intellectual Culture of the Iglulik Eskimos*, Rasmussen asks Aua for the story behind the "Bear song" (238); later, he begs for a fuller version of "Caribou hunting" (239).

31 More specifically, Netsit was Umingmaktuurmiut (of the place where there are musk-ox).

32 Rasmussen's promised "originals" are usually (but not always) included. Ivaluardjuk's "Cold and Mosquitoes" is one exception: the Inuktitut original is not to be found.

33 As Barfield writes: "almost any kind of 'strangeness' may produce an aesthetic effect, that is to say, an effect which, however slight, is qualitatively the same as that of serious poetry. On examination, the sole condition is found to be this, that the strangeness shall have an *interior* significance; it must be felt as arising from a different plane or mode of consciousness, and not merely as eccentricity of expression. It must be a strangeness of *meaning*" (170–171).

34 Imaruittuq, along with Abraham Ulayuruluk, was one of the elders who composed the *ajaja* songs for *Atanarjuat (The Fast Runner)*.

35 The song "Inngirajaalirlanga" ("Let me sing slowly") was performed by Imaruittuq in 1992 for an Isuma CD entitled *Unikkaat Sivunittinnit: Messages from the Past*. Despite a few variations, I believe it is the same song that Imaruittuq performed later at Nunavut Arctic College (Maniq's song, quoted here with the permission of Nunavut Arctic College). The lyrics can be found in Appendix B (I).

36 Thanks to Peter Irniq for explaining the meaning of *ikiaqtagaq* (personal communication).

37 For the lyrics of Imaruittuq's own song, see Appendix B (II). Imaruittuq's own song is similar in theme and expression to Maniq's song.

38 Again, see Appendix B.

39   *-ksaq-* means "material," or "future," as in *pualuksaq* (material for mittens) or *nuliaksaq* (future wife, fiancée) (Harper, *Suffixes* 33).

40   The original is *pija·niajai'kiga*, which Rasmussen translates as "But I often do it badly" (*Netsilik* 517). Piuvkaq connects this anxiety to the fear of failure at the hunt: "It's wonderful / to hunt reindeer: but all too seldom / you succeed, / standing like a bright fire / on the plain" (Lowenstein 45).

41   In translating these verses for a European audience, Rasmussen tended "to 'fill out' the prayers in terms of what he considers more intelligible poetry" (Wiebe 59).

42   In Inuktitut, post-bases (or infixes) such as *–siuq-* (look for) or *–ksaq* (material, future) are roughly equivalent to English words. As a result, an Inuktitut word such as *pisiksaqsiuliqpunga* is in English conveyed in a sentence: "I am searching for a song." *Pisiq* (song) + *-ksaq* (material for) + *-siuq-* (looking, hunting) + *-liq-* (right now) + *punga* (I). Alana Johns points out, however, that like the morphemes in an English word, the post-bases are not usually perceived by native speakers as distinct and easily separated chunks (personal conversation).

43   This statement may have led Edmund Carpenter to declare that "[i]n Eskimo the word to make poetry is the word to breathe; both are derivatives of *anerca*, the soul, that which is eternal: the breath of life" (*Anerca* n.pag.). I have found no other evidence of this usage.

44   Rasmussen notes in *Snehyttens Sange*, however, that hunting songs "are difficult to separate from the songs of mood as so many of the songs touch on game, and the joys and disappointments of the hunter" (qtd. in Lowenstein 107).

45   As may be apparent, the phrase *nunguusimavatigut* uses a construction that is difficult to translate (and to understand). I will try to parse it here. *Nuunguu-* is to finish, use up, or wear out; *sima* is the present perfect tense, and describes a completed action. The ending *–vatigut* indicates that the action is being performed by a third-person plural subject ("they") and is directed towards a first-person plural (indirect) object ("us," or "for us") (Harper, *Grammar* 33).

46   The use of the plural, here, is curious; it seems to indicate that the grammatical subject has changed since the previous line, which was the (singular) song.

47   Imaruittuq says that "*Tainiq* means the title of a song" (219). Schneider translates the term as "the fact of naming oneself" (387). Peter Irniq clarifies, saying that *tainiq* is a "'subject' to sing about" (personal correspondence). In other words, it is the organizing principle of a song. Imaruittuq's own *ikiaqtagaq* (adapted song) contains similar references to titling.

48   The lyrics of Imaruittuq's own song are included in Appendix B (II).

49   In *Intellectual Culture of the Copper Eskimos*, Rasmussen notes that this special vocabulary was "also used by agLErtut—women observing taboo after a birth, miscarriage or menstruation, or death" (108).

50   As Rasmussen explains it, *qilaut* is "a term possibly related to the qilavɔq previously mentioned: the art of getting into touch with spirits apart from the ordinary invocation" (qtd. in Lowenstein 120).

51   A student asked Emile Imaruittuq the following question: "If I take something, and years and years passed before I saw this person and told him I had taken something would that be stealing?" Imaruittuq explained: "During the years that you didn't tell him, it would be stealing. But as soon as you told him, it would no longer be stealing" (Aupilaarjuk et al., *Law* 139).

52   Joanasie Qappik explains that an *inuksuk* like the one used at the Vancouver Olympics (an *inunnguaq* in the shape of a person) is used to signify that there has been a murder—and contains a declaration that no more will occur ("*Taima*"). No doubt the organizers of the Vancouver Olympics were unaware of this denotation.

53 Thanks to Christopher Trott for pointing out *The Journals of Knud Rasmussen*'s departure from the historical record (personal communication). In the screenplay for the film, there is a final scene in which Avva explains his conversion to Rasmussen (who did not go on the trip to Iglulik). However, this scene did not make it into the final version of the film.

54 This discussion would benefit from an analysis of the third feature film to come out of Igloolik: the recently released *Before Tomorrow* by Arnait Video Productions (a sister company of Isuma). This film also makes use of a highly significant theme song, or anthem; initially sung by the character Ningiuq ("old woman" or "grandmother") to put her grandson to sleep, it gradually acquires a more serious connotation.

55 I will use Rasmussen's spelling (Ivaluardjuk) to refer to the historical figure, and Isuma's spelling (Evaluarjuk) to refer to the character in the film.

56 My translation (and transcription). The English-language screenplay gives a version of the song based very closely on Calvert and Worster's English translation in *Intellectual Culture of the Iglulik Eskimos;* these are included in Appendix B (V, VI). As the original was not printed in Rasmussen's *Report*, the song seems to have been translated back into Inuktitut for the film. According to the film's credits, the *ajajas* were composed by Louis Uttak, Paulossie Qulitalik, Atuat Akkitirq, Nathan Qamaniq, Abraham Ulayuruluk (who plays Ivaluardjuk), Clara Quassa, Enuki Kunuk, Julia Amagoalik, Hervé Paniaq, Madeline Ivalu, Eugene Ipakarnak, and Elizabeth Nutarariaq.

57 In the film's opening sequence, the stranger Tuurngarjuaq ("great spirit," now "devil") enters into a competition with the leader, Kumaglak. Kumaglak is killed, and Tuurgarjuaq appoints Kumaglak's son Saurriq leader. This is when things begin to go wrong. The main action of *Atanarjuat* occurs about twenty years later, when the community is still feeling the effects of that fateful night.

58 Lowenstein gives a number of examples of the material nature of songs, such as the following piece by the East Greenland singer Kilimé: "Let me cleave words / sharp little words / like the fire-wood / that I split with my axe" (xxii).

59 The transcription of this conversation is taken, with minor variations, from the film's subtitles (not from the screenplay, which is slightly different).

60 Much more could be said about the use of Flotow's aria in the film. "M'appari tutt'amor" is itself in translation from the German "Ach, so fromm," but neither Italian nor German, of course, is Rasmussen's own language. Furthermore, this aria is a kind of *ikiaqtagaq*—it originally was part of Flotow's opera *L'âme en peine*, but was later transposed into *Martha* (Kobbé 546). In the film, Rasmussen's rendition leads into a recording by Caruso, which accompanies the scene in which Mathiassen is flirting with Avva's daughter Apak; this recording is also the final song used in the film—it is played over a shot, placed in the middle of the credits, of a dog team arriving at a camp, far in the distance.

61 One of the helping spirits is played by Rachel Uyarasuk, who was over 90 years old at the time of filming—and who was a child in the Iglulik area when Umik the Prophet and the members of the Fifth Thule Expedition arrived there (Tungilik and Uyarasuk 5).

62 Some contemporary Inuit artists who draw upon and adapt song traditions include Laina Tullaugak, Tanya Tagaq, and Sylvia Cloutier, or of the up-and-coming spoken-word artist Taqralik Partridge.

CHAPTER FOUR

1 There is apparently some distinction between the literal meaning of *Inuit Qaujimajatuqangit* and the concept that it is meant to convey. Jaypetee Arnakak explains that the invention of the term was a simple translation of the phrase "traditional knowledge," which was inspired (in 1998) by the NWT's Traditional Knowledge

Policy ("Incorporation" 34–35). In contrast, Arnakak explains, IQ has no intention of isolating said knowledge from contemporary realities, contexts, and practices (35). He also clarifies that the Department of Sustainable Development prefers the term *Inuit Qaujimanituqangit*, "for the simple reason that [-niq-] captures the concept in the abstract, as opposed to [-jaq-] which connotes passivity" (35).

2   The principles of IQ vary from place to place, but the ones cited in the Task Force's report (based on Jaypetee Arnakak's work at the Department of Sustainable Development) are as follows: "a) Pijitsirnjiq. The concept of serving (a purpose or community) and providing for (family and/or a community); b) Aajiiqatgiingni. The Inuit way of decision-making. The term refers to comparing views or taking counsel; c) Pilnimmaksarniq. The passing on of knowledge and skills through observation, doing and practice; d) Piliriqatigiingniq. The concept of collaborative working relationships or working together for a common purpose; e) Avatittinnik Kamattiarniq. The concept of environmental stewardship; f) Qanuqtuurniq. The concept of being resourceful to solve problems" ("First Annual Report" 8).

3   "Traditional" is a challenging term, here. Arnakak is likely responding to its connotations of "ancientness"; however, many would contend that tradition, rather than being static and relegated to the past, is continually updated and (in the words of Audra Simpson), "profoundly contemporary." It's possible that the Inuktitut rendering of "traditional knowledge"—*qaujimajatuqangit*—with its use of the infix *–tuqa-* (meaning "old" or "ancient") connotes continued usefulness (Therrien, "Ce que precise" 118) but not the *adaptive* possibility that the concept is meant to include.

4   For a synopsis of Lejeune's notion of the "pact," see Smith and Watson (207).

5   For autobiographical context in Rasmussen's publications, see, for example, the first chapter of *The Netsilik Eskimos: Social Life and Spiritual Culture* (Volume VIII, No.1-2 of the *Report of the Fifth Thule Expedition*), entitled "Eskimo Life: Descriptions and Autobiographies" (7–83).

6   The first Moravian mission was established in Labrador in 1771; in the late nineteenth century, Reverend Edmund Peck introduced James Evans' syllabic writing system to Inuit in Northern Quebec and Cumberland Sound. It quickly gained popularity and is used now (with some variations) in Nunavut and Nunavik (McGrath, *Canadian* 22–23).

7   Inuit writing in the form of letters goes back to the second half of the eighteenth century. See "'What Great Creatures Are These': Early Contact Literature" in Penny Petrone's *Northern Voices: Inuit Writing in English* (55–99).

8   The ship carrying Ulrikab left Hebron, Labrador on 26 August 1880, and by 16 January 1881, the entire family, which included Abraham's wife, Ulrike, their children, Sara and Maria, and Ulrike's nephew Tobias, had died of smallpox. In 2005, Abraham Ulrikab's diary and letters were published in English translation by Hartmut Lutz, with an introduction by the late Iqaluit writer and illustrator Alootook Ipellie. The published diaries were re-translated from a nineteenth-century German translation by Moravian missionary Brother Kretschmer, as the Inuttitut original has been lost (Ulrikab xxvi).

9   *Land of the Good Shadows: The Life Story of Anauta an Eskimo Woman* was co-written with Blackmore's American friend, Heloise Chandler Washburne. See McGrath, *Canadian Inuit Literature* 85.

10   Robin McGrath published *Paper Stays Put* under her former name, Robin Gedalof.

11   McGrath also explores the ways in which oral traditions influence Inuit writing in her 1987 article, "Oral Influences in Contemporary Inuit Literature."

12   Orphans play an important role in the *unikkaaqtuat*, and a number of versions of the Kaujjarjuk story warn against their mistreatment. In most versions, the orphan boy acquires a spirit helper who trains him to become very strong, and he takes bloody revenge on the community. See "The Revenge of the Orphan Boy" in Petrone (17–19), or Selma Van London's "Mythology and Identity Construction Among the Inuit."

13 Thanks to Ooleepeeka Arnaqaq, who first showed me the collection of interviews with Pangnirtung elders.

14 Thanks to Ian MacRae for information about the Igloolik Oral History project.

15 My thanks to Andrew Stewart of Archaeological Services Inc., who gave me access to his collection of reports—several of which he had researched and co-authored—from the Kivalliq region.

16 ITC stands for the Inuit Tapirisat of Canada (the former name of the Inuit Tapiriit Kanatami, or ITK—the Canadian national Inuit organization).

17 Since 1999, Nunavut Arctic College has published multiple bilingual (Inuktitut-English) volumes in its Interviewing Inuit Elders, Memory and History in Nunavut, and Inuit Perspectives on the 20th Century series. It is also publishing a series of books entitled Life Stories of Northern Leaders, which features the recollections of prominent Inuit politicians: Abraham Okpik, John Amagoalik, Paul Quassa, James Arvaluk, and Peter Itinnuar. A subsequent collection, Arnait Nipingit, documents the experience of women leaders (ed. McComber and Partridge).

18 Nutaraaluk is originally from Kinngait (Aupilaarjuk et al., Law 10).

19 The editors of Interviewing Inuit Elders report that students struggled with the process of writing their course papers, which seemed to require them to talk about the elders' stories in a strangely general and objective way (Angmaalik et al. 12).

20 "Just any old story?" is the translation for "Kisumik unikkaaqtuarulutuinnamiik?" (56). But the word "old" found in the translation is a colloquial "usage—"any old." The postbase -rulu- in fact means something along the lines of "darn," and -tuinnaq- refers to ordinariness. Paniaq did not specify an old story; he referred to "just any ordinary long story."

21 Alexina Kublu (Iglulingmiut) was one of the course instructors. Volume 1 of the series contains a number of unikkaaqtuat that she learned from her father, Michel Kupaaq Piugattuk, who unfortunately passed away during the final week of the course (Angmaalik et al. 2).

22 In the ptarmigan myth, a child asks for a bedtime story; her grandmother tells one about baby lemmings and tickles the child, who is so frightened that she turns into a bird (or dies, in some versions) and flies out the window. The distressed grandmother, with her red-rimmed eyes and croaking voice, turns into the ptarmigan. See Inuit Unikkaaqtuangit: Inuit Legends Vol. 2, or Alexina Kublu's "Ingutarjuapiga nauk?" ("Where is my dear grandchild?") in Volume 1 of Interviewing Inuit Elders (Angmaalik et al. 188–191).

23 In her introduction to the book Words of the Real People: Alaska Native Literature in Translation, Ann Fienup-Riordan writes that "Yupik and Iñupiaq people distinguish between two broad, overlapping narrative types.... The first includes legends or tales told by distant ancestors and passed down from generation to generation—what James Ruppert and John Bernet aptly call distant-time stories.... Such legends are designated unipkaaq (singular) among the Iñupiat of north Alaska.... The second broad story category consists of historical narratives related by known persons, labelled quliaqtuaq in North Slope Iñupiaq" (xix). Similarly, in a footnote to the Inuvialuit memoir I, Nuligak, Maurice Métayer explains that there are two types of stories: "unipkat, [which] mingle fantasy and the fantastic with the real" and "kroliat," or "stories he intends to be true and relates in great detail, giving at times a magic interpretation to real-life situations" (Nuligak 68).

24 Dorais writes, "I'm not sure Inuit make any clear-cut distinction between history and myth" (personal correspondence).

25 Thanks to Alana Johns for the information regarding the suffixes that convey hearsay in Inuvialuktun dialects.

26 *"Iilaagaangugaluaq, unikkaaqtuaqsitiunngittualuugama"* (Aupilaarjuk et al., *Maligatuqaliriniup* 191).

27 The story of Ailaq and Papik centres on a family dispute; Papik kills his brother-in-law Ailaq, and then lies to his mother-in-law about it (188).

28 While it would be inaccurate to call the life stories that appear in the Interviewing Inuit Elders publications "traditional" in form (because of the foreign nature of the interview situation), we know from the protocols that the elders emphasized that *inuusirmingnik unikkaat*, or stories based on one's personal experience, is an Inuit genre indeed.

29 For the sake of accuracy, I refer to the author as "Freeman" but to the protagonist as "Minnie"; at the time of the events of the story, Minnie Aodla's name was not yet Freeman.

30 Weetaltuk was an important local leader. An area in Sanikiluaq (the Belcher Islands) is named after him, and Freeman mentions that he navigated for Robert Flaherty (the maker of *Nanook of the North*) in 1913 (69). She also tells of a time when her outspoken cousin came to visit her in Moose Factory, where she was working as a nanny. "You are Weetaltuk's granddaughter," the cousin says, "you can do better than this" (203). At the end of the book, Freeman learns of what happened to her people after her grandfather's death: "the James Bay group had no leader, no one who kept them together... It was as though my group had dispersed into nothing, the proud people were no more. Grandfather had taken it all with him when he died" (201).

31 In the foreword to Maurice Métayer's collection of Copper Eskimo stories, *Tales From the Igloo*, Al Purdy recounts Métayer's interpretation of the legend of "The Magic Drum," in which a skeleton-woman, having emerged from the sea, drums the flesh back onto her bones, and the youth back into the body of the drum-maker: "You see now," says Métayer, "the very important message of this story: a woman is not fully a woman without the love of a man. And a man will never grow old as long as he has the love of a woman" (6). Purdy expresses some dissatisfaction with Métayer's didacticism, emphasizing instead the enjoyment that storytelling brings to both teller and audience (6).

AFTERWORD

1 I would like to thank Leona Carter, Dwayne Donald, Daniel Johnson, and Christine Stewart, all of whom continue to help me reflect on the meaning of living in Treaty 6 territory.

2 This interview with the late Thomas Kimeksun Thrasher, elder brother of Anthony Apakark Thrasher, was recorded by Sam McKegney on 9 June 2011, in Tuktoyaktuk.

BIBLIOGRAPHY

Akilinirmiut Elders, Andrew Stewart, David Toolooktook, and Roy Avaala. *Tibjaliup Kuunnga: Place Names and Oral History of the Beverly Lake Region, Thelon River.* Baker Lake: Akiliniq Planning Committee, 1997.

Akulujuk, Malaya, James Alivatuk, Noah Arnaquq, Katsoo Evic, Aksayook Etoangat, Joanasie Kakee, Jim Kilabuk, Koodloo Pitsualak, Markosie Pitsualak, Paulosie Qappik, and Josephee Sowdloapik. *Stories from Pangnirtung.* Edmonton: Hurtig, 1976.

Alfred, Gerald. *Heeding the Voices of Our Ancestors: Kahnanwake Mohawk Politics and the Rise of Native Nationalism.* Don Mills: Oxford University Press, 1995.

Alia, Valerie. *Names and Nunavut: Culture and Identity in Arctic Canada.* New York: Berghahn Books, 2007.

Amagoalik, John. *John Amagoalik: Changing the Face of Canada.* Edited by Louis McComber. Vol. 2 of Life Stories of Northern Leaders. Iqaluit: Nunavut Arctic College, 2007.

Anawak, Jack. "Condolences to Kusugak Family." Legislative Assembly of Nunavut. *Hansard: Official Report,* 72 (4 December 2003). http://www.assembly.nu.ca/old/english/hansard/final6/Hansard_20031204.pdf.

Anderson, Benedict. *Imagined Communities: Reflections on the Origin and Spread of Nationalism.* London: Verso, 2006.

Angakkuit (Shaman Stories). Directed by Zacharias Kunuk. Igloolik Isuma Productions, 2003.

Angilirq, Paul Apak, Norman Cohn, Zacharias Kunuk, Hervé Paniaq, and Pauloosie Qulitalik. *Atanarjuat: The Fast Runner: Inspired by a Traditional Inuit legend of Igloolik* [Screenplay]. Toronto: Coach House Books and Isuma, 2002.

Angmaalik, Pauloosie, Saullu Nakasuk, Elisapee Ootoova, and Hervé Paniaq. *Introduction.* Edited by Frédéric Laugrand and Jarich Oosten. Vol. 1 of Interviewing Inuit Elders. Iqaluit: Nunavut Arctic College, 1999.

——. *Pigiarutit [Introduction].* Edited by Frédéric Laugrand and Jarich Oosten. Vol. 1 of *Innarnik Apiqsuqattarniq* [Interviewing Inuit Elders]. Iqaluit: Nunavut Arctic College, 1999.

Angutinngurniq, Jose, Mariano Aupilaarjuk, Levi Iluittuq, Ollie Itinnuaq, Luke Nuliajuk, Felix Pisuk, Peter Suvaksiuq, and Pujuat Tapaqti. *Inuit Qaujimajatuqangit: Shamanism and Reintegrating Wrongdoers into the Community.* Edited by Frédéric Laugrand and Jarich Oosten. Vol. 4 of Inuit Perspectives on the 20th Century. Iqaluit: Nunavut Arctic College, 2002.

"a'ppropre/a'pproprie." *Oxford English Dictionary,* 2nd ed. Oxford University Press, 2011. http://www.oed.com.login.ezproxy.library.ualberta.ca/view/Entry/9866

Armstrong, Jeannette C. *Looking at the Words of Our People: First Nations Analysis of Literature.* Penticton, BC: Theytus Books, 1993.

Arnakak, Jaypetee. "Commentary: What Is Inuit Qaujimajatuqangit?" *Nunatsiaq News.* 25 August 2000. http://www.nunatsiaq.com/archives/nunavut000831/nvt20825_17.html.

——. "Incorporation of Inuit Qaujimanituqangit, or Inuit Traditional Knowledge, into the Government of Nunavut." *The Journal of Aboriginal Development* 3, 1 (2002): 33–39.

Arvaluk, James. *James Arvaluk: That's My Vision.* Edited by Noel McDermott. Vol. 4 of Life Stories of Northern Leaders. Iqaluit: Nunavut Arctic College, 2008.

Asch, Michael, ed. *Aboriginal and Treaty Rights in Canada: Essays on Law, Equity, and Respect for Difference.* Vancouver: UBC Press, 1997.

Ashoona, Pitseolak. *Pitseolak: Pictures Out Of My Life.* Edited by Dorothy Harley Eber. Montreal: McGill-Queen's University Press, 2003.

Atanarjuat (The Fast Runner). Directed by Norman Cohn and Zacharias Kunuk. Igloolik Isuma Productions, 2001.

Attagutsiak, Tirisi, Akisu Joamie, Alacie Joamie, Elisapee Ootoova, Malaya Papatsie, and Jayko Pitseolak. *Perspectives on Traditional Health.* Edited by Frédéric Laugrand and Michele Therrien. Vol. 5 of Interviewing Inuit Elders. Iqaluit: Nunavut Arctic College, 2001.

——. *Aanniarniq Aanniaqtailimaniq* [*Perspectives on Traditional Health*]. Edited by Frédéric Laugrand and Michele Therrien. Vol. 5 of *Innarnik Apiqsuqattarniq* [Interviewing Inuit Elders]. Iqaluit: Nunavut Arctic College, 2001.

Aupilaarjuk, Mariano, Isidore Ijituuq, Rose Iqallijuq, Michel Kupaaq, Lucassie Nutaraaluk, Marie Tulimaaq, and Johanasi Ujarak. *Cosmology and Shamanism.* Edited by Bernard Saladin D'Anglure. Vol. 4 of Interviewing Inuit Elders. Iqaluit: Nunavut Arctic College, 2001.

——. *Ukpirijavinituqait Angakkuillu* [*Cosmology and Shamanism*]. Edited by Bernard Saladin D'Anglure. Vol. 4 of *Innarnik Apiqsuqattarniq* [Interviewing Inuit Elders]. Iqaluit: Nunavut Arctic College, 2000.

Aupilaarjuk, Mariano, Emile Imaruittuq, Akisu Joamie, Lucassie Nutaraaluk, and Marie Tulimaaq. *Perspectives on Traditional Law.* Edited by Frédéric Laugrand, Jarich Oosten and Wim Rasing. Vol. 2 of Interviewing Inuit Elders. Iqaluit: Nunavut Arctic College, 2000.

——. *Maligatuqaliriniup Miksaanut Isumagijut* [*Perspectives on Traditional Law*]. Edited by Frédéric Laugrand, Jarich Oosten, and Wim Rasing. Vol. 2 of *Innarnik Apiqsuqattarniq* [Interviewing Inuit Elders]. Iqaluit: Nunavut Arctic College, 1999.

Awa, Joanna. "The Story of a Name." *Nunatsiaq News.* 27 Oct. 2000. http://www.nunatsiaq.com/archives/nunavut001031/letters.html.

Ayaruaq, John. "The Story of John Ayaruaq." *North* 16, 2 (1969): 1–5.

Baikie, Margaret. *Labrador Memories: Reflections at Mulligan.* Happy Valley, NL: Them Days, 1983.

Ballinger, Franchot. "A Matter of Emphasis: Teaching the Literature in Native American Literature Courses. *American Indian Culture and Research Journal* 8, 2 (1984): 1–12.

Barfield, Owen. *Poetic Diction: A Study in Meaning.* London: Faber and Faber, 1952.

"The Bathurst Mandate (Pinasuaqtavut: That Which We've Set Out To Do)." Government of Nunavut, 1999. http://nni.gov.nu.ca/files/05%20Bathurst%20Mandate_Eng.pdf.

Before Tomorrow. Dirs. Marie-Hélène Cousineau and Madeline Ivalu. Arnait Video Productions, 2007.

Bennett, John, and Susan Rowley, eds. *Uqalurait: An Oral History of Nunavut.* Montreal: McGill-Queen's University Press, 2004.

Berger, Thomas R. *The Nunavut Project.* Conciliator's Final Report. Nunavut Land Claims Agreement Implementation Contract Negotiations for the Second Planning Period 2003–2013. Ottawa: Indian and Northern Affairs Canada, 2006.

Berkhofer, Robert F. *The White Man's Indian: Images of the American Indian from Columbus to the Present.* New York: Alfred A. Knopf, 1978.

Berthelsen, Christian. "Greenlandic Literature: Its Traditions, Changes and Trends." *Arctic Anthropology* 23, 1/2 (1986): 339–345.

——. *Grønlandsk Litteratur: Kommeneret Antologi*. Trans. Christian Berthelsen and Per Langgård. Copenhagen: Centrum, 1983.

Bhabha, Homi K., ed. *Nation and Narration*. New York: Routledge, 1990.

Bielawski, Ellen. "Inuit Indigenous Knowledge and Science in the Arctic." *Northern Perspectives* 20, 1 (1992). http://www.carc.org/pubs/v20no1/inuit.htm.

Bilson, Janet Mancini, and Kyra Mancini. *Inuit Women: Their Powerful Spirit in a Century of Change*. Lanham, MD: Rowman and Littlefield, 2007.

Binney, George. *The Eskimo Book of Knowledge*. London: Hudson's Bay Company, 1931.

Blackmore, Lizzie Ford, and Heluiz Chandler Washburne. *Land of the Good Shadows: The Life Story of Anauta, an Eskimo Woman*. New York: AMS Press, 1940.

Blaeser, Kimberly M. "Native Literature: Seeking a Critical Center." In *Looking at the Words of Our People: First Nations Analysis of Literature*, edited by Jeannette Armstrong, 51–62. Penticton, BC: Theytus Books, 1993.

Blake, Dale. "Inuit Autobiography: Challenging the Stereotypes." PhD diss., University of Alberta, 2000.

——. *Study Guide for Inuit Life Writings and Oral Traditions: Inuit Myths*. St. John's: Educational Resource Development Co-operative, 2001.

Blaisel, Xavier, Frédéric Laugrand, and Jarich Oosten. "Shamans and Leaders: Parousial Movements among the Inuit of Northeast Canada." *Numen* 46, 4 (1999): 370–411.

Blondin, George. *Trail of the Spirit: The Mysteries of Medicine Power Reveal*. Edmonton: NeWest Press, 2006.

Boas, Franz. *The Central Eskimo*. Annual Report of the Bureau of Ethnology. Lincoln: University of Nebraska Press, 1964.

——. "Sagen der Eskimos von Baffin-Land." *Verhandlungen der Berliner Gesellschaft für Anthropologie, Ethnologie und Urgeschichte*, edited by Rud. Virchow. Berlin: Verlag von A. Asher and Co., 1888. 398–405.

Bodenhorn, Barbara. "'I'm Not the Great Hunter, My Wife Is': Iñupiat and Anthropological Models of Gender." *Études/Inuit/Studies* 14, 1–2 (1990): 55–74.

Bonesteel, Sarah. *Canada's Relationship with Inuit: A History of Policy and Program Development*. Ottawa: Indian and Northern Affairs Canada, 2006.

Brice-Bennett, Carol. *Our Footprints Are Everywhere: Inuit Land Use and Occupancy in Labrador*. Nain: Labrador Inuit Association, 1977.

Briggs, Jean. "Eskimo Women: Makers of Men." *Many Sisters: Women in Cross-Cultural Perspective*. Edited by Carolyn J. Matthiasson. London: Free Press, 1974. 261–304.

——. "Expecting the Unexpected: Inuit Training for an Experimental Lifestyle." *Ethos* 19, 3 (1991): 259–287.

——. *Inuit Morality Play: The Emotional Education of a Three-Year-Old*. St. John's, NL: Institute of Social and Economic Research, 1998.

——. *Never in Anger: Portrait of an Eskimo Family*. Cambridge: Harvard University Press, 1970.

Bringhurst, Robert. *Everywhere Being Is Dancing: Twenty Pieces of Thinking*. Kentville NS: Gaspereau Press, 2007.

——. *The Tree of Meaning: Thirteen Talks*. Kentville, NS: Gaspereau Press, 2006.

Bringhurst, Robert, trans. *A Story as Sharp as a Knife: The Classical Haida Mythtellers and Their World*. Vancouver: Douglas and McIntyre, 1999.

Brody, Hugh. *Indians on Skid Row*. Ottawa: Information Canada, 1971.

——. "Land Occupancy: Inuit Perceptions." Vol. 1 of Inuit Land Use and Occupancy Project. Edited by Milton Freeman, 185–242. Ottawa: Indian and Northern Affairs, 1976.

——. *The Other Side of Eden.* Vancouver: Douglas and McIntyre, 2000.

——. "Without Stories We Are Lost." In *The Journals of Knud Rasmussen: A Sense of Memory and High-Definition Inuit Storytelling,* edited by Gillian Robinson, 45–56. Montreal: Isuma, 2008.

Brooks, Lisa. "Afterword: At the Gathering Place." *American Indian Literary Nationalism.* Albuquerque: University of New Mexico Press, 2006. 225–52.

——. *The Common Pot: The Recovery of Native Space in the Northeast.* Minneapolis: University of Minnesota Press, 2008.

——. "Digging at the Roots: Locating an Ethical, Native Criticism." In *Reasoning Together: The Native Critics Collective,* edited by Daniel Heath Justice, Christopher B. Teuton, and Craig Womack, 234–64. Norman: University of Oklahoma Press, 2008.

Brown, Leslie and Susan Strega, eds. *Research as Resistance: Critical, Indigenous, and Anti-Oppressive Approaches.* Toronto: Canadian Scholars' Press: 2005.

Burgess, Anthony. "novel." *Encyclopædia Britannica Online Academic Edition.* 23 May 2012. http://www.britannica.com.login.ezproxy.library.ualberta.ca/EBchecked/topic/421071/novel.

Campbell, Lydia. *Sketches of Labrador Life.* St. John's, NL: Killick Press, 2000.

Carlson, Keith Thor, Kristina Fagan, and Natalia Khanenko-Friesen, eds. *Orality and Literacy: Reflections Across Disciplines.* Toronto: University of Toronto Press, 2011.

Carpenter, Edmund. *Anerca.* Toronto: J.M. Dent, 1959.

Carpenter, Mary. "Stories: 'Skeleton Woman,' 'Woman of the Sea.'" In *Echoing Silence: Essays on Arctic Narrative,* edited by John Moss, 225–30. Ottawa: University of Ottawa Press, 1997.

Cavanagh, Beverley. *Music of the Netsilik Eskimo: A Study of Stability and Change.* Ottawa: National Museums of Canada, 1982.

Ce Qu'il Faut Pour Vivre [The Necessities of Life]. Directed by Benoit Pilon. Performance by Natar Ungalaaq. Films Séville, 2008.

Chamberlin, J. Edward. "Close Encounters of the First Kind." In *Myth and Memory: Stories of Indigenous-European Contact,* edited by John Lutz, 15–29. Vancouver: UBC Press, 2007.

——. "'The Corn People Have A Song Too. It Is Very Good': On Beauty, Truth, and Goodness." *Studies in American Indian Literature* 21, 3 (2009): 66–89.

——. "Culture and Anarchy in Indian Country." In *Aboriginal and Treaty Rights in Canada: Essays on Law, Equity, and Respect for Difference,* edited by Michael Asch, 3–36. Vancouver: UBC Press, 1997.

——. "Doing Things With Words: Putting Performance on the Page." In *Talking on the Page: Editing Aboriginal Oral Texts,* edited by Laura J. Murray and Keren Rice, 69–90. Toronto: University of Toronto Press, 1999.

——. "From Hand to Mouth: The Postcolonial Politics of Oral and Written Traditions." In *Reclaiming Indigenous Voice and Vision,* edited by Marie Battiste, 124–41. Seattle: University of Washington Press, 2000.

——. *The Harrowing of Eden.* Toronto: Fitzhenry and Whiteside Ltd., 1975.

——. "Hunting, Tracking and Reading." In *Literacy, Narrative and Culture,* edited by Jens Brockmeier, Min Wang, and David R. Olson, 67–84. Richmond, Eng.: Curzon, 2002.

——. *If This Is Your Land, Where Are Your Stories?: Finding Common Ground.* Toronto: Alfred A. Knopf Canada, 2003.

Chapman, Michael. *Southern African Literatures.* London: Longman, 1996.

Christopher, Neil. *Stories of the Amautalik: Fantastic Beings from Inuit Myths and Legends.* Iqaluit: Inhabit Media, 2009.

Christopher, Neil, ed. *Kappianaqtut: Strange Creatures and Fantastic Beings from Inuit Myths and Legends*. Trans. Louise Flaherty and Robert Jonas. Iqaluit: Inhabit Media, 2007.

——. *Unikkaaqtuat: An Introduction to Inuit Myths and Legends*. Iqaluit: Inhabit Media, 2011.

Coates, Corey. "The First Inuit Autobiography: Text and Context(s)." *The Northern Review* 28 (2008): 261–70.

Coates, Ken, P. Whitney Lackenbauer, Bill Morrison and Greg Poelzer. *Arctic Front: Defending Canada in the Far North*. Toronto: Thomas Allen, 2008.

Cohn, Norman. "Norman Cohn Speaks with Joysanne Sidimus." In *The Journals of Knud Rasmussen: A Sense of Memory and High-Definition Inuit Storytelling*, edited by Gillian Robinson, 263–75. Montreal: Isuma, 2008.

Colakovic, Marina Rojc. *Mytho-Poetic Structure in the Inuit Tale of Kivioq the Wanderer: Inuit Art of Story-Telling in the Light of Oral Literature Theory*. Guelph: McDonald Stewart Art Centre, 1993.

Colombo, John Robert, ed. *Poems of the Inuit*. Ottawa: Oberon Press, 1981.

——. *Songs of the Great Land*. Ottawa: Oberon, 1989.

Cournoyea, Nellie. "Documenting the Oral History of the Inuvialuit." In *Echoing Silence: Essays on Arctic Narrative*, edited by John Moss, 7–13. Ottawa: University of Ottawa Press, 1997.

Cram, Jennifer. "Isumaksaqsiurvik: The First Canadian Collection of Inuit Literature." *Polar Record* 23, 143 (1986): 203–204.

Cruikshank, Julie. *Do Glaciers Listen?: Local Knowledge, Colonial Encounters and Social Imagination*. Vancouver: UBC Press, 2005.

——. "Oral Tradition and Oral History: Reviewing Some Issues." *Canadian Historical Review* 75, 3 (1994): 403–18.

——. *The Social Life of Stories: Narrative and Knowledge in the Yukon Territory*. Vancouver: UBC Press, 1998.

Cruikshank, Julie, ed. *Life Lived Like a Story: Life Stories of Three Yukon Native Elders*. Lincoln: University of Nebraska Press, 1992.

Csonka, Yvon. "Changing Inuit Historicities in West Greenland and Nunavut." *History and Anthropology* 16, 3 (2005): 321–334.

Dahl, Jens, Jack Hicks, and Peter Jull, eds. *Nunavut: Inuit Regain Control of Their Lands and Their Lives*. Copenhagen: International Work Group for Indigenous Affairs, 2000.

d'Anglure, Bernard Saladin. *Être et renaître Inuit: homme, femme ou chamane*. Paris: Gallimard, 2006.

Dauenhauer, Nora Marks, and Richard Dauenhauer, eds. *Haa Kusteeyí, Our Culture: Tlingit Life Stories*. Vol. 3 of Classics of Tlingit Oral Literature. Seattle: University of Washington Press and Sealaska Heritage Foundation, 1994.

——. *Haa Shuka, Our Ancestors: Tlingit Oral Narratives*. Vol. 1 of Classics of Tlingit Oral Literature. Seattle: University of Washington Press and Sealaska Heritage Foundation, 1987

——. *Haa Tuwunáagu Yís, For Healing Our Spirit: Tlingit Oratory*. Vol. 2 of Classics of Tlingit Oral Literature. Seattle: University of Washington Press and Sealaska Heritage Foundation, 1990.

——. "The Paradox of Talking on the Page: Some Aspects of the Tlingit and Haida Experience." *Talking on the Page: Editing Aboriginal Oral Texts*, edited by Laura J. Murray and Keren Rice, 3–42. Toronto: University of Toronto Press, 1999.

Descartes, René. *Meditations on First Philosophy*. Edited by John Cottingham. Cambridge: Cambridge University Press, 1996.

Dobson, Kit. "Indigeneity and Diversity in Eden Robinson's Work." *Canadian Literature* 201 (2009): 54–67.

Dorais, Louis-Jacques, *1000 Inuit uqausingit / 1000 Inuit words / 1000 mots inuit*. Québec: Association Inuksiutiit Katimajiit and Groupe d'études inuit et circumpolaires (GETIC), Université Laval, 1990.

——. "À Propos d'Identité Inuit." *Études/Inuit/Studies* 18, 1–2 (1994): 253–60.

——. *From Magic Words to Word Processing: A History of the Inuit Language*. Iqaluit: Nunavut Arctic College, 1993.

——. *The Language of the Inuit: Syntax, Semantics, and Society in the Arctic*. Montreal: McGill-Queen's University Press, 2010.

——. *La parole Inuit: langue, culture et société dans l'arctique nord-américain*. Paris: Peeters, 1996.

Dorais, Louis-Jacques, ed. *Inuit Identities in the Third Millenium/Identités inuit au troisième millénaire/Inutuinnauniq Aqraguni (Ukiuni) 2000-Nginni*. Québec: Association Inuksiutiit Katimajiit, Inc., 2001.

Dreque, Dracc [Gideon Enutsia Etorolopiaq]. *Iliarjuk: An Inuit Memoir*. Surrey, BC: Libros Libertad, 2007.

Dumont, Marilyn. "Popular Images of Nativeness." *Looking at the Words of Our People: First Nations Analysis of Literature*, edited by Jeannette Armstrong, 46–50. Penticton: Theytus Books, 1993.

Dybbroe, Susanne. "Questions of Identity and Issues of Self-Determination." *Études/Inuit/Studies* 20, 2 (1996): 39–53.

Eakin, Paul John. *Fictions in Autobiography: Studies in the Art of Self-Invention*. Princeton: Princeton University Press, 1985.

——. *How Our Lives Become Stories: Making Selves*. Ithaca: Cornell University Press, 1999.

Eber, Dorothy Harley. *Images of Justice: A Legal History of the Northwest Territories and Nunavut as Traced through the Yellowknife Courthouse Collection of Inuit Sculpture*. Montreal: McGill-Queen's University Press, 1997.

——. *When the Whalers Were up North: Inuit Memories from the Eastern Arctic*. Kingston: McGill-Queen's University Press, 1989.

——. *Encounters on the Passage: Inuit Meet the Explorers*. Toronto: University of Toronto Press, 2008.

Eekoomiak, Norman. *An Arctic Childhood*. Oakville, ON: Chimo, 1980.

Eigenbrod, Renate. *Travelling Knowledges: Positioning the Im/Migrant Reader of Aboriginal Literatures in Canada*. Winnipeg: University of Manitoba Press, 2005.

Eigenbrod, Renate and Jo-Ann Episkenew, eds. *Creating Community: A Roundtable on Canadian Aboriginal Literature*. Penticton: Theytus, 2002.

Ekho, Naqi and Uqsuralik Ottokie. *Childrearing Practices*. Edited by Jean Briggs. Vol. 3 of Interviewing Inuit Elders. Iqaluit: Nunavut Arctic College, 2000.

——. *Nutaqqirijjusituqait [Childrearing Practices]*. Edited by Jean Briggs. Vol. 3 of *Innarnik Apiqsuqattarniq* [Interviewing Inuit Elders]. Iqaluit: Nunavut Arctic College, 2000.

Eliot, T.S. "Tradition and the Individual Talent." *The Sacred Wood: Essays on Poetry and Criticism*. London: Methuen, 1964. 47–59.

Exile. Dir. Zacharias Kunuk. Isuma Igloolik Productions, 2008.

Fabian, Johannes. *Time and the Other: How Anthropology Makes its Object*. New York: Columbia University Press, 1983.

Fagan, Kristina. "Tewatatha:wi: Aboriginal Nationalism in Taiaiake Alfred's Peace, Power, Righteousness: An Indigenous Manifesto." *The American Indian Quarterly* 28, 1 (2004): 12–29.

Field, Edward. *Eskimo Songs and Stories: Collected by Knud Rasmussen on the Fifth Thule Expedition.* New York: Delacorte, 1973.

Fienup-Riordan, Ann. "The Real People: The Concept of Personhood Among the Yukon Eskimos of Western Alaska." *Études/Inuit/Studies* 10, 1–2 (1984): 261–270.

——. "'We Talk to You Because We Love You': Learning from Elders at Culture Camp. *Anthropology and Humanism* 2 (2001): 173–187.

Fienup-Riordan, Ann, and Lawrence Kaplan, eds. *Words of the Real People: Alaska Native Literature in Translation.* Fairbanks: University of Alaska Press, 2007.

Finley, Robert. "The Riddle's Charm." *Dalhousie Review* 77, 3 (1997): 313–22.

"The First Annual Report of the Inuit Qaujimajatuqangit (IQ) Task Force." Government of Nunavut, 12 Aug. 2002. http://www.inukshukmanagement.ca/IQ%20Task%20 Force%20Report1.pdf.

Foley, John Miles. *How to Read an Oral Poem.* Urbana: University of Illinois Press, 2002.

Fossett, Renée. *In Order to Live Untroubled: Inuit of the Central Arctic, 1550–1940.* Winnipeg: University of Manitoba Press, 2001.

Freeman, Milton, ed. *Inuit Land Use and Occupancy Project: A Report.* Ottawa: Ministry of Supply and Services Canada, 1976.

Freeman, Minnie Aodla. *Life Among the Qallunaat.* Edmonton: Hurtig, 1978.

Freeman, Victoria. "The Baffin Writers' Project." *Native Writers and Canadian Writing*, edited by William H. New, 266–71. Vancouver: UBC Press, 1990.

Freiwald, Bina Toledo. "'Covering Their Familiar Ways with Another Culture': Minnie Aodla Freeman's *Life among the Qallunaat* and the Ethics of Subjectivity." In *Postmodernism and the Ethical Subject*, edited by Barbara Gabriel and Suzan Ilcan, 273–301. Montreal: McGill-Queen's University Press, 2004.

French, Alice Masak. *My Name is Masak.* Winnipeg: Peguis Publishers, 1977.

——. *The Restless Nomad.* Winnipeg: Pemmican Publications, 1991.

Frobisher. By John Estacio. Libretto by John Murrell. Southern Alberta Jubilee Auditorium, Calgary. Rec. 27 Jan. 2007. CBC Radio 2, 2007.

Gallop, Jane. "The Historicization of Literary Studies and the Fate of Close Reading." *Profession* (2007): 181–6.

Gagnon, Melanie, ed., with Iqaluit Elders. *Inuit Recollections on the Military Presence in Iqaluit.* Vol. 2 of Memory and History in Nunavut Series. Iqaluit: Nunavut Arctic College, 2002.

Gatti, Maurizio, ed. *Littérature amérindienne du Québec: écrits de la langue française.* Montréal: Hurtubise, 2004.

Gedalof [McGrath], Robin. *An Annotated Bibliography of Canadian Inuit Literature.* Ottawa: Indian and Northern Affairs Canada, 1979.

Gedalof [McGrath], Robin, ed. *Paper Stays Put: A Collection of Inuit Writing.* Edmonton: Hurtig, 1980.

Giffen, Naomi Musmaker. *The Rôles of Men and Women in Eskimo Culture.* New York: AMS Press, 1975.

Gingell, Susan. "Teaching the Talk that Walks on Paper: Oral Traditions and Textualized Orature in the Canadian Literature Classroom." In *Home-Work: Post-Colonialism, Pedagogy, and Canadian Literature*, edited by Cynthia Sugars, 285–300. Ottawa: University of Ottawa Press, 2004.

Goody, Jack. *The Interface Between the Written and the Oral.* Cambridge: Cambridge University Press, 1987.

Goudie, Elizabeth. *Woman of Labrador.* Toronto: Martin, 1973.

Gould, Glenn. *The Idea of North.* Ideas. CBC Radio, Toronto. 27 Dec. 1967.

Government of Nunavut. "Nunavut: A New Government, A New Vision." http://www.gov.nu.ca/english/about/newvision%20Jan%2008.pdf.

Grace, Sherrill. *Canada and the Idea of North.* Montreal: McGill-Queen's University Press, 2002.

Graff, Gerald. *Professing Literature: An Institutional History.* Chicago: University of Chicago Press, 2007.

"Grammar» -vik (affix)." *Inuktitut Tusaalanga.* Pirurvik Centre, 2012. http://www.tusaalanga.ca/node/1136.

Grant, Shelagh. *Arctic Justice: On Trial for Murder, Pond Inlet, 1923.* Montreal: McGill-Queen's Press, 2005.

Grey, Minnie and Marianne Stenbaek, eds. *Voices and Images of Nunavimmiut: Vol. 1: Stories and Tales.* Montreal and Hanover: International Polar Year Press, 2011.

——. *Voices and Images of Nunavimmiut: Vol. 2: Way of Life.* Montreal and Hanover: International Polar Year Press, 2011.

Guemple, Lee. "Gender in Inuit Society." In *Women and Power in Native North America,* edited by Laura F. Klein and Lillian A. Ackerman, 17–27. Norman: University of Oklahoma Press, 1995.

"Guiding Principles of Inuit Qaujimajatuqangit." Poster. Government of Nunavut, n.d. http://www.piqqusilirivvik.ca/apps/UPLOADS/fck/file/IQ%20poster.pdf.

Hallendy, Norman. *Inuksuit: Silent Messengers of the Arctic.* Vancouver: Douglas and McIntyre, 2001.

Harper, Kenn. "Charles Dickens and the Inuit." *Nunatsiaq News.* 14 Nov. 2008. http://www.nunatsiaq.com/opinionEditorial/columns.html.

——. *Give Me My Father's Body: The Story of Minik, the New York Eskimo.* New York: Washington Square Press, 2000.

——. "Inuit Writing Systems in Nunavut: Issues and Challenges." In *Inuit Regain Control of Their Lands and Their Lives,* edited by Jens Dahl, Jack Hicks, and Peter Jull, 91–100. Copenhagen: IWGIA Document.

——. *Some Aspects of the Grammar of the Eskimo Dialects of Cumberland Peninsula and North Baffin Island.* Ottawa: National Museums of Canada, 1974.

——. *Suffixes of the Eskimo Dialects of Cumberland Peninsula and North Baffin Island.* Ottawa: National Museums of Canada, 1979.

Harrison, Phyllis, ed. *Q-Book [Qaujivallirutissat].* Ottawa: Northern Administration Branch, Welfare Division: 1964.

Harry, Margaret. "Literature in English by Native Canadians (Indians and Inuit). *Studies in Canadian Literature* 10, 1 (1985). 146–153.

Henderson, Ailsa. *Nunavut: Rethinking Political Culture.* Vancouver: UBC Press, 2007.

Henderson, Heather. "North and South: Autobiography and the Problems of Translation." In *Reflections: Autobiography and Canadian Literature,* edited by K.P. Stitch, 61–8. Ottawa: University of Ottawa Press, 1988.

Hoffman, Charles. *Drum-Dance: Legends, Ceremonies, Dances and Songs of the Eskimos.* Agincourt, ON: Gage, 1974.

Holm, Tom, J. Diane Pearson, and Ben Chavis. "Peoplehood: A Model for the Extension of Sovereignty in American Indian Studies." *Wicazo Sa Review* (2003): 7–24.

Hot, Aurélie. "Écrire et lire la langue inuit: choix linguistiques contemporains à Iqaluit et Igloolik, Nunavut." PhD diss., Université Laval, 2010.

Houston, James, ed. *Songs of the Dream People: Chants and Images from the Indians and Eskimos of North America*. New York: Atheneum, 1972.

Huhndorf, Shari. "'Atanarjuat, the Fast Runner': Culture, History, and Politics in Inuit Media. *American Anthropologist* 105, 4 (2003): 822-826.

——. *Going Native: Indians in the American Cultural Imagination*. Ithaca: Cornell University Press, 2001.

——. *Mapping the Americas: The Transnational Politics of Contemporary Native Culture*. Ithaca: Cornell University Press, 2009.

Hulan, Renée. *Northern Experience and the Myths of Canadian Culture*. Montreal: McGill-Queen's University Press, 2002.

Hutcheon, Linda. "Adventures in Literary Historyland." Keynote address, The Cambridge History of Postcolonial Literature Conference, Toronto, 19 Sept. 2008.

——. *The Politics of Postmodernism*. London: Routledge, 2002.

Hutcheon, Linda. "Interventionist Literary Histories: Nostalgic, Pragmatic, or Utopian? *Modern Language Quarterly* 59, 4 (1998): 401-417.

Hymes, Dell. *Now I Only Know So Far: Essays in Ethnopoetics*. Lincoln: University of Nebraska Press, 2003.

Igloliorte, John. *An Inuk Boy Becomes a Hunter*. Halifax: Nimbus, 1994.

"Igloolik (IKCC): Inuit Knowledge and Climate Change (IKCC): Assessing, Mitigating, and Communicating Health Risks." *Climate Telling*. Institute for Circumpolar Health Research, 2012. http://climatetelling.ca/community/igloolik-ikcc/#.

Imaruittuq, Emile. "Pisiit, Songs." *Perspectives on Traditional Law*, edited by Frédéric Laugrand, Jarich Oosten, and Wim Rasing, 201-19. Vol. 2 of Interviewing Inuit Elders. Iqaluit: Nunavut Arctic College, 2000.

Innuksuk, Rhoda, and Susan Cowan, eds. *We Don't Live in Snow Houses Now: Reflections of Arctic Bay*. Ottawa: Canadian Arctic Producers, 1978.

Inuit Circumpolar Council. "Final Report—First Inuit Circumpolar Conference, 1977." Eben Hopson Memorial Archives. http://www.ebenhopson.com /icc/ICCBooklet.html.

"Inuit Qaujimajatuqangit." Department of Human Resources, Government of Nunavut. 2005. http://www.gov.nu.ca/hr/site/beliefsystem.htm.

Inuit Unikkaaqtuangit: Inuit Legends. CBC North Radio One, Iqaluit, 2002.

Inuit Unikkaaqtuangit: Inuit Legends Vol. 2. CBC North Radio One, Iqaluit, 2004.

The Inuit Way: A Guide to Inuit Culture/Inuit Piusingit: Inuit Iliqqusingnni Qaujigiaruti. Ottawa: Pauktuutit Inuit Women's Association of Canada, 2006.

Inuksuk, Aipili. "Tuniit in Life and Legend." *Inuktitut Magazine* 66 (1987): 33-6.

Inuksuk, Meeka, ed. *Unikkaaqtuat Unikkaallu Sanirajarmit Katitaujut [Stories from Hall Beach]*. Iqaluit: Nunavuumit Marrungnit Uqausilingnut Illinniaqtittinirmit Katujjiqatigiinggit [Nunavut Bilingual Education Society], 2005.

"Inuktitut Linguist Dies in Toronto." *Nunatsiaq News*. 8 Feb. 2002. http: //www.nunatsiaq. com/archives/nunavut020208/news/nunavut/20208_13.html.

Inuktitut Living Dictionary. Government of Nunavut: Department of Culture, Language, Elders and Youth. http://www.livingdictionary.com.

Ipellie, Alootook. *Arctic Dreams and Nightmares*. Penticton: Theytus Books, 1993.

——. "Thirsty for Life: A Nomad Learns to Write and Draw." In *Echoing Silence: Essays on Arctic Narrative*, edited by John Moss, 93-101. Ottawa: University of Ottawa Press, 1997.

———. "Walking Both Sides of an Invisible Border." In *The Journals of Knud Rasmussen: A Sense of Memory and High-Definition Inuit Storytelling*, edited by Gillian Robinson, 57–83. Montreal: Isuma, 2008.

Ipellie, Alootook, ed. *Kivioq: Inuit Fiction Magazine*. Ottawa: Baffin Writers' Project, 1990.

Iqalujjuaq, Levi. *Recollections of Levi Iqalujjuaq: The Life of a Baffin Island Hunter*. ICI Autobiography Series, 1988.

Irniq, Peter. Email to Keavy Martin. 21 Feb. 2009.

———. "Healthy Community." *Arctic* 61: Supplement 1 (2008): 48–61.

———. "Mourning the Death of Titirarti." *Nunatsiaq News*. 15 Feb. 2002. http://www.nunatsiaq.com/archives/nunavut020201/news/editorial/letters.html

Irqugaqtuq, Bernard. "The Autobiography of a Pelly Bay Eskimo." *Eskimo* 14, 22–25; 15, 14–18; 16, 7–10.

Issenman, Betty Kobayashi. *Sinews of Survival: The Living Legacy of Inuit Clothing*. Vancouver: UBC Press, 1997.

Itinnuar, Peter. *Peter Itinnuar: Teach an Eskimo How to Read*. Edited by Thierry Rodon. Vol. 5 of Life Stories of Northern Leaders. Iqaluit: Nunavut Arctic College, 2008.

Jenness, Diamond. *Eskimo Administration: I. Alaska*. Technical Paper No. 10. Montreal: Arctic Institute of North America, 1962.

———. *Eskimo Administration: II. Canada*. Technical Paper No. 14. Montreal: Arctic Institute of North America, 1964.

———. *Eskimo Administration: III. Labrador*. Technical Paper No. 16. Montreal: Arctic Institute of North America, 1965.

———. *Eskimo Administration: IV. Greenland*. Technical Paper No. 19. Montreal: Arctic Institute of North America, 1967.

———. *Eskimo Administration: V. Analysis and Reflections*. Technical Paper No. 21. Montreal: Arctic Institute of North America, 1968.

———. *Eskimo Folk Lore*. Vol. XIII of *Report of the Canadian Arctic Expedition 1913–1918*. Ottawa: King's Printer, 1924.

Jenness, Diamond, and Helen H. Roberts. *Songs of the Copper Eskimos*. Vol. XIV of Report of the Canadian Arctic Expedition 1913–18. Ottawa: F.A. Acland, 1925.'

Johnson, Terrence. "Edward Field." *glbtq: An Encyclopedia of Gay, Lesbian, Bisexual, Transgender, and Queer Culture*. Edited by Claude J. Summers. 2002. 26 Apr 2007. http://www.glbtq.com/literature/field_e.html.

The Journals of Knud Rasmussen. Directed by Zacharias Kunuk and Norman Cohn. Igloolik Isuma Productions, 2006.

Justice, Daniel Heath. "'Go Away, Water!': Kinship Criticism and the Decolonization Imperative." In *Reasoning Together: The Native Critics Collective*, edited by Daniel Heath Justice, Christopher B. Teuton, and Craig Womack, 147–168. Norman: University of Oklahoma Press, 2008.

———. *Our Fire Survives the Storm: A Cherokee Literary History*. Minneapolis: University of Minnesota Press, 2006.

Justice, Daniel Heath, Christopher B. Teuton, and Craig Womack, eds. *Reasoning Together: The Native Critics Collective*. Norman: University of Oklahoma Press, 2008.

Kakkik, Maaki, Frederic Laugrand, and Jarich Oosten, eds. *Keeping the Faith*. Vol. 3 of Memory and History in Nunavut. Iqaluit: Nunavut Arctic College, 2003.

Kalluak, Mark, ed. *How Kabloonat Became and Other Inuit Legends*. Yellowknife: Program Development Division, Government of the Northwest Territories, 1974.

Kaplan, Lawrence D., and Ann Fienup-Riordan, eds. *Words of the Real People: Alaska Native Literature in Translation.* Fairbanks: University of Alaska Press, 2007.

Kappianaq, George Agiaq, and Cornelius Nutarak. *Travelling and Surviving on Our Land,* edited by Frédéric Laugrand and Jarich Oosten. Vol. 2 of Inuit Perspectives on the 20th Century Series. Iqaluit: Nunavut Arctic College, 2001.

Kappianaq, George Agiaq, Felix Pisuk, and Salome Ka&&ak Qalasiq. *Dreams and Dream Interpretation,* edited by Stephane Kolband and Sam Law. Vol. 3 of Inuit Perspectives on the 20th Century Series. Iqaluit: Nunavut Arctic College, 2001.

Kennedy, Michael P.J. "Alootook Ipellie: The Voice of an Inuk Artist." *Studies in Canadian Literature/Études en littérature canadienne* 21, 2 (1996): 155–64.

——. "Captured Words: Inuit Creative Voice in English for the Twenty-First Century." *Proceedings: 14ᵗʰ Inuit Studies Conference.* Calgary: University of Calgary, 2004. 137–152.

——. "Sea Goddess Sedna: An Enduring Pan-Arctic Legend from Traditional Orature to the New Narratives of the Late Twentieth Century." In *Echoing Silence: Essays on Arctic Narrative,* edited by John Moss, 211–24. Ottawa: University of Ottawa Press, 1997.

Killulark, John. *Three Legends/Pingasut Unipkaaqtuat.* Baker Lake: Inuit Heritage Centre, n.d.

King, Thomas. "Godzilla vs. Post-Colonial." *World Literature Written in English* 30, 2 (1990): 10–6.

——. *The Truth About Stories.* Toronto: House of Anansi, 2003.

Kiviuq. Dir. John Houston. Halifax: Triad Film Productions, 2007.

"Kiviuq's Journey." Edited by Kira Van Deusen. 2008. http://www.unipka.ca.

Kleivan, Inge. "A New History of Greenlandic Literature." *Études / Inuit / Studies* 19, 1 (1995): 127–136.

Kobbé, Gustav. *The Complete Opera Book.* London: Putnam, 1935.

Krupat, Arnold. "*Atanarjuat, the Fast Runner* and Its Audiences." *Critical Inquiry* 33, 3 (2007): 606–631.

——. *For Those Who Come After: A Study of Native American Autobiography.* Berkeley: University of California Press, 1985.

Krupat, Arnold and Brian Swann, eds. *Recovering the Word: Essays on Native American Literature.* Berkeley: University of California Press, 1987.

Kublu, Alexina. "Stories." *Introduction.* Edited by Jarich Oosten and Frédéric Laugrand. Vol. 1 of Interviewing Inuit Elders. Iqaluit: Nunavut Arctic College, 1999. 152–91.

Kulchyski, Peter. "Colonization of the Arctic." *Encyclopedia of the Arctic.* Edited by Mark Nuttall, 405–11. New York: Routledge, 2005. 405–11.

——. *Like the Sound of a Drum: Aboriginal Cultural Politics in Denendeh and Nunavut.* Winnipeg: University of Manitoba Press, 2005.

——. "Nunavut Final Agreement." In *Encyclopedia of the Arctic.* Edited by Mark Nuttall, 1529–32. New York: Routledge, 2005. 1529–32.

——. "Violence, Gender and Community in *Atanarjuat.*" In *Film, History and Cultural Citizenship,* edited by Tina Chen and David Churchill, 131–142. New York: Routledge, 2007.

Kulchyski, Peter, Don McCaskill, and David Newhouse, eds. *In the Words of Elders: Aboriginal Cultures in Transition.* Toronto: University of Toronto Press, 2003.

Kulchyski, Peter, and Frank James Tester. *Kiumajut (Talking Back): Game Management and Inuit Rights, 1900–70.* Vancouver: UBC Press, 2007.

——. *Tammarniit (Mistakes): Inuit Relocation in the Eastern Arctic, 1939–63.* Vancouver: UBC Press, 1994.

Kunuk Family Reunion. Directed by Zacharias Kunuk. Igloolik Isuma Productions, 2004.

Kunuk, Zacharias. "Zacharias Kunuk Speaks with Joysanne Sidimus." In *The Journals of Knud Rasmussen: A Sense of Memory and High-Definition Inuit Storytelling*, edited by Gillian Robinson, 251–61. Montreal: Isuma, 2008.

Kunuk, Zacharias, and Norman Cohn. "The Journals of Knud Rasmussen: Original Screenplay." In *The Journals of Knud Rasmussen: A Sense of Memory and High-Definition Inuit Storytelling*, edited by Gillian Robinson, 287–438. Montreal: Isuma, 2008. 287–438.

Kusugak, Michael. *The Curse of the Shaman: A Marble Island Story.* Toronto: Harper Trophy Canada, 2006.

Lalonde, Christine, Leslie Boyd Ryan, Doug Steiner, Kananginak Pootoogook, and Ningeokuluk Teevee. *Uuturautiit: Cape Dorset Celebrates Fifty Years of Printmaking.* Ottawa: National Gallery of Canada, 2009.

Langgard, Karen. "Does Greenlandic Literature call for a Specific Greenlandic Literary Theory?" In *Cultural and Social Research in Greenland 95–96: Essays in Honour of Robert Petersen*, edited by B. Jacobsen. Nuuk, Ilisimatusarfik/Atuakkiorfik. 1996.

LaRocque, Emma. *When the Other Is Me: Native Resistance Discourse, 1850–1990.* Winnipeg: University of Manitoba Press, 2010.

Laugrand, Frédéric. "Écrire pour prendre la parole: Conscience historique, mémoires d'aînés et régimes d'historicité au Nunavut." *Anthropologie et Sociétés* 26, 2–3 (2002): 91–116.

Laugrand, Frédéric, and Jarich Oosten. *The Sea Woman: Sedna in Inuit Shamanism and Art in the Eastern Arctic.* Fairbanks: University of Alaska Press, 2008.

———. *Inuit Shamanism & Christianity: Transitions and Transformations in the Twentieth Century.* Montreal and Kingston: McGill-Queen's University Press, 2010.

Laugrand, Frédéric, and Jarich Oosten, eds. *The Ethnographic Recordings of Inuit Oral Traditions by Father Guy Mary-Rousselière (OMI).* Translated by Gloria Putumiraqtuq. Iqaluit: Nunavut Arctic College, 2009.

Laugrand, Frédéric, Jarich Oosten, and François Trudel, eds. *Apostle to the Inuit: The Journals and Ethnographic Notes of Edmund James Peck–The Baffin Years, 1894–1905.* Toronto: University of Toronto Press, 2006.

———. *Representing Tuurngait.* Vol. 1 of Memory and History in Nunavut Series. Iqaluit: Nunavut Arctic College, 2000.

Laugrand, Frédéric, Jarich Oosten, and Wim Rasing. "Introduction: Tirigusuusiit, Piqujait and Maligait: Inuit Perspectives on Traditional Law." Volume 2: Perspectives on Traditional Law. Iqaluit: Nunavut Arctic College, 2000.

Lauritzen, Philip. *Oil and Amulets: Inuit: A People United at the Top of the World.* Edited by R.E. Buehler. St. John's, NL: Breakwater, 1983.

Leacock, Eleanor Burke. *Myths of Male Dominance: Collected Articles on Women Cross-Culturally.* New York: Monthly Review Press, 1981.

Legaré, André. "The Construction of Nunavut: The Impact of the Nunavut Project on Inuit Identity, Governance, and Society." PhD diss., University of Saskatchewan, 2010.

———. "The Spatial and Symbolic Construction of Nunavut: Towards the Emergence of a Regional Collective Identity." *Études/Inuit/Studies* 25, 1–2 (2001): 141–68.

Lejeune, Philippe. *Le pacte autobiographique.* Paris: Editions du Seuil, 1975.

———. *On Autobiography.* Translated by Katherine Leary. Minneapolis: University of Minnesota Press, 1989.

Le Mouël, Jean-François. *Music of the Inuit: The Copper Eskimo Tradition.* Gentilly: Auvidis, 1994.

Lerena, María Jesús Hernáez. "'Changing Silk Gowns for Survival Suits': A Written Conversation with Robin McGrath." *British Journal of Canadian Studies* 21, 2 (2008): 2057–2074.

Lewis, Richard, ed. *I Breathe a New Song: Poems of the Eskimo.* New York: Simon and Schuster, 1971.

Leyerle, John. "The Interlace Structure of Beowulf." *University of Toronto Quarterly* 37, 1 (1967): 1–17.

"Live From the Set: The Journals of Knud Rasmussen." 2005. http://www.sila.nu/live.

Lopez, Barry. *Arctic Dreams: Imagination and Desire in a Northern Landscape.* New York: Scribner, 1986.

Lotz, Jim, and Pat Lotz, eds. *Pilot Not Commander: Essays in Memory of Diamond Jenness.* Ottawa: Saint Paul University, 1971.

Lowe, Ronald. *Siglit Inuvialuit Ilisarviksait: Basic Siglit Inuvialuit Eskimo Grammar.* Inuvik: Committee for Original Peoples Entitlement, 1985.

Lowenstein, Tom, trans. *Eskimo Poems from Canada and Greenland: From Material Originally Collected by Knud Rasmussen.* Pittsburgh: University of Pittsburgh Press, 1973.

Lutz, Maija M. *The Effects of Acculturation on Eskimo Music of Cumberland Peninsula.* Ottawa: National Museums of Canada, 1978.

Lynge, Aqqaluk. *Taqqat Uummammut Aqqutaannut Takorluukkat Apuuffiannut/The Veins of the Heart to the Pinnacle of the Mind.* Translated by Ken Norris and Marianne Stenbaek. Montreal and Hanover: International Polar Institute, 2008.

Lyons, Scott Richard. "Rhetorical Sovereignty: What Do American Indians Want from Writing?" *College Composition and Communication* 51, 1 (2000): 447–68.

——. *X-Marks: Native Signatures of Assent.* Minneapolis: University of Minnesota Press, 2010.

MacDonald, John, ed. *The Arctic Sky: Inuit Astronomy, Star Lore, and Legend.* Toronto: Royal Ontario Museum/Nunavut Research Institute, 1998.

Malinowski, Bronislaw. "The Language of Magic." In *The Importance of Language,* 72–90. Englewood Cliffs, NJ: Prentice Hall, 1962.

Mamnguqsualuk, Victoria. *Keeveeok, Awake!: Mamnguqsualuk and the Rebirth of Legend at Baker Lake.* Edmonton: The Boreal Institute for Northern Studies, 1986.

Mannik, Hattie, ed. *Inuit Nunamiut: Inland Inuit.* Ottawa: Parks Canada Archives, 1993.

Maracle, Lee. *Oratory: Coming to Theory.* North Vancouver: Gallerie, 1990.

Markoosie [Patsauq]. *Harpoon of the Hunter.* Montreal: McGill-Queen's University Press, 1970.

Mary-Rousselière, Guy, ed. *Beyond the High Hills: A Book of Eskimo Poems.* Cleveland: World Publishing Corporation, 1961.

——. "The 'Tunit' According to Igloolik Traditions." *Eskimo* 35 (1955): 14–20.

Mathiassen, Therkel. *Archaeology of the Central Eskimos.* Report of the Fifth Thule Expedition. Vol. 4. Copenhagen: Gyldendal, 1927.

——. *Material Culture of the Iglulik Eskimos.* Vol. VI, No. 1 of *Report of the Fifth Thule Expedition 1921–24.* Copenhagen: Gyldendal, 1928.

——. *Report on the Expedition.* Vol. I, No. 1 of *Report of the Fifth Thule Expedition 1921–24.* Copenhagen: Gyldendal, 1945.

McCall, Sophie. "'I Can Only Sing This Song to Someone Who Understands It': Community Filmmaking and the Politics of Partial Translation in *Atanarjuat, the Fast Runner.*" *Essays on Canadian Writing* 83 (2004): 19–46.

——. *First Person Plural Aboriginal Storytelling and the Ethics of Collaborative Authorship.* Vancouver: UBC Press, 2011.

McComber, Louis and Shannon Partridge, eds. *Arnait Nipingit: Voices of Inuit Women in Leadership and Governance.* Iqaluit: Nunavut Arctic College, 2011.

McDermott, Noel. *Akinirmut Unikkaaqtuat: Stories of Revenge.* Iqaluit: Nunavut Bilingual Education Society, 2006.

McGrath, Robin. *Canadian Inuit Literature: The Development of a Tradition.* Ottawa: National Museums of Canada, 1984.

——. "Circumventing the Taboos: Inuit Women's Autobiographies." In *Undisciplined Women: Tradition and Culture in Canada,* edited by Pauline Greenhill and Diana Tye, 223–33. Montreal: McGill-Queen's University Press, 1997.

——. "The Development of Inuit Literature in English." In *Minority Literature in North America: Contemporary Perspectives,* edited by Hartmut Lutz and Wolfgang Karrer, 193–203. Frankfurt am Main: Verlag Peter Lang, 1990.

——. "Editing Inuit Literature: Leaving the Teeth in the Gently Smiling Jaws." *Inuit Art Quarterly* (1987): 3–5.

——. "Monster Figures and Unhappy Endings in Inuit Literature." *Canadian Journal of Native Education* 15, 1 (1988): 51–8.

——. "Oral Influences in Contemporary Inuit Literature." In *The Native in Literature: Canadian and Contemporary Perspectives,* edited by Thomas King, Cheryl Calver and Helen Hoy, 159–73. Oakville: ECW Press, 1987.

——. "Reassessing Traditional Inuit Poetry." In *Native Writers and Canadian Writing,* edited by William H. New, 19–28. Vancouver: UBC Press, 1990.

McGregor, Heather. *Inuit Education and Schools in the Eastern Arctic.* Vancouver: UBC Press, 2010.

McKegney, Sam. *Magic Weapons: Aboriginal Writers Remaking Community After Residential School.* Winnipeg: University of Manitoba Press, 2007.

McLeod, Neal. "Coming Home Through Stories." In *(Ad)Dressing Our Words: Aboriginal Perspectives on Aboriginal Literatures,* edited by Armand Garnet Ruffo, 17–36. Penticton: Theytus Books, 2001.

——. *Cree Narrative Memory: From Treaties to Contemporary Times.* Saskatoon: Purich, 2007.

McMahon-Coleman, Kimberly L. "Dreaming an Identity Between Two Cultures: The Works of Alootook Ipellie." *Journal of Postcolonial Writing* 28, 1 (2006): 108–125.

Métayer, Maurice, trans. *Contes de mon iglou.* Montreal: Éditions du Jour, 1973.

——. *Tales From the Igloo.* Edmonton: Hurtig, 1972.

Métayer, Maurice, ed. *Unipkat: Tradition esquimaude de Coppermine, Territoires-du-Nord-Ouest, Canada.* 3 vols. Quebec: Centre d'études nordiques, Université Laval, 1973.

Mihesuah, Devon Abbott and Angela Cavender Wilson, eds. *Indigenizing the Academy: Transforming Scholarship and Empowering Communities.* Lincoln: University of Nebraska Press, 2004.

Mitchell, Marybelle. *From Talking Chiefs to a Native Corporate Elite: The Birth of Class and Nationalism among the Canadian Inuit.* Montreal: McGill-Queen's University Press, 1996.

Momaday, N. Scott. *House Made of Dawn.* New York: Harper, 1977.

Moquin, Heather. "Breathing Out 'The Songs that Want to be Sung': A Dialogue on Research, Colonization and Pedagogy Focused on the Canadian Arctic." PhD diss., University of Glasgow, 2010.

Morice, Rev. Adrian G. *Thawing out the Eskimo*. Translated by Mary T. Loughlin. Boston: The Society for the Propagation of the Faith, 1943.

Moses, Daniel David, and Terry Goldie, eds. *An Anthology of Canadian Native Literature in English*. 3 Edited by Don Mills, ON: Oxford University Press, 2005.

Moss, John, ed. *Echoing Silence: Essays on Arctic Narrative*. Ottawa: University of Ottawa Press, 1997.

Murray, Laura J., and Keren Rice, eds. *Talking on the Page: Editing Aboriginal Oral Texts*. Toronto: University of Toronto Press, 1999.

Nagy, Murielle. "Time, Space and Memory." In *Critical Inuit Studies: An Anthology of Contemporary Arctic Ethnography*, edited by Pamela Stern and Lisa Stevenson, 71–88. Lincoln: University of Nebraska Press, 2006.

Nanook of the North. Directed by Robert Flaherty. Les Frères Revillon, 1922.

Nappaaluk, Mitiarjuk. *Sanaaq*. Trans. Bernard Saladin d'Anglure. Paris: Stanké, 2002.

——. *Sanaaq: Sanaakkut Piusiviningita Unikkausinnguangat*. Edited by Bernard Saladin d'Anglure. Québec: Association Inuksiutiit Katimajiit, 1984.

Nattiez, Jean-Jacques. "La danse à tambour chez les Inuit igloolik (nord de la Terre de Baffin)." *Recherches Amérindiennes au Québec* 18, 4 (1988): 37–48.

Neuhaus, Mareike. *That's Raven Talk: Holophrastic Readings of Contemporary Indigenous Literatures*. Regina: CPRC Press, 2011.

New, William H., ed. *Encyclopedia of Literature in Canada*. Toronto: University of Toronto Press, 2002.

Norris, Stephen P. "Sustaining and Responding to Charges of Bias in Critical Thinking." *Educational Theory* 45, 2 (1995): 199–211.

Nuliajuk: Mother of the Sea Beasts. Directed by John Houston. Halifax: Triad Film Productions, 2001.

Nuligak [Bob Cockney]. *I, Nuligak*. Trans. Maurice Metayer. Toronto: Peter Martin Associates, 1966.

The Nunavut Handbook: Travelling in Canada's Arctic. Iqaluit: Ayaya Marketing and Communications, 2004.

Nungak, Zebedee, and Eugene Y. Arima, eds. *Inuit Stories/Légendes Inuits: Povungnituk*. Ottawa: Canadian Museum of Civilization, 1988.

Okpik, Abraham. *We Call It Survival: The Life Story of Abraham Okpik*. Edited by Louis McComber. Vol. 1 of Life Stories of Northern Leaders. Iqaluit: Nunavut Arctic College, 2005.

Oman, Lela Kiana. *The Epic of Qayaq: The Longest Story Ever Told by My People*. Ottawa: Carleton University Press, 1995.

Ong, Walter. *Orality and Literacy: The Technologizing of the Word*. London: Methuen, 1982.

Oosten, Jarich, and Cornelius Remie, eds. *Arctic Identities: Continuity and Change in Inuit and Saami Societies*. Leiden: Research School CNWS, School of Asian, African and Amerindian Studies, Universiteit Leiden, 1999.

Ortiz, Simon J. "Towards a National Indian Literature: Cultural Authenticity in Nationalism." In *American Indian Literary Nationalism*, edited by Robert Allen Warrior, Jace Weaver, and Craig Womack, 225–52. Albuquerque: University of New Mexico Press, 2006.

Owlijoot, Pelagie. *Guidelines for Working with Inuit Elders*. Iqaluit: Nunavut Arctic College, 2008.

Partridge, Taqralik. "Quiet Is Not Silent." Perf. DJ Madeskimo, Philippe Brault, Guido del Fabbro, and Taqralik Partridge. CBC Radio, 27 June 2008.

Patiq, Joe. "Tunijjuaq." *Inuktitut* (1987): 39–40.

Pelly, David F, ed. *Hanningajuq Project: A Project of the Baker Lake Hunters and Trappers Organization 2003–2004*. Baker Lake: Baker Lake Hunters and Trappers Organization, 2005.

——. *Hanningajuq Project Synthesis*. Baker Lake: Baker Lake Hunters and Trappers Organization, 2005.

Perkins, David. *Is Literary History Possible?* Baltimore: Johns Hopkins University Press, 1992.

Petrone, Penny, ed. *Northern Voices: Inuit Writing in English*. Toronto: University of Toronto Press, 1988.

Philip, Neil, ed. *Songs Are Thoughts: Poems of the Inuit*. Toronto: Doubleday Canada, 1995.

Pisilik Anglikamaunut Atuktaujuk / The Eastern Arctic Hymnbook of the Diocese of the Arctic. N.p.: Anglican Church of Canada, 1970.

Pitseolak, Peter, and Dorothy Harley Eber. *People from Our Side: A Life Story with Photographs and Oral Biography*. Edmonton: Hurtig, 1975.

Pratt, Mary-Louise. *Imperial Eyes: Travel Writing and Transculturation*. London: Routledge, 1992.

Purdy, Al. "Lament for the Dorsets." In *Selected Poems*, 71–72. Toronto: McClelland and Stewart, 1972.

Qaggiq. Directed by Zacharias Kunuk. Igloolik Isuma Productions, 1989.

Qallunaat: Why White People Are Funny. Directed by Zebedee Nungak and Mark Sandiford. Beachwalker Films and National Film Board of Canada, 2006.

Qapirangajuq: Inuit Knowledge and Climate Change. Directed by Zacharias Kunuk and Ian Mauro. Igloolik Isuma Productions, 2010.

Qikiqtani Inuit Association. "Tuniit/Tunitjuat." *Inuit Myths and Legends*. http://www.inuitmyths.com/tuniit.htm.

Qirniq, Simon. "The Death of the Tuniit." *Inuktitut* (1987): 37–39.

Qitsualik, Rachel. "In the Bones of the World." *Nunatsiaq News*, 12 July 2002. http://www.nunatsiaq.com/archives/nunavut020705/news/editorial/ columns.html#nunani_july12.

——. "Is It 'Eskimo' or 'Inuit'?" *Indian Country Today*, 11 Feb. 2004. http://www.indiancountry.com/content.cfm?id=1076511949

——. "*Nalunaktuq*: The Arctic as Force, Instead of Resource." CBC News, 31 Aug. 2006. 31 May 2012. http://www.cbc.ca/news/background/canada2020/essay-qitsualik.html.

——. "Skraeling." *Our Story: Aboriginal Voices on Canada's Past*. Toronto: Doubleday Canada, 2004. 36–66.

——. "Word and Will——Part Two: Words and the Substance of Life." Nunatsiaq News, 12 November 1998. http://www.nunatsiaqonline.ca/archives/nunavut981130/nvt81113_09.html.

Quassa, Paul. *Paul Quassa: We Need to Know Who We Are*. Edited by Louis McComber. *Life Stories of Northern Leaders*, Vol. 3. Iqaluit: Nunavut Arctic College, 2008.

Qumaq, Taamusi. *Je veux que les Inuit soien libres de nouveau: Autobiographie 1914–1993*. Québec: Presses de l'Université de Québec, 2010.

——. *Sivulitta Piusituqangit [An Encyclopedia of Inuit Traditional Life]*. Québec: Association Inuksiutiit Katimajiit, 1988.

Rankin, Sharon. *A Bibliography of Canadian Inuit Periodicals*. Québec: Presses de l'Université du Québec, 2011.

Rasmussen, Knud. *Across Arctic America: Narrative of the Fifth Thule Expedition*. Fairbanks: University of Alaska Press, 1999.

——. *Intellectual Culture of the Copper Eskimos*. Translated by William Worster and W.E. Calvert. Vol. IX of *Report of the Fifth Thule Expedition 1921–24*. Copenhagen: Gyldendal, 1932.

——. *Intellectual Culture of the Iglulik Eskimos*. Translated by William Worster and W.E. Calvert. Vol. VII, No. 1 of *Report of the Fifth Thule Expedition 1921–24*. Copenhagen: Gyldendal, 1929.

——. *The Mackenzie Eskimos: After Knud Rasmussen's Posthumous Notes*. Edited by H. Ostermann. Translated by William Worster and W.E. Calvert. Vol. X, No. 2 of *Report of the Fifth Thule Expedition 1921–24*. New York: AMS Press, 1942.

——. *The Netsilik Eskimos: Social Life and Spiritual Culture*. Translated by William Worster and W.E. Calvert. Vol. VIII, No. 1–2 of *Report of the Fifth Thule Expedition 1921–24*. Copenhagen: Gyldendal, 1931.

——. *The People of the Polar North: A Record*. Edited by G. Herring. London: K. Paul, 1908.

——. *Den store Slæderejse*. København: Gyldendal, 1956.

Rasmnssen, Knud, ed. *Iglulik and Caribou Eskimo Texts*. Translated by William Worster and W.E. Calvert. Vol. VII, No. 3 of *Report of the Fifth Thule Expedition 1921–24*. Copenhagen: Gyldendal, 1930.

——. *Schneehüttenlieder; Eskimoische Gesänge*. Translated by Aenne Schmücker. Essen: Hans v. Chamier, 1947.

——. *Snehytttens Sange*. København: Gyldendal, 1930.

Renan, Ernest. "Qu'est-ce qu'une nation?" Edited by A. Guézou. *La collection électronique de la Bibliothèque Municipale de Lisieux*. 1997. http://ourworld.compuserve.com/homepages/bib_lisieux/nation01.htm.

——. "What Is a Nation?" Translated by Martin Thom. *Nation and Narration*, edited by Homi K. Bhabha, 8–22. New York: Routledge, 1990.

Richler, Noah. *This Is My Country, What's Yours?: A Literary Atlas of Canada*. Toronto: McCelland and Stewart, 2006.

Rideout, Denise. "Nunavut's Inuit Qaujimajatuqangit Group Gets StartEdited by" *Nunatsiaq News*, 2 Feb. 2001. http://www.nunatsiaqonline.ca/archives/nunavut010228/nvt10202_08.html

Robinson, Gillian, ed. *Isuma Inuit Studies Reader: An Inuit Anthology*. Montreal: Isuma, 2004.

——. *The Journals of Knud Rasmussen: A Sense of Memory and High-Definition Inuit Storytelling*. Montreal: Isuma, 2008.

Rothenberg, Jerome, ed. *Shaking the Pumpkin: Traditional Poetry of the Indian North Americas*. Albuquerque: University of New Mexico Press, 1991.

——. *Technicians of the Sacred: A Range of Poetries from Africa, America, Asia, Europe and Oceania*. Berkeley: University of California Press, 1985.

Ruffo, Armand Garnet, ed. *(Ad)Dressing Our Words: Aboriginal Perspectives on Aboriginal Literatures*. Penticton: Theytus Books, 2001.

Sahlins, Marshall. *The Original Affluent Society*. Chicago: Aldine-Therton, 1972.

Said, Edward W. "Yeats and Decolonization." In *Nationalism, Colonialism and Literature*, 69–95. Minneapolis: University of Minnesota Press, 1990.

Sarris, Greg. *Keeping Slug Woman Alive: A Holistic Approach to American Indian Texts*. Berkeley: University of California Press, 1993.

Saul, John Ralston. *A Fair Country: Telling Truth About Canada*. Toronto: Viking Canada, 2008.

Schneider, Lucien. *Ulirnaisigutiit: An Inuktitut-English Dictionary of Northern Quebec, Labrador and Eastern Arctic Dialects*. Québec: Les Presses de l'Université Laval, 1985.

Schwartz, Joanne. "Transmitting Oral Culture to the Page: The Emergency of Inuit Children's Books." *International Board of Books for Young People*. http://www.ibby.org/index.php?id=1135.

Serkoak, David, with Ann Meekitjuk Hanson and Peter Irniq. "Inuit Music." In *The Nunavut Handbook: Travelling in Canada's Arctic*, 79–81. Iqaluit: Ayaya Marketing and Commuications, 2004.

Simon, Mary. *Inuit: One Future—One Arctic*. Peterborough: Cider Press, 1996.

——. "Sovereignty from the North." *The Walrus* (Special Arctic Issue) (November 2007): 32–4.

Simpson, Audra. "Mohawk Interruptus." Native American and Indigenous Studies Association, Mohegan Sun Casino. 5 June 2012.

Smith, Linda Tuhiwai. *Decolonizing Methodologies: Research and Indigenous Peoples*. London: Zed Books, 1999.

Smith, Sidonie, and Julia Watson. *Reading Autobiography: A Guide for Interpreting Life Narratives*. Minneapolis: University of Minnesota Press, 2001.

Sontag, Susan. *Against Interpretation, and Other Essays*. New York: Farrar, 1966.

Spalding, Alex. *Aivilik Adventure: A Reminiscence of Two Years Spent with the Inuit of the Old Culture*. Toronto: A. Spalding, 1994.

——. *Inuktitut: A Multi-dialectal Outline Dictionary (with an Aivilingmiutaq Base)*. Iqaluit: Nunavut Arctic College: 1998.

——. *Learning to Speak Inuktitut: A Grammar of North Baffin Dialects*. London, ON: Centre for Research and Teaching of Canadian Native Languages, University of Western Ontario, 1979.

——. *The Polar Bear: and Other Northern Poems*. Toronto: A. Spalding, 1993.

——. "Wordsworth as a Pastoral Poet." PhD Diss., McMaster University, 1974.

Spalding, Alex, ed. *Eight Inuit Myths/Inuit Unipkaaqtuat Pingasuniarvinilit*. Ottawa: National Museums of Canada, 1979.

Spivak, Gayatri Chakravorty. "Can the Subaltern Speak?" In *Marxism and the Interpretation of Culture,* edited by Cary Nelson and Lawrence Grossberg, 271–313. Urbana: University of Illinois Press, 1988.

Stenbaek, Marianne. "Arqaluk Lynge——Poet and Politician." *Scandinavian-Canadian Studies/Études Scandinaves au Canada* 3 (1988): 133–42.

——. "Cultural Change Among the Inuit During the Last Forty Years: Some Reflections." *Arctic* 40 (1987): 300–9.

Stern, Pamela, and Lisa Stevenson, eds. *Critical Inuit Studies: An Anthology of Contemporary Arctic Ethnography*. Lincoln: University of Nebraska Press, 2006.

Stern, Pamela R. *Daily Life of the Inuit*. Santa Barbara: Greenwood, 2010.

——. "Learning to Be Smart: An Exploration of the Culture of Intelligence in a Canadian Inuit Community." *American Anthropologist* 101, 23 (1999): 502–514.

Stevenson, Marc G. *Inuit, Whalers, and Cultural Persistence: Structure in Cumberland Sound and Central Inuit Social Organization*. Toronto: Oxford University Press, 1997.

Stott, Jon C. "Form, Content, and Cultural Values in Three Inuit (Eskimo) Survival Stories." *American Indian Quarterly* 10, 3 (1986): 213–226.

Sugars, Cynthia. *Home-Work: Postcolonialism, Pedagogy and Canadian Literature*. Ottawa: University of Ottawa Press, 2004.

Sutherland, Patricia D., ed. *Contributions to the Study of the Dorset Paleo-Eskimos*. Ottawa: Canadian Museum of Civilization, 2005.

Tagoona, Armand. *Shadows*. Toronto: Oberon Press, 1975.

Tales of the Netsilik. By Raymond Luedeke. Roy Thomson Hall, Toronto, 26 Mar. 2008.

Tedlock, Dennis. *The Spoken Word and the Work of Interpretation*. Philadelphia: University of Pennsylvania Press, 1983.

Tester, Frank James. "Can the Sled Dog Sleep? Postcolonialism, Cultural Transformation and the Consumption of Inuit Culture." *New Proposals: Journal of Marxism and Interdisciplinary Inquiry* 3, 3 (2010): 7–19.

Tester, Frank James, and Peter Irniq. "Inuit Qaujimajatuqangit: Social History, Politics and the practise of Resistance." *Arctic* 61: Supplement 1 (2008): 48–61.

Teuton, Christopher. *Deep Waters: The Textual Continuum in American Indian Literature*. Lincoln: University of Nebraska Press, 2010.

——. "Theorizing American Indian Literature: Applying Oral Concepts to Written Traditions." *Reasoning Together: The Native Critics Collective*, edited by Daniel Heath Justice, Christopher B. Teuton, and Craig Womack, 193–215. Norman: University of Oklahoma Press, 2008.

Therrien, Michèle. *Le Corps Inuit (Québec Arctique)*. Paris: Société d'Études Linguistiques et Anthropologiques de France, 1987.

——. "Ce que precise la langue inuit au sujet de la remémoration." *Anthropologie et Sociétés* 26, 2–3 (2002): 117–135.

Thrasher, Anthony Apakark. *Thrasher: Skid Row Eskimo*. Toronto: Griffin House, 1976.

——. Unpublished ms., 1973.

Thériault, Yves. *Agaguk*. Montreal: Quinze, 1981.

Timpson, Annis May. "Rethinking the Administration of Government: Inuit Representation, Culture, and Language in the Nunavut Public Service." In *First Nations, First Thoughts: The Impact of Indigenous Thought in Canada*, edited by Annis May Timpson, 199–228. Vancouver: UBC Press, 2009.

Treuer, David. *Native American Fiction: A User's Manual*. Saint Paul: Graywolf Press, 2006.

Trott, Christopher. "Mission and Opposition in North Baffin Island." *Journal of the Canadian Church Historical Society* 40, 1 (1998): 31–55.

Tulugarjuk, Leo, and Neil Christopher. *Ilagiinniq: Interviews on Inuit Family Values*. Iqaluit: Inhabit Media, 2011.

Tungilik, Victor, and Rachel Uyarasuk. *The Transition to Christianity*. Edited by Jarich Oosten and Frédéric Laugrand. Vol. 1 of Inuit Perspectives on the 20th Century. Iqaluit: Nunavut Arctic College, 1999.

Ulrikab, Abraham. *The Diary of Abraham Ulrikab*. Edited by Hartmut Lutz. Ottawa: University of Ottawa Press, 2005.

Umeek (E. Richard Atleo). *Tsawalk: A Nuu-chah-nulth Worldview*. Vancouver: UBC Press, 2004.

Unikkaat Sivunittinnit: Messages from the Past. Igloolik Isuma Productions, 1992.

Vail, Leroy and Landeg White. "The Invention of 'Oral Man': Anthropology, Literary Theory and Western Intellectual Traditions." In *Power and the Praise Poem: Southern African Voices in History*, edited by Leroy Vail and Landeg White, 1–39. Charlottesville: University Press of Virginia, 1991.

Van Deusen, Kira. *Kiviuq: An Inuit Hero and His Siberian Cousins*. Montreal: McGill-Queen's University Press, 2009.

Van Herk, Aritha. *Places Far From Ellesmere: Explorations on Site: A Geografictione*. Red Deer: Red Deer College Press, 1990.

Van London, Selma. "Mythology and Identity Construction Among the Inuit." In *Arctic Identities: Continuity and Change in Inuit and Saami Societies,* edited by Jarich Oosten and Cornelius Remie, 109–34. Leiden: Research School CNWS, School of Asian, African and Amerindian Studies, Universiteit Leiden, 1999.

Vascotto, Norma Mae Kritsch. "The Transmission of Drum Songs in Pelly Bay, Nunavut, and the Contributions of Composers and Singers to Musical Norms." PhD diss., University of Toronto, 2001.

Wachowich, Nancy, in collaboration with Apphia Agalakti Awa, Rhoda Kaukjak Katsak, and Sandra Pikujak Katsak. *Saqiyuq: Stories from the Lives of Three Inuit Women.* Montreal: McGill-Queen's University Press, 1999.

Warrior, Robert Allen. "Organizing Native American and Indigenous Studies." *PMLA* 123, 5 (2008): 1683–91.

——. *Tribal Secrets: Recovering American Indian Intellectual Traditions.* Minneapolis: University of Minnesota Press, 1994.

Warrior, Robert Allen, Jace Weaver, and Craig Womack. *American Indian Literary Nationalism.* Albuquerque: University of New Mexico Press, 2006.

Weaver, Jace. *That the People Might Live: Native American Literatures and Native American Community.* New York: Oxford University Press, 1997.

Weber, Max. "Politics as a Vocation." In *From Max Weber: Essays in Sociology,* translated by Hans Heinrich Gerth and Charles Wright Mills, 77–128. London: Routledge, 1998.

Webster, David, ed. *Oral Histories: Baker Lake, Northwest Territories 1992–1993.* Baker Lake: n.p., 1993.

Weetaltuk, Eddy. *E9–422: Un Inuit, de la Toundra à la guerre de Corée.* Paris: Carnets Nord, 2009.

Weetaluktuk, Jobie. "Editorial." *Inuktitut Magazine.* 78 (1995): 3–4.

Wenzel, George W. "From TEK to IQ: *Inuit Qaujimajatuqangit* and Inuit Cultural Ecology." *Arctic Anthropology* 41, 2 (2004): 238–250.

White, Hayden. "The Historical Text as Literary Artifact." In *The Norton Anthology of Theory and Criticism,* edited by Vincent B. Leitch, 1712–29. New York: W.W. Norton and Company, 2001.

Wiebe, Rudy. "Songs of the Canadian Eskimo." *Canadian Literature* 52 (1972): 57–69.

Williamson, Robert G. *Eskimo Underground: Socio-Cultural Change in the Canadian Central Arctic,* Occasional Papers II. Uppsala: Institutionen för Allmän och Jämförande Etnografi vid Uppsala Universitet, 1974.

Wilson, Angela Cavender. "Power of the Spoken Word: Native Oral Traditions in American Indian History." In *Rethinking American Indian History,* edited by Donald L. Fixico, 101–116. Albuquerque: University of New Mexico Press, 1997.

Wiseman, Marcus. "The Struggle for Survival of the Inuit Culture in English Literature." MA thesis, McGill University, 1984.

Womack, Craig. "A Single Decade: Book-Length Native Literary Criticism between 1986 and 1997." In *Reasoning Together: The Native Critics Collective,* edited by Daniel Heath Justice, Christopher B. Teuton, and Craig Womack, 3–104. Norman: University of Oklahoma Press, 2008. 3–104.

——. *Art as Performance: Story as Criticism: Reflections on Native Literary Aesthetics.* Norman: University of Oklahoma Press, 2009.

——. *Red on Red: Native American Literary Separatism.* Minneapolis: University of Minnesota Press, 1999.

——. "Theorizing American Indian Experience." In *Reasoning Together: The Native Critics Collective,* 353–410.

INDEX

A

adaptation: by Inuit, 6, 14–15; and Inuit Qaujimajatuqangit, 3, 100; in Inuit stories, 7–8, 50; in *The Journals of Knud Rasmussen* (film), 97

Amarook, Michael, 14

Anauta (Lizzie Ford Blackmore), 102.

Anaviapik, Simon, 20–21

Anawak, Jack, 145n23

Anderson, Benedict, 16

angakkuq/angakkuit, 59, 65, 82

Angmarlik, Pauloosie, 107

"Angusugjuk and the Polar Bears" (Kusugaq): *ihuma* in, 56–57, 58; read as allegory, 49–50; read as parable, 50–54; telling of, 47–49

Aniksak, Margaret Uyauperk, 50

Apess, William, 45

appropriation, 86–87

Arnakak, Jaypetee, 43, 100

Arnaktauyok, Germaine, 105

assimilation, 18–19, 26

Atanarjuat (film), 4, 89, 93–94, 151n57

Atoat, 24

Aua. *See* Avva

Aupilaarjuk, Mariano, 86, 98

autobiographies. *See* Indigenous autobiography/memoir

Avva: conversion of, 64–65, 89, 91, 97; relations with Rasmussen, 66, 92, 94–95, 101; singing of, 81; trip north, 90

B

Barfield, Owen, 67

Before Tomorrow (film), 151n54

Blaeser, Kimberley M., 44–45

Blake, Dale, 115

Briggs, Jean, 55–56

Bringhurst, Robert, 40

Brooks, Lisa, 12

Burgess, Anthony, 60

C

Campbell, Lydia, 102

Carpenter, Edward, 75–76

Chamberlin, J. Edward, 17, 20, 24, 35, 44, 58, 111

Christianity: and adaptability, 8; and *The Journals of Knud Rasmussen*, 64–65, 89–90, 91, 97; and memoirs, 102; and songs, 65–66

climate change, 1–2, 23

"Cold and Mosquitoes," 69–71, 79, 82, 92, 129–31, 133

colonization: critique of in "Skraeling," 33, 34; and Inuit-Tuniit stories, 24–25, 29; and southern institutions, 4, 6

commodification, 68, 95–96

critical thinking, 54–58, 62, 119–20

Cruikshank, Julie, 101

The Curse of the Shaman: A Marble Island Story (Kusugak), 58–63

D

Dauenhauer, Nora Marks, 44, 109

Dauenhauer, Richard, 44, 109

decontextualization of songs and stories: by Europeans, 9, 67–68, 74–76, 77, 96–97; by Inuit, 91, 93–94